READING SEMINAR XI

*SUNY Series in Psychoanalysis
and Culture*

Henry Sussman, Editor

READING SEMINAR XI

LACAN'S *FOUR FUNDAMENTAL CONCEPTS OF PSYCHOANALYSIS*

Including the first English Translation of
"Position of the Unconscious"
by Jacques Lacan

EDITED BY

Richard
Feldstein

Bruce
Fink

Maire
Jaanus

The Paris Seminars in English

STATE UNIVERSITY OF NEW YORK PRESS

Cover painting reproduced by
courtesy of the Trustees, The National Gallery, London
Hans Holbein, the Younger: *Jean de Dinteville and
Georges de Selve ('The Ambassadors').*

Published by
State University of New York Press, Albany

Printed in the United States of America

For information, address State University of New York
Press, State University Plaza, Albany, N.Y., 12246

Production by Diane Ganeles
Marketing by Theresa Swierzowski

Library of Congress Cataloging-in-Publication Data

Reading Seminar XI : Lacan's Four Fundamental Concepts of
    Psychoanalysis : the Paris Seminars in English / edited by Richard
    Feldstein, Bruce Fink, and Maire Jaanus.
        p.   cm.—(SUNY series in psychoanalysis and culture)
    Includes index.
    ISBN 0-7914-2147-3 (alk. paper).—ISBN 0-7914-2148-1 (pbk. :
alk. paper)
    1. Lacan, Jacques, 1901– Quatre concepts fondamentaux de la
psychanalyse—Congresses.   2. Psychoanalysis—Congresses.
I. Feldstein, Richard.   II. Fink, Bruce, 1956– . III. Jaanus,
Maire.   IV. Title: Lacan's Four Fundamental Concepts of
Psychoanalysis.   V. Series.
BF173.R3656   1995
150.19'5—dc20   93-50120
                                                                    CIP

10 9 8 7 6 5 4 3 2 1

CONTENTS

v

PREFACE

Bruce Fink

Psychoanalysis is not a science. Not yet, at any rate—not in the sense in which "science" is currently understood. Unlike the "hard" sciences, it is a praxis constituted by certain aims, ends, and desires. Since the demise of alchemy, desire has been excluded from the sciences, despite the historian's and the biographer's keen awareness of the importance of the individual scientist's motives and personality.

Some people have tried to render psychology scientific by asking patients to fill out questionnaires and take standardized tests before, during, and after therapy to provide "objective" criteria for evaluating the psychotherapeutic process. As important as such information about whether or not analysands feel they are being or have been helped may be to *Consumer Reports*-type publications, they establish nothing about the epistemological status of psychoanalysis itself. Instead they relegate psychoanalysis to the status of public opinion polls.

While any field of study can produce statistical data (whether the effect of advertising on TV viewers, the popularity of presidential candidates, visitors' reactions to zoo exhibits, etc.), the type of scientificity proper to psychoanalysis derives from the formulation of the psychoanalytic process in generic—i.e., abstract theoretical—terms. Each moment or movement in analytic treatment can be understood in terms of identification, alienation, separation, fantasy, and so on, each of these terms being formulated and developed within psychoanalytic theory.

This kind of formalization—which Lacan takes as far as providing a sort of algebra with which to formulate certain aspects of analytic experience (S_1 and S_2 standing for the most elementary matrix of language, $\math$ for the subject split into conscious and unconscious, *a* for the cause of desire, and so on), constituting a form of mathematization which is not quantifiable, but provides restrictive "formulas" or formulations which reduce experience to its bare psychoanalytic essentials—allows one to compare the various forms of psychotherapy and psychoanalysis, predict their outcomes, and critique their methods.

A critique of methods, however, requires a well-developed theory of the aims of analysis. Physics and chemistry can do without aims. Game theory— the "conjectural science" with which Lacan most closely associates psychoanalysis—begins with an aim, but a rather simplistic, unchanging one: winning. Psychoanalysis is a practice, and as such requires a praxis whereby aims and theory constantly interact. This is what Lacan provides, and it is quite rare in the history of psychoanalysis: a sustained attempt to examine ever further the aims of analysis on the basis of advances in theory, and to develop ever further theorization on the basis of revised views of analysis' aims.

The aims of psychoanalysis have faded into the background—they are considered too obvious and well known to warrant discussion. To most analysts, psychoanalysis seeks to alleviate the patient's symptoms and readapt him or her to social reality. Yet neither Freud nor Lacan ever adopts or endorses any such aims. Psychoanalysis' aims have, to Lacan's mind, more to do with psychoanalytic theory itself and the patient's predicament. If the analysand sustains that s/he never gets what s/he wants because s/he always does something to sabotage things, the knots in his or her desire need to be undone. If that doesn't lead to satisfaction, perhaps that implies something about the nature of desire itself—namely, that desire has no object, pursuing instead its own maintenance and furtherance: more desire, ever greater desire. Yet in fantasy, the analysand is fixated on a specific object which arouses his or her desire. How is that fixation to be transformed? What is the analyst to aim at with regards to that object which causes the analysand's desire: Putting a new object in its place (is it even substitutable?), i.e., maintaining the basic structure of that fantasy while displacing its object, leaving intact the fixation? Changing the subject-object relationship altogether—i.e., reconfiguring the fantasy? What does transforming or "traversing" fantasy—putting the subject in the place of the object—lead to? A desiring subject. And isn't that state of pure desirousness what is required of the analyst in order to avoid the identification trap whereby the analysand identifies with the analyst and tries to become like him or her?

By formulating fantasy as a relationship ($\lozenge$) between the subject ($\math$) and that object (*a*) which causes his or her desire ($\math\ \lozenge\ a$), Lacan is able to indicate how the analyst can elude the role of the all-knowing, judgmental

Other, repository of all social values, and come to play the role of object *a* instead, thereby orchestrating a change in the subject's fantasy. By defining the three orders of the symbolic, imaginary, and real, Lacan is able to discern three possible corresponding positions of the analyst in the analytic relationship—Other, other, or object *a*—and indicate the kinds of dangers the first two involve by analyzing case histories in the literature where such positions have clearly been adopted. This conceptual advance in turn clarifies the analyst's aim, and allows him or her to better maneuver into the position of object *a*—desirousness.

In Lacan's work, theory informs analysis' aims and practice and vice-versa. Analysis is not pragmatic in its aims, if pragmatism means compliance with social, economic, and political norms and realities. It is a praxis of jouissance, and jouissance is anything but practical. It ignores the needs of capital, health insurance companies, socialized health care, public order, and "mature adult relationships." The techniques psychoanalysts must use to deal with it wreak havoc on the principle that time is money and on accepted notions of "professional conduct." While therapists in our society are expected to interact with their patients in ways which are clearly for their own *good* (always understood in terms of what is socially acceptable at a particular historical moment), analysts act instead for their analysands' *Eros*.

In 1963, a great deal of pressure was put on Lacan to change his practice or stop training analysts if he wanted to remain part of the French psychoanalytic institute, the *Société française de psychanalyse*, of which he had been a member for many years. He refused, and Seminar XI is a product of that refusal. It marks a turning point in Lacan's life and in his teaching as well. While presenting many continuities with the work that had gone before, Seminar XI also represents a break: a break from Freud, which is by no means anti-Freudian in thrust—from the reliance on one of Freud's articles or books as the crux of each and every seminar, and from such great dependence on Freud's conceptualizations, Lacan allowing himself ever greater theoretical latitude thereafter—and a break from the association Freud had formed, the International Psychoanalytical Association (IPA). In 1964 Lacan founded his own school, the *École freudienne de Paris* (EFP), initiating his search for new institutional forms and procedures. His concern with the teaching or "transmission" and "transmissibility" of psychoanalysis came to the fore, resulting, for example, in ever greater formalization and in a procedure for evaluating analytic transmission known as the "pass."

Each of the speakers whose papers are collected in this volume presents this turning point in Lacan's work in his or her own way, emphasizing theoretical and/or clinical aspects of Lacan's "break" from Freud, and from the "early Lacan" as well. Rather than summarize them here, I prefer to let them make their own cases. Instead, let me provide a little background on this collection.

Richard Feldstein, professor of English at Rhode Island College, editor of the journal *Literature and Psychology*, and author of numerous books on psychoanalysis and cultural theory, came up with the idea of holding several-week-long seminars in English in Paris, with the members of the *École de la Cause freudienne* (ECF, the school of psychoanalysis Lacan founded shortly before his death) giving the lion's share of the lectures. He approached Jacques-Alain Miller—head of the ECF, chairman of the Department of Psychoanalysis at the University of Paris VIII, and general editor of all of Lacan's seminars—who put him into contact with me (I was finishing my analytic training at the ECF at the time). With the assistance of Ellie Ragland, professor of English at the University of Missouri-Columbia and author of two books on Lacan, Roger Williams University instructor Kate Mele, whose organizational energy and enthusiasm were indispensable, and the organizational and moral support of many members of the ECF, we organized two "Lacan Seminars in English," the first in June 1989 (cf. the companion volume to this one) on Lacan's Seminars I and II, and the second in July 1990 on Seminar XI.

The members of the ECF who generously gave of their time by lecturing to the participants, and whose contributions are collected here, include Jacques-Alain Miller, Colette Soler, Éric Laurent, François Regnault, Marie-Hélène Brousse, Pierre-Gilles Gueguen, Jean-Pierre Klotz, Antonio Quinet, and Anne Dunand; the first five of them are also professors in the Department of Psychoanalysis at the University of Paris VIII, Saint-Denis. Contributions by ECF members Vincent Palomera, Dominique Miller, Claude Léger, Françoise Koehler, and Françoise Gorog will appear in the companion volume to this one. Lectures by many other members of the ECF and other Lacan Seminar faculty could not be included in the present volume due to inadequate tape recordings: our sincere apologies to Dominique Laurent, Michael Turnheim, Henry Sullivan, Silvia Rodríguez, Darian Leader, Mark Bracher, Leonardo Rodríguez, and Russell Grigg.

Maire Jaanus is a professor of English at Barnard College, author of *Literature and Negation*, and one of the editors of this volume. Robert Samuels is a Lacanian analyst teaching and practicing in New York City, and author of *Between Philosophy and Psychoanalysis: Lacan's Reconstruction of Freud*. Hanjo Berressem is a professor of English at the University of Aachen in Germany, and author of *Pynchon's Poetics*. Slavoj Žižek is a researcher at the Institute for Sociology in Ljubljana, Slovenia, and author of numerous books on Lacan, politics, and film.

On behalf of the three editors of the present volume, I would like to thank all of the speakers here for their gracious generosity in speaking to us in what was for many of them a foreign tongue, and so clearly and elegantly formulating Lacan's views for us. Special thanks go to Dr. Françoise Gorog, who organized a very stimulating daylong series of talks and case presentations at Sainte-Anne Hospital (her case presentation is included in the companion volume to this one), and to the whole of her staff who gave us a very warm welcome two years in a row. Judith Miller helped provide us with classroom space at the *Collège freudien* and the ECF, and welcomed us into her home, as did Françoise Gorog, Colette Soler, and Jean-Jacques Gorog. Jacques-Alain Miller, apart from lecturing and inviting us into his home, made the whole of the seminar possible by supporting the idea and its realization every step of the way.

Many people assisted in many ways in the preparation of the manuscript: Héloïse Fink, Ashley Hoffman, Tom Ratekin, Arielle Jarmuth, Jennifer Rutherford (who transcribed Jacques-Alain Miller's talks), Craig Saper, Beatriz Sanchez-Guadarrama, Yan Shen, Suzette Thibeault, Sara Williams, Paula Delfiore, Ling Xiao Hong, Susan Beller, Ann Murphy, and Rituja Mehta. On behalf of all of the editors, I would like to express heartfelt thanks for what was often an extremely fastidious task, for this volume represents no ordinary collection of papers. Unlike most conferences and conventions where at least a majority of the contributors are native speakers of the language in which the conference is held, or where interpreters render a talk in the speaker's native tongue into that of the people in the audience, we decided to invite primarily French speakers to address an English-speaking (primarily non-French-speaking) audience. This allowed for greater contact between speakers and participants, but vastly complicated the work of the editors of this volume.

The transcription of the tapes of the lectures was a formidable undertaking. Each lecture was then extensively edited, our goal being less to preserve the "letter" of the talks than to ensure their comprehensibility. In no case have we tried to make the text say something other than what it seemed the speaker meant to say; we have, however, sought to eliminate Gallicisms, grammatical formulations based on French structure, repetitions, and inaccuracies. A modicum of informality is lost thereby, but we feel that the gains in understanding far outweigh the losses. While the essence of communication remains miscommunication, we have nevertheless managed to remove some of the more obvious obstacles.

Questions and answers during and after lectures were particularly difficult to transcribe, and have been left out despite their important contribution to the conference as a whole. Wherever possible, references to the English editions of Lacan's work have been provided, but we have taken numerous liberties with the existing translations of Seminar XI and the *Écrits*—their inadequacies are becoming ever more glaring as our understanding of Lacan's work grows. Page references to Seminar XI always correspond to Alan Sheridan's 1978 English translation published by Norton. "*Écrits* 1966" refers to the French edition published by Seuil in Paris, while "*Écrits*" alone refers to Alan Sheridan's 1977 English translation published by Norton.

The reader will note that we have included at the end of this volume the first English translation ever to appear in print of Lacan's article from the *Écrits*, "Position of the Unconscious." It is a perfect companion piece to Seminar XI, as it takes up a considerable number of the subjects covered therein—the unconscious, the drives, alienation and separation, transference, the "lamella," and so on—at a still higher level of abstraction. And it is quoted and/or alluded to in many of the papers presented in this volume.

Originally written in 1960, "Position of the Unconscious" was considerably reworked for its 1964 publication in *VIᵉ Colloque de Bonneval : l'Inconscient* (Paris: Desclée de Brouwer, 1966), and further reworked for its 1966 publication in the *Écrits*. Thus it presents a slice of Lacan's more "mature" work in which the real has truly come into its own, object *a* is viewed as a part of the subject's libido located outside of his or her own body, and sexual difference is articulated in terms suggestive of Lacan's 1970s formulas of sexuation.

The article is, strictly speaking, unreadable, once again confirming Lacan's appraisal of his *Écrits* in Seminar XX: they were not meant to be read ("*ils n'étaient pas à lire*" [29]). Indeed, they were not written in such a way as to facilitate the reader's task. Rather they were written to be *worked over*—unabridged dictionaries and an immense library in hand (including all of Lacan's seminars and his other *Écrits*)—mulled over, diagrammed, pieced together, dreamt about, and reformulated in non-Lacanian French. Their translation into other languages is obviously impossible, at one level, when not altogether ridiculous.

Some will, no doubt, feel that what is to be gleaned from this particular *Écrit* does not justify the effort of working it over and over and over. Others will, I hope, find the text an inexhaustible source of provocative formulations that stick with them even if they aren't the least bit sure what they mean:

> [T]he signifier as such, whose first purpose is to bar the subject, has brought into him the meaning of death. (The letter kills, but we learn this from the letter itself.) That is why every drive is virtually a death drive.

> [P]sychoanalysts are part and parcel of the concept of the unconscious.

> [The subject] was first produced at the other's summoning.

> The subject, the Cartesian subject, is the presupposition of the unconscious. . . . The Other is the dimension required in order for speech

to affirm itself as truth. The unconscious is, between the two of them, their cut in act.

The effect of language is to introduce the cause into the subject. Through this effect, he is not the cause of himself; he bears within himself the worm of the cause that splits him. For his cause is the signifier, without which there would be no subject in the real.

Jacques-Alain Miller and Seuil have been kind enough to allow us to include this "piece" by Lacan here; the royalties associated with it and with the cover photo were generously covered by Barnard College, which financed the index of this book as well.

It should be noted that, while many of the papers (including "Position of the Unconscious" by Lacan) presented here refer to the "subject" as he or him, not she or her, this is largely a byproduct of the translation process: in French, the noun "subject" is masculine, and thus all references back to it require masculine pronouns and possessive pronouns. (This is no doubt also in part due to older English-language conventions—it should be kept in mind that few of the lecturers learned English fewer than twenty years ago!) While we have not changed these references in every case, *it should be understood that references to the subject* (unless a particular subject is being discussed) *always imply a subject of either sex*.

PART I

EXCOMMUNICATION

CONTEXT AND CONCEPTS

Jacques-Alain Miller

Seminar XI, which you are studying this year, was the first of Lacan's seminars I participated in and the first I edited. Lacan arrived on the fifteenth of January 1964, at the *École normale supérieure*, in what was called the *Salle Dussane*, the theater of the *École normale* named after a famous French actress of the *Comédie française*, and said "Ladies and gentlemen, in this series of lectures, which I have been invited to give by the *École Pratique des Hautes Études*, I shall be talking to you about the fundamentals of psychoanalysis."

It was the very first time I saw him and heard him speak. When he finished his lecture that day he asked the students of the *École normale* to come and introduce themselves to him. I went with my friends, and he asked our names. He then asked us to write them down with our addresses, and we shook hands. If I remember correctly, I asked him a question about an error in one of his schemas that had been reproduced in a psychology journal, and he responded affirmatively. Two or three times during that year, between January and June 1964, he met with three or four of us privately at the *École normale* for small question and answer sessions. For instance, when he says on page 149 at the end of chapter 12 in Seminar XI, "Last time, I ended with a formulation which, I later realized, was well received," he was alluding to one of those private meetings where we questioned him about his formulation, "transference is the enactment of the reality of the unconscious."

Ten years later I edited Seminar XI. I did not do it for the public. I really did it for him in response to a challenge. Please excuse me for reminiscing. Many of Lacan's students had asked him if they could edit his seminars by the time I started in 1973, but they always tried to rearrange the stenography or intertwine what he said with their own considerations, and he was never really satisfied. He was always grumbling that it would not do, even when he allowed a few summaries to appear here and there. He had just rejected the complete manuscript of one of his seminars, edited by a former student at the *École normale* (who had spent a year working on it) when I said to him that it ought to be done step by step. It ought, I said, to be done sentence by sentence, every lecture constituting a chapter, nothing being left out or moved around. Today this seems quite natural, but at the time it had not yet occurred to people that everything Lacan said was worth writing down and studying.

When I said that it ought to be done that way, he gazed at me. You have all, I imagine, read something about the gaze. He gazed at me, which had some weight, and all he said was, "prove it." Before he said "prove it," I had no idea that I wanted to do it myself. I discovered it at that very moment. "Prove it" is the formulation of a challenge. I believe he recognized that desire in me, and at the same time, proving it was an invitation to prove myself. Furthermore, he was astute enough to say it in the language of logic, for it was a challenge formulated in that language. Thus he recognized my logical side as well. He took me at my word and asked for a commitment: "don't just say it, do it." As a matter of fact, I could prove it only by doing it.

It was also a matter of proving that I could satisfy him, who was so well known for being unsatisfied. I jumped at the challenge, not knowing that I was thereby deciding, as it were, my fate. Not knowing what I was saying, I claimed that it would be finished in one month. I worked night and day for a month and finished in time. I gave him the first draft of twenty chapters from the seminar, which I had converted from the stenography. He read it and was satisfied. Shortly afterwards I began to revise the draft, discussing a few points with him before completing it. He eventually offered to let me do the whole series of his seminars, which I had no idea I wanted to do. As you know, I'm still not through with it, and I am sometimes reproached for not doing it quickly enough.

Again and again, I come back to this seminar, which in some ways is particularly dear to me, but in other ways is not because the commitment I made at that time still weighs upon me. Be that as it may, I come back to this seminar frequently. It was not until the course I gave in 1981–1982, many years after having attended and rewritten Seminar XI, that I was satisfied with my understanding of alienation and separation, which you find in chapters 16 and 17 entitled "The Subject and the Other." And it was not until my course in 1982–1983 that I was satisfied that I had grasped the chapters on the drive. In my course, "From the Symptom to Fantasy and Back Again," I tried to reconstruct various parts of Seminar XI. Every year, at one moment or another, I would look at the seminar from a new perspective. I attended it as a student, edited it as a professor, and commented on it publicly as a psychoanalyst. Thus it has been with me during various periods of my life.

This past year I spoke about it in my course, emphasizing the sense in which it is a debate with Freud. Even more than that, a quarrel with Freud is secretly going on in the text. I believe I grasped this aspect better now because we have been having some institutional problems in the *École de la Cause freudienne* lately; these circumstances have made me see just how embattled Lacan was in 1964 when he gave this seminar. It is not just the seminar of a thinker—Lacan was also a fighting man at the time. He was trying to prove himself, and we see this at the very beginning when he asks, "Am I qualified to [give this seminar]?" He expands on his qualifications, mentioning his having given his seminars for ten years, but then goes on to say, "I consider the problem deferred for the time being."

It is the seminar of someone beginning anew. There is a cut between his ten previous seminars and this one. The ten previous seminars had been given in Sainte-Anne Hospital in a lecture hall that held fifty and later one hundred people. For Seminar XI, he left the psychiatric hospital for a lecture hall at the *École normale*, 45 rue d'Ulm, right near the Pantheon. His lecture hall there opened directly onto the street, and, whereas for the ten previous years one had to register to get into the psychiatric hospital, with this seminar things were quite different. Anyone from the Latin Quarter could come inside and listen. It was not just fifty or one hundred selected people; the numbers grew to three hundred. Some years later, at the *Faculté de Droit* near the Pantheon, six hundred people came to listen to him lecture.

But it was not just a matter of changing places; it was also a matter of changing audiences. The previous seminars were given to an audience of clinicians, while this seminar was the first to address the general public—not only clinicians but students, professors, and others in the humanities. There was a specific audience as well: the students of the *École normale*. When Lacan began by asking whether or not psychoanalysis is a science, he was clearly addressing a few of us who were, at that time, students of Althusser's. Althusser had suggested that Lacan come to the *École normale* and they had had some discussions. Lacan was always very attentive to those in his audience who spoke, and thus he did, at least in the beginning, try to relate to us.

The seminar for that year. was announced as "The Names-of-the-Father," but apart from the first lecture, Lacan decided not to give that seminar because of institutional problems in the analytic group he was part of at that time. A split had occurred, and under pressure from the International Psychoanalytical Association (IPA), some of his old companions decided to forbid him from being a training analyst. I will not mention them. I believe they are all forgotten or unknown. In any case, he decided to cancel his seminar and never give one on the same exact subject again. In the following years he reiterated again and again that he had not given his seminar on the names-of-the-father, and would never give it, because he believed people were not prepared to hear what he had to say, or perhaps because nobody deserved to attend such a seminar. At the beginning of my course in November I proposed, however, that he gave the seminar in a disguised way, and that instead of the names-of-the-father, we have Freud's fundamental concepts. Secretly it *was* delivered.

Lacan founded his own school in 1964. Previously he had just wanted to be readmitted into the IPA. Let me remind you that Lacan was not thrown out of the IPA. In 1953, he decided with some colleagues to leave the French institute, the *Société psychanalytique de Paris,* because it was moving in an authoritarian direction he could not accept. They left the French institute and asked that their new group be accredited by the IPA. A similar situation arose in New York, for example, when, following a split, a second group was recognized by the IPA and later even a third one. In many cities in the United States there are two different institutes, both of which are recognized by the IPA. But in 1963, Marie Bonaparte, who was on the central committee and friendly with Anna Freud, Hartmann, and the others, convinced them to send a letter to Lacan saying that they were awfully sorry, but since Lacan had left the French institute, he was no longer a member of the IPA. Lacan and his colleagues were very surprised by this answer. I found this letter in Lacan's archives and published a photo of it. It was signed by Ruth Eissler, the wife of Kurt Eissler, who determined a lot in the history of psychoanalysis. But for ten years after 1953, Lacan and his friends tried to prove that they were worthy of being asked back into the fold. In 1963 they received a definite "no" from the IPA and split from the group. At that point, Lacan, who had never wanted to create his own school, did so, and he called it the *École freudienne* (Freudian School) to prove he was not a dissident. Despite not being accepted back into the IPA, he had no intention of following Jung's or Adler's path, and remained faithful to Freud. Lacan's *École freudienne* was founded on the 21st of June, which falls textually between chapters 19 and 20 of Seminar XI.

So that was the context of Lacan's institutional battle. Lacan is very discreet about it in his lectures. It is only in the first chapter that we are given a context for the dispute; in it he asks a fundamental question concerning Freud's responsibility for what had occurred in the IPA. The latter was created by Freud, and Lacan's opinion is that Freud wanted the IPA as it is today, that Freud himself wanted an institution to preserve his work faithfully, to preserve the letter of his work, even at the risk of condemning analytic experience to a standstill. We have no proof that Sigmund Freud was betrayed by the IPA. We know, for instance, that he desperately tried to have his American students accept non-medical doctors as analysts, and he discussed this in "The Question of Lay Analysis." Freud's correspondence attests to his desperation at having been foiled by his American students who were prepared to split with him rather than accept lay analysts. In that sense we may say that Freud was betrayed and that he gave up because he had no power. Or that he had to choose between what he wanted, i.e. the truth of analytic experience, and the worldwide spread of psychoanalysis. He chose worldwide spread over truth. As he wrote to one of the faithful, "I would rather have an international movement because we may be forced into exile." He had astonishing foresight.

Thus Lacan does not follow the usual approach of saying that Freud was betrayed by the IPA. He says, on the contrary, that the IPA corresponds to something in Freud: a preference for what Lacan calls a formal preservation of his message, rather than the living spirit of psychoanalysis. What is thrown into question in this seminar is the way in which Freud himself organized the cult of the dead father. For instance, when Lacan explains that Freud was oriented in the discovery of the field of the unconscious by his self-analysis, he asks, "And what is his self-analysis, if not the brilliant mapping of the law of desire hinging on the Name-of-the-Father?" (48) This sentence stresses a link between Freud's self-analysis and the Oedipus complex, which is the relationship between the law of desire and the Name-of-the-Father. Do not think that in saying this, Lacan is saying that's all there is to it. He stresses this point in the seminar precisely because he's trying to go beyond the link between the law of desire and the Name-of-the-Father. He stresses the fact that the result of Freud's self-analysis is a limitation in Freud's perspective. Lacan throws the Name-of-the-Father into question, and this questioning of Freud is presented as, "I'm going to talk about the four fundamental concepts of psychoanalysis."

He announced the title of the seminar as *The Fundamentals of Psychoanalysis* (you'll find this in the first pages). But, as he immediately presented the four concepts, we in the audience used to refer to the seminar as *The Four Fundamental Concepts*. Later Lacan accepted this title from his audience.

The Four Fundamental Concepts of Psychoanalysis appears to be a tribute to Freud, since the four concepts are taken directly from his work. Just as Lacan at that time calls his institute the "Freudian School," in his seminar he uses the term "Freudian concepts" just to prove that he is not a dissident. But within this "tribute" he tries to go beyond Freud. Not a beyond Freud which leaves Freud behind; it is a beyond Freud which is nevertheless in Freud. Lacan is looking for something in Freud's work of which Freud himself was unaware. Something which we may call "extimate," as it is so very intimate that Freud himself was not aware of it. So very intimate that this intimacy is extimate. It is an internal beyond.

Here and there in the text you find elements of a reanalysis of Freud, a questioning of the limitations of Freud's self-analysis. In doing this, Lacan tries to understand his own position as an outcast in the international psychoanalytic movement. He is not fighting in his own name alone, because he believes that his rejection by the IPA is part of something larger. He says, "I am referring to something that I can only call the refusal of the concept." (18) Refusal is perhaps not the best translation. In French it's *le refus du concept* (perhaps "rejection" of the concept is better than "refusal"). It means something along the lines of putting something outside, like repression. He identifies what he presents in the first chapter as an excommunication, and theorizes it as a rejection of the concept. That's why he stresses the Freudian concepts, but at the same time here and there we can hear something other than a celebration of the Freudian concepts. For instance, in the first chapter, when he asks those seemingly rhetorical questions, we may hear something else. "What are the formulations in psychoanalysis concerned with? What motivates and modulates this 'sliding away' (*glissement*) of the object? Are there psychoanalytic concepts that we are now in possession of? How are we to understand the almost religious maintenance of the terms proposed by Freud to structure analytic experience? Was Freud really the first, and did he really remain the only theoretician of this supposed science to have introduced fundamental concepts? Were this so, it would be very unusual in the history of the sciences." (10)

Lacan raises epistemological questions about psychoanalytic concepts, but in doing so he is really asking whether Freud's concepts are to remain the only worthwhile ones in psychoanalysis. It is clear—as is true in the case of Lacan's "Seminar on 'The Purloined Letter' "—that in giving a seminar on the four fundamental concepts of psychoanalysis he is introducing other concepts which, strictly speaking, are not found in Freud's work, and which Lacan considers his own. Whereas, during the first ten years of his seminar Lacan always took up a text of Freud's (the first year it was Freud's technical writings, the third year it was the Schreber case, in *The Ethics of Psychoanalysis* it was *Civilization and its Discontents*), this time he does not do so. He takes on Freud as such, and in the following years of his seminar he never again takes up a text of Freud's in the same way. Here and there he discusses a text, but he does not build his whole seminar around one of Freud's articles or books. Instead, every year he builds on one of his own schemas or concepts.

Within these epistemological questions and this celebration of Freud, we thus see not a debasement of Freud, but what might be called a substitution. A kind of rewriting of Freud, a version of Freud that Lacan adopts; but this is done secretly, or at least discreetly, because at the same time he has to prove himself to be Freud's true heir. This might be referred to as the strategy of the seminar.

In some sense I knew this from the outset. But I was only really able to formulate it clearly this year.

In the limited time we have left, let us consider the four fundamental concepts. First, the unconscious. This Freudian concept has been completely neglected by ego-psychologists to the extent that, to them, the unconscious is not even a fundamental concept. They do not know what to do with the unconscious because they consider Freud's first topography—unconscious, preconscious, and conscious—to have been completely superseded by the second topography—ego, superego, and id. Hence they discard the first topography altogether.

Lacan revitalizes the Freudian concept of the unconscious, introducing thereby the concept of the subject. Indeed, he introduces the unconscious as a subject, for the subject is not a Freudian concept even if, when Freud says *Ich*, he is sometimes referring to the subject. When Freud says *das Ich*, he is often referring to the ego. The subject is a Lacanian concept, a reordering of Freud's work.

When Lacan takes up the second fundamental concept, repetition, he introduces the connection between S_1 and S_2, which is the articulation of things. When he presents transference, it is through a combination of the first and second—subject and knowledge—which is the subject supposed to know. And with the concept of drives he introduces jouissance.

What I am suggesting is another reading of Seminar XI. It may be read at two levels. On the one hand, it is a revitalization or celebration of Freud and, on the other, it's the introduction of a new way of speaking about psychoanalysis, a refoundation of psychoanalysis.

With his four fundamental concepts, it is as if Lacan were presenting the unconscious in four distinct ways. Indeed, there are four distinct representations of analytic experience—four distinct ways of grasping what is going on in an analysis. It is not at all an abstract seminar; it is a seminar that is very close to actual analytic practice.

The seminar poses the question, "What is talking?" How do we grasp the phenomenon of talking in analysis? Lacan privileges the gaps. He chooses to define the unconscious—and it's only one definition among many—as "impediment, failure, split." Here he is very close to Freud's first discovery, a discovery rejected by ego-psychologists who think that Freud did not know as much as they do. "Impediment, failure, split. In a spoken or written sentence something stumbles. Freud is attracted by these phenomena, and it is there that he seeks the unconscious. There, something other demands to be realized—which appears as intentional, of course, but of a strange temporality. What occurs, what is *produced*, in this gap, is presented as *the discovery*. It is in this way that the Freudian exploration first encounters what occurs in the unconscious." (25)

Here Lacan is very close to *The Interpretation of Dreams*, *The Psychopathology of Everyday Life*, and *Jokes and their Relation to the Unconscious*. At the same time, what he says is very practical. Freudian analysts are attracted to these phenomena and, when they occur, it is easy to say, "that's it." Lacan makes this same point in the preface to the English language edition of Seminar XI that he wrote in 1976: "When the space of a lapsus no longer carries any meaning (or interpretation), only then is one sure that one is in the unconscious. *One knows*." (vii) Thus even though he is stressing another point, a gap in meaning, he is also trying to focus on the times one is led to say, "that's it." Lacan presents that moment as precisely the one in ordinary discourse when we would say, "that's not it." In analytic experience something is inverted, and we say, "that's it" when a miss or a failure occurs. That is what Lacan calls the subject. He tries to present the unconscious as something that is both a modality of nothingness and a modality of being. It is a strange kind of being that appears when it ought not to: precisely when a strange intention is being realized. Lacan chose to stress the unconscious as subject, a subject which has no substance, which is a stumbling, since something does not fit but expands to fill desire itself.

In some ways, when Lacan says "subject," it is equivalent to saying "desire"—something which does not fit. But that is not the whole of the Freudian unconscious because the unconscious also appears as repetition. That is what Lacan presents as the network of signifiers. The unconscious is also an articulation of signifiers, and we can see Freud practically producing this field of investigation by noticing in his patients' speech what appears again and again in their dreams and parapraxes. Freud thereby invents his own Rosetta stone, pinpointing his own version of Champollion's cartouche. Just as Freud notices repetitive occurrences, Lacan first stresses the unconscious as a stumbling, but also emphasizes the repetition of the unconscious that always says the same thing.

It is important to stress the unconscious as repetition, because it is completely different from stressing the unconscious as resistance, which is so fundamental in ego-psychology. The thesis that Lacan develops in this book is that the unconscious does not resist so much as it repeats. In some ways, resistance disappears in this text. It does not appear at all as a fundamental concept, or even as a secondary concept. Lacan stresses repetition

instead of resistance, and when he speaks of transference he stresses deception, not resistance. Lacan says:

> As you saw with the notion of cross-checking, the function of return,
> *Wiederkehr*, is essential. It is not only *Wiederkehr* in the sense of that
> which has been repressed—the very constitution of the field of the uncon-
> scious is based on *Wiederkehr*. Freud bases his certainty on that. (47–8)

And he says:

> . . . there is only one method of knowing that one is there, namely, to map
> the network. And how is a network mapped? One goes back and forth over
> one's ground, one crosses one's path, one cross-checks it again and again,
> and in the seventh chapter of *The Interpretation of Dreams* there is no
> other confirmation of one's *Gewissheit*, one's certainty, than this—'Speak
> of chance, gentlemen, if you like. In my experience I have observed noth-
> ing arbitrary in this field, for it is cross-checked in such a way that chance
> is eliminated.' (45)

This is another perspective on the unconscious: the unconscious is not
merely a gap, but repetition; and through this cross-checking, a network is
constituted.

Let us move on to the unconscious as transference. Transference is
one aspect of the unconscious and (I did not discover this until the seven-
ties, *à la* "The Purloined Letter"), in Seminar XI, transference and repetition are treated as two distinct concepts. That was not a common theory of
transference; for a long time Freud himself considered transference to be a
modality of repetition, a repetition of primary love for the fundamental
object in the patient's infancy. That is, first you love your father, for example, and that is all you want. You have a primary love object, which you
supposedly transfer onto the analyst by repeating past relationships. What
is fundamental in Lacan's construction is the complete splitting and separation of these two concepts in order to propose a new theory of transference.
Lacan says this very precisely: "repetition is something the true nature of
which"—i.e., repetition as a network of signifiers—"is always veiled in analysis, because of the identification of repetition with transference in analysts'
conceptualization." (54) This was a true breakthrough which Lacan had not
arrived at before. In the *Écrits* you find various attempts to theorize transference in which transference is viewed as a modality of repetition. Here we
have a breakthrough which ought to surprise everyone, in that these two
concepts are completely distinguished.

Lacan connects transference with psychical reality, for instance, when
he defines transference as "the enactment of the reality of the unconscious." But it takes on its true meaning only when you distinguish reality

from the real. So when Lacan says, "transference is the enactment of the reality of the unconscious," he is not saying the enactment of the real of the unconscious; as you will see, that is a fundamental distinction. He shows that *the reality of the unconscious is always ambiguous and deceptive, whereas repetition is connected to the real, which does not deceive.* When Lacan talks about anxiety in Seminar X, he distinguishes anxiety from all other affects, saying that in analysis and in life, anxiety is the only affect which does not mislead or deceive. He shows how anxiety is connected to what he calls the real. It is a function that one may not grasp, but it does not deceive.

To understand Seminar XI, you have to connect transference with reality as deceptive, and repetition with the real as that which does not mislead. When you present the unconscious as transference, you present it as something which misleads and deceives—a view that is very much present in Freud's work. For instance, when Freud discusses his patients' dreams regarding analysis, he points to his patients' attempts to satisfy something in their analyst by dreaming. If you take the plasticity and mobility of dreams seriously, you have to admit that the unconscious is not truth itself without at the same time being a lie: the analytic concept of truth is connected with lying. That is what Lacan means when he says that truth has a fictional structure, and this is borne out in his lectures on transference here.

Fourth, you have the unconscious as drive. This was always present in Lacan's work, and he develops the point later in *Television*. The subject, at some level, is always happy, is always enjoying himself. As Freud says in *Beyond the Pleasure Principle*, one way or another, be it through apparent unhappiness or displeasure, the subject obtains satisfaction. Even if we try to go beyond the pleasure principle, this beyond stresses something which is an internal beyond of the pleasure principle. Freud explained this very precisely: when the pleasure principle fails, the reality principle is triggered. Thus while the pleasure principle may fail, the reality principle takes upon itself the task imposed by the pleasure principle. The reality principle takes the place of and carries on the task of the pleasure principle when the latter fails. The reality principle is actually a more cumbersome way of obtaining satisfaction. When you are dreaming and you have a nightmare, you open your eyes and connect with reality because the dream has failed to protect your sleep, which is the fundamental task of dreaming (true, a dream fulfills a wish, but first and foremost it serves to protect sleep). The pleasure principle has failed, and so you open your eyes, as Lacan says, to continue dreaming with your eyes open. That's why Lacan says that reality is fantasy. We receive data through sense perception, but with the exception of this supposed pure data, reality is fantasy. Thus we must distinguish the reality that is equal to fantasy from what we call the real, which refers to that which is satisfied by the overwhelming and all-powerful pleasure principle: something that does not change, which requires all our dreaming and all our waking, but that is nevertheless pleasure.

Freud draws a distinction between the goal and the aim of the drive. You may or may not have the object of the drive—food, for example, in the case of the oral drive. Nevertheless, as Freud says, the object itself is unimportant. It may be this or that, but what remains the same is what is satisfied in the circuit of the drive. Even if you don't have the goal, you realize the aim, which is jouissance.

I have presented various ways to schematize these four fundamental concepts. The first concept, the unconscious as subject, is grounded in hysteria because the clinical structure of hysteria presents this privileging of desire. Repetition is better illustrated by obsessive neurosis; that is why Lacan refers to the "Rat Man's" repetition compulsion. In Seminar XI, you can read the chapters on the unconscious in relation to the Dora case, and the chapters on repetition in relation to the Rat Man case. The chapters on transference refer to the lies of hysteria, whereas the chapters on the drives refer essentially to that part of analytic experience which does not lie. In this trajectory we move from the unconscious to the id—which is why Lacanians unify Freud's first and second topographies. We go from the unconscious, which refers to the distinction unconscious/preconscious/conscious, to the drives which refer to the id.

What I would like to show you, however, is the homologous structure present in Lacan's conceptualization of all four of these terms. In some sense, he is really speaking of the same thing in four different ways.

First, he presents the unconscious by what he calls its formations: dreams, parapraxes, etc. In the case of parapraxes, you bungle what you want to say or do. You make a mistake, and that is precisely where the analyst may say, "that's right." Therein lies the truth: not in what you wanted to say, but in what you effectively said or did. Thus we have a reversal of values: you missed your goal, but your true aim was achieved. This is what Lacan presents at the end of Seminar XI as the distinction between goal and aim. This structure is already there in Lacan's presentation of the unconscious, in this strange inversion of values which is the cornerstone of analytic experience.

Repetition. Again and again, something is repeated. (The true translation of the title of Seminar XX, *Encore*, should be *Again* or *More*). What Lacan makes apparent in the section on "The Unconscious and Repetition" in Seminar XI is that you repeat because you have not fulfilled your aim. You have fulfilled something, but it is not what it ought to be. In *Encore* he says that you obtain satisfaction, but it is never the satisfaction it ought to be. That is why Lacan developed the notion of the real as that which always comes back to the same place for the subject, but which the subject does not encounter. He takes repetition as the repetition of a failure, not of a success, and this has even given rise to the concept of "failure neurosis."

That is why, for instance, Lacan distinguishes between repetition and other types of behavior. (143) Freud's concept of repetition, *Wiederholung*, has nothing to do with habit or stereotypical behavior because Freud speaks of *Wiederholung* in reference to something that is always missed, and that is lacking. Thus we can better understand what Freud meant by his "latency period": you have a primary object with which you repeatedly attempt to establish a relationship. Repetition is always connected to a lost object—it is an attempt to refind the lost object yet, in so doing, to miss it. And what is that lost object? It is illustrated in analytic theory by the mother as the fundamental primary object which, through the operation of the Name-of-the-Father, is always forbidden and lost. Lacan says that the mother is the fundamental *Ding*, the thing that is always lost and that repetition tries to recover and yet always misses.

Lacan speaks of the real as always connected with a mistake and an impossible encounter. (53) And where do we meet this real? What we have in the discovery of psychoanalysis is an encounter, an essential encounter, an appointment to which we are always summoned with a real that eludes us. It is an appointment with some thing that is never there at the meeting place. Consider the importance of appointments, meetings, and dates in the realm of love; there can be no love story with the real because you try to make a date, and repeatedly reschedule the date, but something else appears.

This is the encounter with the real that is beyond automaton, the return or insistence of signs. The real is that which lies behind automaton. That is where Lacan introduces repetition. It is not repetition that is important, but what is missed.

Thus you can see that there is a homologous relationship between Lacan's discussion of repetition and his presentation of the unconscious as subject. It is always a question of what is missed, and what in this mistake, lies or appears.

I will present the third point, transference, very briefly as we are running out of time. Here too Lacan introduces the dialectic of goal and aim. He presents transference as the fundamental deception of the unconscious, using the example of the statement, "I am lying." I will not go into all the steps of his presentation, but he shows the patient as someone who says, "I am lying" which, except in logical treatises, means "I am deceiving you." And the analyst may say at that moment, "by telling me that you are deceiving me, you are telling the truth." Lacan, in the schema you find in the chapter, "Analysis and Truth," illustrates once again this reversal of values at the very moment that you say that you are not telling the truth. Even if you lie in your dream, there are ways of interpreting your dream whereby the truth emerges. Thus here again we find the same structure as before.

The fourth concept is the drive. Lacan shows, for example, that eating is not merely a manifestation of the oral drive. The object or goal of the drive is food. But the aim of the drive is jouissance, which may very well be satisfied without any food. Anorexia, for instance, illustrates the full range of the oral drive, for the anorexic eats nothing and derives oral jouissance therefrom which is elevated to the level of being lethal—to the level of the death drive. Anorexia represents the ultimate in oral jouissance.

PART II

SUBJECT AND OTHER

ALIENATION AND SEPARATION (I)

Éric Laurent

I have chosen to speak on the concepts of alienation and separation in Seminar XI. The subtitle of chapter 16 is "Alienation," but none of the other chapters is entitled or even subtitled "Separation." I adopted this title because one of the cuts or breaks this seminar produced when it was delivered in 1964 was the introduction of alienation and separation as two operations constituting the subject. That represented a break, though it was probably not deciphered as such in those years, and a new alliance as well.

It represented a break because, at that time, what was well known to Lacan's audience was that he was applying categories derived from structuralist linguistics to psychoanalysis. Prevalent in those years was Lacan's stress on metaphor and metonymy as two operations constituting the unconscious or the work of the unconscious. We have a sign of that, for instance, in a text by François Lyotard which criticizes Lacan, by emphasizing that the unconscious, as elaborated by Freud in *The Interpretation of Dreams*, cannot be reduced to metaphor and metonymy. (Lacan replied to this criticism in *Radiophonie*, an interview aired by the Belgian Broadcasting System.) What Lacan was being criticized for was his use of these categories, derived in part from Jakobson's work. It was not fully understood in 1964 that Lacan's introduction of the concepts of alienation and separation indicated a break with those of metaphor and metonymy and his previous mapping of the unconscious.

Alienation and separation, introduced here as operators derived from formal logic, mark a further step away from Lacan's former emphasis on "full speech," with its connection to phenomenology and existentialism, the

dominant philosophies of that era. With the linguistic operations of metaphor and metonymy, he had taken one step, and with the formal sciences
and categories derived from a linguistic approach involving formal languages, not natural ones, he took a further step. Alienation and separation
are directly related to the two basic operations of first order logic.

In the first line of chapter 16, Lacan indicates the epistemological
horizon of his work—that of constituting psychoanalysis as a science. This
project goes as far as trying to define the exact nature of a science that
could include psychoanalysis. Lacan is speaking from an epistemological
point of view (to paraphrase one of Quine's titles) when he stresses that, if
psychoanalysis is to be constituted as the science of the unconscious, one
must begin with the notion that "the unconscious is structured like a
language." That is what Jacques-Alain Miller has called Lacan's main thesis.

But, the second paragraph introduces a curious deduction therefrom:
"From this I have deduced a topology." (203) How does one deduce a topology from the axiom that the unconscious is structured like a language?
This was always quite difficult to understand for Lacan's audience. It does
not seem natural. Linguists have proposed virtually no topologies that ac-
commodate the axiom of a system structured like a language.

Still more mysterious is how a topology can account for the constitution of a subject. The subject is a concept which seems to escape any
topological or logical definition. Furthermore, Lacan adds that his topology
responds to criticisms that he was neglecting the dynamic point of view in
psychoanalysis. He says:

> At a time that I hope we have now put behind us, it was objected that in
> giving precedence to structure I was neglecting the dynamics so evident
> in our experience. It was even said that I went so far as to ignore the
> principle affirmed in Freudian doctrine that this dynamics is, in its es-
> sence, through and through, sexual. (203)

We have here three steps: first, the unconscious is structured like a
language; second, a topology can be derived therefrom that accounts for the
constitution of the subject; and third, the subject in turn accounts for what
is known in psychoanalysis, though not in Lacan's teaching, as the dynamic
point of view. This subject is linked with the drives or instincts and cannot
be separated therefrom. One of the objectives of chapter 16 and the two
that follow is to substitute a topological viewpoint for the so-called dynamic
viewpoint. Lacan tries to show that these two points of view are identical,
and that what Freud presents, using energy metaphors derived from nineteenth century mechanics, has to be revised from a formal twentieth century standpoint. That standpoint, far from instituting a logic that excludes

time, includes a temporal function. Yet there is always a problem introducing time into a formal logical system.

Hegel tried to establish a logic that could include time, but his views were widely repudiated by formal logic. What Lacan tries to establish is precisely that, from his standpoint, distinct from Hegel's, a temporal function can be introduced within the "logification" of operations constituting the subject. And with that temporal function, the dynamics of transference can be thoroughly accounted for.

Jacques-Alain Miller was the first in the Lacanian community to draw out the consequences of the substitution of alienation and separation, as the new pair of opposites, for the old pair, metaphor and metonymy, especially in "The Other Lacan" (*D'un autre Lacan*), a lecture he gave in Caracas in 1980 (*Ornicar?* 28, 1984). Thanks to Miller's lecture, we can now note the importance of the mention of metonymy at the end of chapter 16:

> In this interval intersecting the signifiers, which forms part of the very structure of the signifier, is the locus of what, in other registers of my exposition, I have called metonymy. (214)

This substitution also, as I said earlier, represents a new alliance. Before the consequences of this substitution were understood, there was, in Lacan's audience, a separation between the practicing analysts and the academics. The academics were delighted by the use of metaphor/metonymy, which they knew how to handle; they saw the importance of that use and were enthralled by a new approach that stressed a method well known in literary criticism, for instance. The practicing analysts were delighted to see that all the mechanisms pointed out in *The Interpretation of Dreams* could be spoken of in terms of metaphor/metonymy, but did not see very clearly how to do anything with that, apart from sticking with the mechanisms of dream interpretation. These two separate audiences were brought together by Lacan when he defined the process of analysis, analytic treatment, in terms of alienation and separation, and the final phase of analysis, the end of the experience, in terms of separation.

Lacan founded his own school, the *École freudienne de Paris*, in 1964 and Seminar XI is the first seminar he gave to his trainees. Three years later, he made a proposition to define in his school in some precise way the end or final phase of an analysis (*Scilicet* 1, 1968). In that 1967 proposition, he introduced a new category, the "pass"—alienation and separation—to define the category of being in analysis, the ontology psychoanalysis can provide through which human sexuality can be grasped. This ontology links the subject and his desire to a want-to-be, to a lack of being, and at the same time attributes substance only to jouissance, the only substance Lacan recognizes.

Trying to define alienation in chapter 16, Lacan points out that he needs the concepts of the subject and the Other, defining the Other as "the locus in which is situated the signifying chain that governs which aspect(s) of the subject may become present." (203) This definition links the Other and the subject in a way that clearly constitutes an alienation: the subject as such can only be known in the place or locus of the Other. There is no way to define a subject as self-consciousness.

This is a point Lacan introduced long before his logical impulse. It started at the beginning of his teaching, when he opposed Sartre; Sartre was trying to establish a subject defined as an impasse in its self-consciousness.

In Sartre's play, *No Exit*, three people are in a room. Each one has committed a crime, is a murderer in one way or another, and can see the hell, torment, or tormenting logic in which the other two are trapped, but cannot admit that he himself was at fault and is tormented by guilt without being able to determine whence that guilt came. He can only know in what sense he is guilty through the two others. At the end of the play (these are not the last words, which are "let's go on," but nearly the last) is the well known sentence, "Hell is other people." In fact, we cannot know ourselves as subjects; there is no self-consciousness of ourselves—we are obliged to know ourselves via others.

Lacan replied in a very specific way to Sartre's play in an article published in 1945 entitled "Logical Time and the Assertion of Anticipated Certainty" (*Newsletter of the Freudian Field* 2, 1988). It is not a play; it is a logical construction, a logical game or puzzle, in which three people are in a room. It is a prison and they are condemned to death. In Sartre's play they are dead and condemned. In Lacan's presentation they are condemned to death, but there is a way out. The way out is explained by the prison warden. He tells them the following: each one of them has a disk on his back which may be either black or white. There are three white disks and two black disks in all, from which the warden has chosen three—one for each prisoner. They cannot see their own disk, but they can see the disk of the two other prisoners in the room with them. They must attempt to figure out the color of their disk without talking among themselves, and the first to walk out the door and logically explain his conclusion shall be set free.

It is exactly the same logic as in Sartre's play. Lacan reduces the Sartrian metaphor of original sin to a disk that everyone is wearing, and reduces Sartre's view that one can have no direct access to one's own guilt, and that one is condemned to live with one's bad faith, to the fact that one cannot see the color of the disk one is wearing.

Having received this information from the warden, the three prisoners are locked in a room. Since there are three white disks and only two black ones, if a prisoner sees two black disks, he knows that he obviously has a white one. Thus each of the three prisoners first tries to see the other two prisoners' disks and then watches their movements. If one of them moves towards the exit, the other two know he has seen two black disks and thus that their disks must be black. They too can move towards the door and declare their disks blacks, and thus, within that structure with the three prisoners, revealing movements are produced.

Lacan stresses that truth, in this experiment, while attained independently by each individual, has the structure of a collective calculus: it can only be attained through the others. When he says that truth can only be attained *"par les autres"* (through the others), this is a direct response to Sartre's "hell is other people." The structure of the three condemned people and one lacking disk is exactly the Oedipal structure of the father, mother, and child trapped in their private hell. They can only calculate because one element is missing: the phallus. No one has it, but the three of them have to take that symbol into account to define their positions as father, mother, and child. If any one of them makes an error, thinking that he or she is the one that is missing—if the father thinks he is *the* father, if the mother thinks she is *Woman*, if the child thinks it is the phallus for its mother— then they all get stuck in their calculation. No one will find a way out. They will be stuck in eternal repetition.

But if they admit that that element is fundamentally missing—that everyone has to define his or her position with respect to that symbol— then they have a chance to attain what are known as truth values in analysis, that is, desire values. The solution to the impasse of sexual definition is the fact that there is no inscription of man and woman in the unconscious. There are only inventions that try to make up for that fundamental failure or lack in the unconscious.

This is probably the reason why Lacan, in "Science and Truth" (*Newsletter of the Freudian Field* 3, 1989), speaks of the phallus as a *gnomon*—a Greek term referring directly to Greek mathematics and the calculation of harmonic series—i.e., as a link between subject and other. That link in a chain, that is both a chain of signifiers and a chain of calculations, was introduced by Lacan at the beginning of his teaching to illustrate the dynamics of analytic treatment. It is true that the recognition of how one is defined as a subject—through the recognition and calculation of one's identifications—can alleviate the sense of guilt one brings to analysis. The fact that one cannot find one's way out of the private hell in which one is trapped has to do with the fact that it was there from the very beginning.

What Lacan adds in chapter 16 is the fact that drives arise in the subject. He says, "it is in this living being, called to subjectivity, that the drive is essentially manifested." (203) Thus subject and drive are situated in the same place, which seems in a sense paradoxical. But Lacan had previously made a play on words, using the letter "S" to designate the subject, which is pronounced the same way as Freud's *Es*, the id, which is the locus of the drives.

Drives cannot be represented as the Other *qua* whole. Drives are only partial, as Freud says, and Lacan reinterprets that by saying that the logic of the whole cannot appear in the Other ($\bar{\forall}$). There is no way to inscribe the quantifier "for all" or "the whole of" in the Other. No such quantifier can function in that place. $\bar{\forall}$ equals not all. Not all of the subject can be present in the Other. There is always a remainder. Lacan develops this in a way that alludes to the further development he provides in the seminar on feminine sexuality entitled *Encore*.

In Seminar XI, Lacan says:

> Aristophanes' myth illustrates man's pursuit of his complement in a moving, yet misleading, way, by suggesting that it is the other, one's sexual other half, that the living being seeks in love. For this mythical representation of the mystery of love, analytic experience substitutes the search by the subject, not for his sexual complement, but for that part of himself, lost forever, that is constituted by the fact that he is only a sexed living being, and that he is no longer immortal. (205)

Lacan reminds us that Aristophanes' myth of the original splitting of human beings explains love's longing to find its other half. This myth obscures the true meaning of longing: there is always a remainder in the subject's sexual representation in the Other. The two lacks that Lacan locates at the beginning of his lecture, and develops all the way through it, overlap. I will first present the two lacks and then explain them before we return to the text.

To present them I will use the formulations Jacques-Alain Miller has provided in his own commentary, because they are the simplest and most accurate in bringing out Lacan's essential point. To articulate the subject and the Other, a figure is supplied in Lacan's text. (211) Lacan links the subject and the Other, and situates being on one side and meaning on the other.

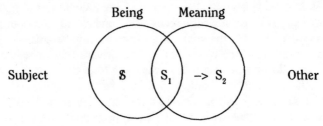

The first lack is related to the fact that the subject cannot be wholly represented in the Other: there is always a remainder, a remainder which defines the subject's sexually defined being. Not all of the subject can be presented here. The fundamentally partial character of the drives introduces a lack, which Lacan designates by drawing a bar through the subject ($).

But then we have, more profoundly, a second lack. Unfortunately, in this seminar there is no graph or formalization of separation. Jacques-Alain Miller has, however, provided such a formalization in his lectures. To understand the second lack, the Other can be abbreviated as follows: $S_1 \longrightarrow S_2$. This indicates that you need at least two signifiers to define the structure of the Other.

Once the subject is constituted, however, what has to be taken into account is the fact that there is a remainder—a remainder which is both within the subject as sexually defined and within the Other. To illustrate this, we can place the two signifiers in one part of the circle, object a where the unary signifier (S_1) was in my last figure, and the subject ($$) in the other circle.

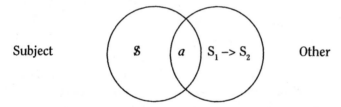

We have two ways of defining the subject's lack, one of which is due to the fact that in alienation, at the very moment at which the subject ($) identifies with a signifier, he is represented by one signifier for another ($S_1 \longrightarrow S_2$). For instance, a "bad boy" is represented as a "bad boy" in relation to his mother's ideal. Thus "bad boy" (or any other identification that served at one time as a master signifier) serves the subject as a guideline his whole life long. He is defined as such and behaves as such. At the very moment at which the subject identifies with such a signifier, he is petrified. He is defined as if he were dead, or as if he were lacking the living part of his being that contains his jouissance.

Whenever you isolate one of the subject's identifications, what you then need to do is find the fantasy ($ $\Diamond$ a$) that goes with it, the fantasy that brings him some jouissance. How can he obtain some jouissance, some sexual being, when he is defined as a "bad boy" in relation to the woman he loves? What is the object—oral, anal, scopic, or invocatory—at stake in fantasy that brings him jouissance? Object a is the other part of the subject (and that is the second way of defining the subject's lack).

Thus we have one lack (S_1 in the first figure) here and another lack there (*a* in the second figure). In the first lack, when the subject is defined by a master signifier, a part of the subject is left out of the total definition. Even if he is a "bad boy," he is other things as well. Then we have a second lack, in which the subject tries to inscribe a representation of jouissance within the Other in the text of his fantasy, and tries to define himself through that fantasy ($\mathcal{S} \lozenge a$). When he tries to define himself in that way, he creates another lack: the fact that his jouissance is only partial.

Lacan, then, as I said, tries with these categories, which seem so abstract, to provide a mapping of the course of analytic treatment. Implications can be derived from these categories—implications for the handling of interpretation in analytic treatment. He says:

> One of the consequences of alienation is that interpretation is not limited to providing us with significations of the paths followed by the psyche that we have before us. This range is no more than a prelude. Interpretation is directed not so much at meaning as at reducing signifiers to their non-meaning so as to find the determinants of the whole of the subject's behavior. (212)

The distinction Lacan tries to make here is of the utmost importance. Interpretation is conceived of as the enumeration of all of a signifier's sexual significations. Let's take the case of a patient who's obsessed by the number three. He has a number fixation. That creates problems for him, especially if he is an accountant. Every time he goes through columns of numbers he misses the threes. Then he has to check how many threes he has missed, and this can take up a great deal of his time. You could start by exploring or mapping all the sexual significations of the number three. What happened when he was three years old? What happened in his Oedipal triangle? Was he attracted, for instance, to a *ménage à trois*? There may be a whole set of significations.

That is only the first step, but it is a necessary first step—you have to map all the significations, and explore in precise detail all the circumstances in the patient's life where three functioned as a master signifier and draw out their significations. But once that mapping is done, you have to lead the subject somewhere else—to a place where every signifier has this function ($\mathcal{S} \longrightarrow a$) for him. After all, $S_1 \longrightarrow S_2$ leaves him without a true sexual referent that could give him his place.

Once you've gone through all the symptoms defined by that obsession with numbers, then you have to explore another dimension of the subject. Apart from the symptoms, he must define himself with respect to a precise fantasy. It is through a nonsensical chain of master signifiers, linked together in a certain way, that the fantasy is defined which determines his sexual behavior or his self-identity.

In the course of this discussion, Lacan refers to a colloquium held in the town of Bonneval in 1960,[1] where a confrontation took place between Lacan's students and psychiatrists and psychoanalysts of other persuasions. The meeting was organized by Henry Ey, one of the great figures in French psychiatry, and Lacan gave a lecture entitled "Position of the Unconscious," which was published in the French edition of the *Écrits*. At that colloquium, Laplanche and Leclaire made presentations, and Leclaire gave a well-known paper in which he showed how a Lacanian analysis could be worked through.

Leclaire discussed a patient named Philippe who had a series of obsessive symptoms. The patient was especially obsessed with unicorns (*licorne* in French). The question is how come we aren't all obsessed with unicorns, for we have lots of reasons to be obsessed with unicorns. Philippe had obsessions that could be traced to the fact that he was defined, not as a bad boy, but rather as "poor Philippe" (*pauvre Philippe*). His mother always referred to him as "poor Philippe" and the connection of the sound of "au" in "*pauvre*" and "o" in "*licorne*" was stressed by Leclaire, who showed that "*pauvre Philippe*" was the sound that put Philippe to bed. It was connected with the dream he had of a unicorn with the voice of his mother putting him to sleep, saying "*pauvre Philippe*." Leclaire noted that the unicorn represented the mother's phallus and Philippe's refusal to accept his mother's castration. In his dream he ensured that his mother was not poor from the phallic point of view.

From the standpoint of meaning, the link between the obsession and the dream (the central dream in Philippe's life), Leclaire pointed out that Philippe could be defined in terms of a chain that could be written as follows: Poôr (d) J'e - Li (Poordjeli) including "poor Philippe," the "je" (I) of the subject, and "li" from Philippe, *licorne*, and *lit* (bed). All that could be included in a sort of chain, absurd in this juxtaposition, but it was the chain of the master signifiers in Philippe's life.

Lacan says:

> I ask you to refer to what my student Leclaire contributed, at the Bonneval Colloquium, in application of my theses. You will see in his contribution that he isolated the unicorn sequence, not, as was suggested in the discussion [following his talk], in its dependence on meaning, but precisely in its irreducible and insane character as a chain of signifiers. (212)

What Lacan does not say is that, to Leclaire's way of thinking, that marked the end of the interpretive process. Leclaire presented it as the end of the analysis, while Lacan stresses the fact that it is only a prelude. Once you have isolated a certain number of master signifiers in a patient's life, there is *another* problem. How can "poor Philippe" define himself, not by the phallus but rather by the remainder of the phallic operation, i.e. by his partial objects or rather object *a* (Lacan introduces object *a* as a logification of the partial object)?

The subject has to be driven through yet another labyrinth, not that of his identifications, but that of the ways he obtains jouissance—the ways he transforms the other he loves into an object. If we only isolate one chain (S_1 —> S_2), we neglect the fact that poor Philippe loves women in a certain way. How? Does he treat a woman like a breast, setting the tone for his love affairs: clinging, demanding, being rejected, and always coming back? That would be an oral-style love affair, the woman's love being transformed into a breast one clings to. Or does he adopt an anal approach to women, falling in love, and then fleeing like a madman once the object he loves is reduced to an anal object that smells? Or a scopic approach, never seeing, in the object he loves, how that object deceives him blatantly, openly; not seeing the impasse into which he always falls; always falling in love instantly; placing great importance on the moment of being love-struck? Or does he reduce his loved one to a voice, a voice that gives him orders or leaves him with a compulsion to hear from her once more?

All of these approaches to love can be derived from the same chain of master signifiers, and one has to learn in one's analysis not only how one's identification is lacking and that the chain of master signifiers is not a new name for the subject (even in Philippe's case), as the subject's proper name is always lacking; one also has to see that one is not represented by one's love—one does not completely inscribe one's love in the locus of the Other. One must always find that other lack—the fact that as authentic as one's love is, one is always confronted with that same remainder—a remainder in the true sense of the term: one that reminds him of the fact that he is not represented, that there is a limit, that there is only partial representation. It reminds him of the jouissance he experienced through his oral demands and anal demands, and what he tried to obtain from his mother—her gaze or voice—which is not directly linked with need. You need to eat, you need to shit. You don't apparently need the Other's gaze or voice, but you nevertheless desire it more than you know.

Note

1. See *L'inconscient*, VIe Colloque de Bonneval, ed. Henri Ey, Desclée de Brouwer, 1966.

ALIENATION AND SEPARATION (II)

Éric Laurent

Today I will pursue the theme of alienation and separation I began with last week, stressing some of the clinical consequences thereof. I will start with pages 249 and 250 in chapter 19, "From Interpretation to Transference," because these pages contain an explicit statement by Lacan about an error that Jean Laplanche, one of his students at that time, made concerning Lacan's theory of interpretation. The error made by Laplanche (who was not an imbecile) arose because something in Lacan's work seemed to authorize Laplanche's position. Here is Lacan's statement:

> Consequently, it is false to say, as has been said [by Laplanche], that interpretation is open to any and all meanings under the pretext that it is but a question of the connection of one signifier to another. (249–50)

In the heyday of metaphor and metonymy, Laplanche stressed the fact that, while metaphor is an effect of the signification produced by the substitution of one signifier for another, and metonymy is the fact that these signifiers are linked on the same level with an effect of signification, any effect produced is admitted into the formula. You have no constraint on the metaphoric or metonymic aspects of interpretation and, as in jazz age epistemology, "anything goes."[1]

It seemed like anything that produced an effect was acceptable, and at that time some of Lacan's followers thought that Lacan's "expressionist" character and Baroque ways were based on the notion that the most important thing was to produce an effect of any kind. Many people tried to imitate

him and to obtain the same effect in the analytic situation; thus they theorized analytic treatment on the basis of these assumptions.

In contrast, when Lacan established his own school of psychoanalysis
and assumed responsibility for training analysts, he denounced such assumptions and stressed that you cannot say that anything goes. "Interpretation is not open to any and all meanings." (250) I will comment upon this.
Why does he stress this in the lecture in which he introduces alienation and
separation?

As we saw last time, the union of the subject with the Other leaves a
loss: if the subject tries to find him or herself in the Other, s/he can only
find him or herself as a lost part. S/he is petrified by a master signifier and
loses some part of his or her being. Alienation (that is, the fact that the
subject, having no identity, has to identify with something) masks or over-
laps the fact that, more deeply in a sense, the subject defines him or herself
not only in the signifying chain, but, at the level of drives, in terms of his or
her jouissance as related to the Other. If we adopt the schemas that Jacques-
Alain Miller first developed, we have:

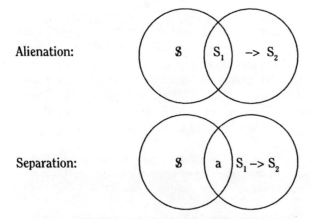

Alienation:

Separation:

In Freudian terms, alienation masks the fact that the object of jouissance
as such is lost, as Freud pointed out in his famous 1925 article, "Negation."
These two formulas or logical operations that produce the subject can be
read vertically in a sense. First, alienation—the fact that the subject is
produced within the language that awaits him or her and is inscribed in the
locus of the Other. The subject finds him or herself divided, dismembered
between the partial drives, and partial as there is always a loss.

These formulas can be read in another way. The subject is fundamentally an object of the Other's jouissance, and his or her first status as an
infant is to be a lost part of that Other, that real Other (generally the
mother). S/he begins life in the place of object *a*, and then has to identify

with that lost part and enter the chain of signifiers. S/he will try, as Lacan said, to "assume his or her primary identifications," a phrase used in the *Écrits*. His or her primary identification, in one sense, is with the master signifier. In a deeper sense, his or her primary identification is with an object which s/he will define in the end. It is the complete identification— what *s/he* was, as such, in the Other's desire, not only at the symbolic level of desire, but as the real substance at stake for jouissance. S/he can only try to recover or identify it within the development of the chain of signifiers.

Thus you can read these schemas both ways. First alienation and then separation, or first separation and then alienation. Logically speaking, alienation comes first. In the analytic situation, separation comes first. When Lacan says, "interpretation is not open to any and all meanings," he is far from authorizing the "anything goes" theory or "the most popular interpretation" theory that some analysts developed (one tries an interpretation, and if it doesn't work, one tries another, and yet another, mapping out the whole range until one reaches the one most "popular" with the analysand, the ones s/he accepts).

Instead you have to address the true meaning of what the analysand says within the signifying chain, and the true meaning analytic interpretation has to address is not an effect of signification but rather the product or remainder of the first encounter between the subject and the Other—the remainder of that experience, *das Erlebnis* in Freudian terms, the remainder of jouissance.

Lacan goes on:

> Interpretation is not open to any and all meanings. That would be to concede to those who criticize analytic interpretation for being uncertain that, in effect, any and all interpretations are possible, which is patently absurd. While I have said that the effect of interpretation is to isolate in the subject a kernel, a *Kern*, to use Freud's own term, of non-sense, that does not mean that interpretation is in itself nonsense. (250)

Freud used the word "*Kern*" especially in speaking of *der Kern unseres Wesens* (the core of our being). Lacan adopted the term and described the *Kern* of the subject as a signifier isolated in its deeper meaning—separated from meaning, the binary signifier standing for anything that makes sense, thus separating out in the chain of signifiers what remains at the level of nonsense: the master signifier, S_1.

This is an intuition that Lacan formulated in many ways in his teaching: one's basic identifications have no meaning at all, they simply *are*. One can explore the meanings they have, but one must not neglect the fact that, in the end, they make no sense. Lacan, for example, often referred to Freud's formulation of the fetish in the case of the man who, in order to become interested in a woman, had to detect a certain "shine on the nose" (in German, *Glanz auf der Nase*). Freud traced this back to the fact that the patient had had an English nurse. Out of sexual curiosity, he tried to "glance" at her, but she told him that somehow his nose would be punished if he tried to look at her when he was not allowed to. Hence *Glanz* and glance were linked to the nose. In this way one can make sense of something that, in its deeper aspects, made no sense at all. That is just the way it is. One cannot explain why all of this man's sexual life was devoted to the transliteration of English into German. It has a nonsensical side, and that is exactly what Lacan tries to isolate when he stresses the master signifier, "*Glanz*" in this case. Only afterwards does he discuss all the explanations; whatever makes sense can be interpreted.

It is true that in an analysis you have to do the same work that was done by Freud. You try to trace things back and elicit the memories that were linked to the original sexual aspects of the patient's life. In a deeper sense, at the end you've got the kernel, which has been isolated as nonsensical. In the case of Freud's patient, it is precisely in this *Glanz* (glance) that Freud detects what the boy was at the origin of his life. He was a gaze, and what structured his relationship with the Other was the fact that he identified with that gaze, that is, a partial drive. His jouissance was once and for all fixated within that gaze. It was a necessary condition for him to attain an erection, to take into account his phallic situation. The *Glanz auf der Nase* was a fetish. It was defined in part by a partial drive and also conditioned phallic signification for that subject.

$$a = \textit{Glanz auf der Nase}$$
$$S_1 \quad \varphi \quad \text{phallic signification}$$

You can see in this example that interpretation is not open to any and all meanings. In the end, you have to point out the partial drive that is at stake. Lacan also defined it in another seminar when he said interpretation has to aim at the object, between the lines, so to speak, because the only way to aim at the object is not to comment on it directly. Analytic interpretation could, in certain schools of psychoanalysis, involve explaining to the patient that when he was a small boy, he wanted to look at his English nurse—which was considered very bad—and so he was anxious that he would be punished by losing his nose, and yet even now he is looking. You could comment on that and lecture your patient about it. That would be a mistake. Why? Why not lecture the patient? Isn't a lecture the shortest way to the aim?

It isn't the shortest because the subject always appears as a fading subject, and if you lecture him like that, the only effect is to fixate the subject on that jouissance, which leads to acting out. Thus you have to evoke things—you have to aim at the object between the lines, using the subject's chain of signifiers and equivocation. As Cicero first said, a concept tries to take hold of or grasp an object. But in psychoanalysis you cannot grab hold of an object. You can, however, aim at it. Using signifiers, you have to target that point. You cannot hit it directly.

These propositions, made by Lacan in Seminar XI, were then formalized in Seminar XVII (1968–1969) when he proposed his formulas for the four discourses.

$$\frac{S_1}{\mathcal{S}} \quad \overset{\longrightarrow}{} \quad \frac{S_2}{a} \qquad \begin{matrix} \text{alienation} \\ \\ \text{separation} \end{matrix}$$

There he combines in a single formula the definition of alienation and that of separation when he concludes, so to speak, the first part of his teaching. Here we have a shorthand formula for what Freud calls "unconscious formations," not productions but formations, form being implied on the one side, all other aspects of fantasy (the place where "Es" was, where jouissance is) being implied on the other. Writing the four discourses in 1969 appears to be the result of the development of an earlier insight in Lacan's teachings and the inclusion of different aspects into a single formula.

At the same time, however, it was also related to the debate taking place in 1968, the year in which France's student rebellion led to political trouble that lasted a month and a half. The exact status of these troubles has not yet been established. What were they exactly? There was a wave of student rebellions throughout the world, from the USA (Kent State, etc.) to China (where the first stage of the cultural revolution was the student rebellion). In both the capitalist and socialist systems there were curious events that lasted two or three years, like a chain reaction, and their meaning has yet to be exactly defined.

It was precisely at that time that a debate was taking place at the intellectual level. One of the main points of that debate separated Foucault and Derrida, for instance. As some of you are very familiar with Derrida's and Foucault's work, I will try to be brief and show how Lacan viewed the debate and what, in a sense, Foucault and Derrida owe to Lacan.

Derrida accentuates the fact that the subject is defined through the process of alienation and stays alienated, while Foucault stresses the fact that the deeper meaning of what one says has to do with one's *pratique de jouissance,* one's practice, how one obtains jouissance.

For Derrida, there can always be dissemination. It is always possible to find another meaning. A new signifier can always produce a new development in the chain, and thus in the end the subject is always considered as a void or empty place. Foucault denounced Derrida as metaphysical, as accepting that place in its indeterminacy, and tried to propose a way to eliminate that indeterminacy, defining the jouissance at stake.

Thus went the debate between knowledge and power (*savoir et pouvoir*), common in the 1960s. The debate was organized by the operations Lacan defines. Derrida criticized Foucault, a year before Lacan's seminar, in a lecture on the cogito and the history of madness.[2] Derrida's lecture is a very harsh critique of Foucault's history of madness published a few years before.[3] Foucault did not say anything during the lecture, nor did he reply after the publication of *Writing and Difference.* He waited until the second edition of *Madness and Civilization* in 1972. At the end of the book, he added a very harsh rejoinder to Derrida's critique.

Let me quote a passage from a biography of Foucault (*Michel Foucault, Life and Work*) in which Foucault develops his points very clearly. In these extracts, he says about Derrida:

> I wouldn't say that it's metaphysics or its closure that is hidden in the textualization of his discursive praxis. I'd go much further. I would say [. . .] that what very visibly manifests itself is a little pedagogue who teaches the student that there is nothing outside of the text. It is a pedagogy that gave the voice of the masters the unlimited sovereignty that permits them to indefinitely repeat the text.

It is quite harsh to call Derrida—the most eminent representative and teacher of the *École normale supérieure* and quite a good teacher of phenomenology, who in the past decades transmitted phenomenology to philosophers at the *École normale supérieure*—a little pedagogue. It's rather insulting. Foucault and Derrida stopped talking to each other for ten years over it. That finally changed when Derrida was in prison in Czechoslovakia. He was framed by the Czech police when he went to visit and salute the people who had signed the charter of the Czech dissenters; the police planted some hashish on him, said he was a drug dealer, tried to ruin his reputation, and imprisoned him. In France there was a huge protest to free Derrida, in which Foucault joined, for which Derrida thanked him over lunch. But that was ten years later. There was quite a break between the two.

I mention this break just to show you that, in a certain way, it can be deduced from the operations Lacan proposes in Seminar XI. Foucault, who was gay, stressed the fact that what is at stake in one's experience is that one speaks from one's own jouissance; Foucault was very well aware that his theory was, in a way, a theory of his own sexual practice, and that it could not be attacked simply by calling him a pervert or something like that. It was, rather, an authentic attempt to define *his* rebellion against the master signifiers, against conformity. His theory referred to the fact that, in the end, it is object *a* which is at stake when one thinks, whether it be in analysis or in the academy.

Derrida wanted to leave aside the fact that the place of object *a* is always full. It is this same place that is at stake when, at the end of the sixteenth lecture of Seminar XI (on May 27, 1964), Jacques-Alain Miller, then twenty years old, asked Lacan a question:

> Do you not wish to show that the alienation of a subject who has received the definition of being born in, constituted by, and ordered in a field that is exterior to him, is to be distinguished radically from the alienation of a consciousness-of-self? In short, are we to understand—Lacan against Hegel? (215)

And Lacan replied, "what you have just said is very good, it's exactly the opposite of what Green just said to me." Green, a French psychoanalyst who was vice-president of the IPA ten years ago, attended Lacan's seminar for a year or two in the 1960s, and then wrote a book entitled *The Living Discourse*, stressing that Lacan did not take into account the living aspect of the thing because he left biology out of psychoanalysis. Green was very funny on this question, because as Lacan told the anecdote:

> [Green] came up to me, shook my paw, at least morally, and said, "the death of structuralism, you are the son of Hegel." I don't agree. In saying Lacan *against* Hegel, I think you are much closer to the truth, though of course it is not at all a philosophical debate. (215)

What was at stake? It is true that Lacan was *against* Lévi-Strauss' structuralism which tried to eliminate the subject. Lacan reintroduced the subject into structuralism, and also introduced a logic that could admit a certain temporality. In that sense, Green was trying to say, it is the death of structuralism; you are the son of Hegel, since you introduce time and the subject—that's pure consciousness.

Jacques-Alain Miller's question points out that, far from leaving that place empty, Lacan defines it precisely with the Freudian fantasy or lust object, with its full charge of jouissance. The energetic aspects that Freud formulated mechanistically in the context of 19th century physics are reformulated by Lacan within the context of formal logic. That can be seen in Lacan's comments at a lecture given by Foucault in February 1969, a well known lecture entitled "What is an Author?"[4] In this lecture, Foucault made many references to a return to Freud without naming Lacan. The French academy was still Marxist at that time and attacked Foucault, who was quite famous for the role he had played at Vincennes and for his links with the student rebellion, because structuralism and his brand of structuralism, stressing discourse and structure, left the subject behind ("subject", in the old sense of the term, i.e., man). In his lecture, Foucault showed that the modern author is best defined by Beckett's texts, in which, in the end, the possible identity of he who speaks is dissolved.

Lacan makes the following comment:

> Structuralism or not, there is no question, in the field vaguely determined by that label, of the negation of the subject. The point is the dependence of the subject—which is extremely different, especially as concerns the return to Freud—on something truly elementary that I try to isolate with the term "signifier." Thirdly, I will limit my remarks here to the following: I do not consider it legitimate for it to be written that these structures do not march in the street. Because if there is something proved by the events that occurred in May, it is precisely that the structures do go marching in the street. The fact that someone wrote that "structures do not march in the street" (it was written by someone marching), in the place itself where this marching took place, proves only that in the structure of the act, the act misrepresents itself.[5]

What was at stake in the writing of Lacan's four discourses or in Foucault's discursive practice was the fact that structures "march in the street," because structure implies a quota of jouissance, and people die for it. Lacan wrote the university discourse—with knowledge located in the position of master —

$$\frac{S_2}{S_1} \longrightarrow \frac{a}{\$}$$

That discourse produces the subject who goes marching in the streets, as there is a necessary link between the student rebellion and the university. The academy has existed since the twelfth century, and there have always been student rebellions. There is a necessary connection there. Under many different regimes and conditions, from that time until now, what has been constant is the fact that students rebel. Lacan does not accept the Marxist explanation that the students are rebellious because they are not involved

in production. They are rebellious, he says, because they are made that way
by the university discourse.

Now if we turn back to Seminar XI, Lacan stresses the consequence of
this in psychoanalysis:

> Leclaire's work illustrates particularly well the move from meaning-based
> interpretation to signifying non-sense, when he proposes, on the subject
> of his obsessive neurotic patient, the so-called *Poordjeli* formula, which
> links the two syllables of the word *licorne* (unicorn), thus enabling him to
> introduce into this sequence a whole chain in which his desire is ani-
> mated. Indeed, you will see in what he will publish later that things go
> much further still. (250)

In this same lecture, Lacan refers to the fact that the first part of the article
was written by Laplanche, and the second part concerning the presentation
of this "Poordjeli" formula regarding the man with the unicorn was written
by Leclaire. In fact, however, Leclaire's book did not show how things go
much further still, though Lacan's article, "Position of the Unconscious,"
did. Lacan showed that one has to go further, because there is a chain in
which desire is animated—alive—and Lacan speaks quite a few times in the
Écrits of the *life* of desire. It is not desire, but jouissance that has to be
considered, and they have to be considered in opposition to each other.

There is another clinical consequence that Lacan develops in this same
lecture. Lacan comments on the proposition made by one of his students,
Maud Mannoni, regarding the clinical definition of mental deficiency:

> Inasmuch, for example, as the child, the mentally-deficient child, takes
> the place, on the blackboard, at the bottom right, of this S, with regard to
> this something to which the mother reduces him, in being no more than
> the support of her desire in an obscure term, which is introduced into
> the education of the mentally-deficient child by the psychotic dimension.
> (237–8)

That "obscure term" to which the mother reduces the child is object *a*. In
Lacan's "Notes on the Child," published in *Ornicar?*, written by Lacan to
another one of his students, the head of a hospital child psychology ward,
Lacan refers directly to the fact that, in a series of phenomena like mental
deficiency, psychosis, and other phenomena of this kind, the child is reduced to this object and to realizing the mother's fantasy. This passage in
Seminar XI paves the way for his comments on the child, written in 1969.

Thus the clinical consequence of Lacan's work on alienation and separation in Seminar XI was the fact that, after 1964, Lacan stressed ever
more, in his conception of psychosis, object *a*'s role as the object to which

the psychotic subject is reduced. This was not present in Lacan's 1958 article on Schreber's *Memoirs,* published in the *Écrits.* From 1964 on, Lacan stressed the clinical importance of the extent to which a child is reduced to the obscure object of its mother's desire and the fact that all of this is important in the clinical understanding of childhood psychosis.

Notes

1. Cf. Paul Feyerabend's *Against Method,* Verso, 1979.

2. In *Writing and Difference,* Chicago, 1978.

3. *Madness and Civilization: A History of Insanity in the Age of Reason,* New York, 1973.

4. In Michel Foucault, *Language, Counter-Memory, Practice,* ed. D.F. Bouchard, Cornell, Ithaca, 1977.

5. These remarks are not found in the English edition. The interested reader can find them in the *Bulletin de la Société française de Philosophie,* 63, No. 3 (1969).

THE SUBJECT AND THE OTHER (I)

Colette Soler

I would like to welcome you to the second seminar in Paris, and I want to thank the people who have organized this seminar on behalf of the Department of Psychoanalysis at the University of Paris VIII. The first seminar was organized last June by Richard Feldstein and Ellie Ragland in America and by Bruce Fink in Paris. This year's seminar has been organized once again by Richard Feldstein, Bruce Fink, and Ellie Ragland, and in Paris this year by Anne Dunand and Bob Samuels. I would like to thank them, because I know how many difficulties arise in organizing a conference of this kind.

My theme is "The Subject and the Other," but before I begin I want to say something about Seminar XI itself, because it is not just any old seminar. It is a very important seminar from several points of view. First of all, it was given at a crucial moment in psychoanalytic history. Lacan started this seminar in January 1964, about a month after leaving the International Psychoanalytical Association (IPA). Thus it was a propitious moment historically speaking, and it was also a propitious moment in Lacan's life. Lacan at that time had been planning another seminar, the title of which was the *Names-of-the-Father*. He interrupted that seminar because of his exclusion from the IPA, and began Seminar XI: *The Four Fundamental Concepts of Psychoanalysis*.

It was also a propitious moment in Lacan's teaching. It marked the end of Lacan's return to Freud, and with this seminar Lacan began to surpass Freud's teaching and criticize something in Freud's analytic position. That is very important, because the new elaborations which start with

39

this seminar permit us to understand Lacan's view of the end of psychoanalytic treatment. That must be kept in mind when we read the text.

Today I will primarily speak about the subject. If we truly want to know
what psychoanalysis is and how it differs from any form of psychotherapy,
we have to "know what the term 'subject' means," as Lacan says. (37) What
does the term "subject" mean? Lacan provides a thesis: the subject is the
Cartesian subject, i.e. the subject of the *cogito* or "I am thinking." Lacan
says, "In order to understand Freud's concepts, one must begin with the
notion that it is the subject who is called upon—the subject of Cartesian
origin." (47) And before that he says:

> the Freudian field was possible only a certain time after the emergence of
> the Cartesian subject, insofar as modern science began only after Descartes
> made his inaugural step.
>
> The fact that one can call upon the subject to return to his home in the
> unconscious depends on this step . . . . (47)

You see that in these lines, there are in reality two theses. The first thesis is
that science—the science we know now—physics, for example, began with
Descartes. That is to say, the subject of science is the subject of the *cogito*.
This first thesis is not Lacan's invention; it is a philosophical thesis established years ago, above all by Hegel. To Hegel, Descartes marked the beginning of modern times. Heidegger also emphasized the homogeneity between
science (especially what he called the essence of science) and modern meta-
physics, i.e., Descartes. I am not going to develop this philosophical thesis,
but it is nevertheless useful to remember here that Lacan adopts a thesis
which is not his own.

The second thesis is that the subject of psychoanalysis is the Cartesian
subject, i.e., the subject that conditions science. Thus, we first have to
understand in what way Freud is Cartesian and why. We have to understand
what similarity exists between Freud and Descartes. Lacan uses the term
"similarity." (36) Later we will see a dissymmetry between Freud and
Descartes. To the clinician or psychotherapist who intends to cure patients,
it may seem a bit strange to hear that the subject he cures is the Cartesian
subject; the clinician may think that it is a philosophical thesis and possibly
also an old-fashioned thesis, because Freud's work is almost one hundred
years old now. Therefore, we have to see in what way Freud is Cartesian and
why.

Secondly, you know Descartes' famous line, *cogito ergo sum:* "I am
thinking, therefore I am." We immediately see the characteristics of the
subject of the cogito. The subject of the cogito is the subject of thought. It
is only because he thinks that he is certain about himself. He is a subject of

thought, and at the same time, a subject of certainty. ("Of the Subject of Certainty" is a chapter title in Seminar XI.) The subject of certainty is precisely the subject of the cogito. But what is his or her certainty? S/he is certain only about his or her own existence; s/he is not certain about his or her essence or essential being. His or her certainty is a certainty of existence as presence, presence of the subject. S/he is certain about existence as *real* presence, and Lacan stressed that the cogito aims at the real.

My third point is that the subject of thought or the subject of certainty is not the subject of truth because his or her certainty is completely independent of truth. The cogito suspends any consideration of truth. My thoughts can be true or false—never mind; they can be hallucinations, dreams, mistakes—never mind; when I am thinking, I am.

Given these three characteristics of the subject of the cogito, we can observe that the patient who asks for therapy is very different from the subject of the cogito, or so it seems. What is a patient who asks for therapy like? S/he is someone who suffers, firstly. The cogito of the patient, if you will, is "I am suffering, therefore I am." Thus it is not the subject of truth who asks for psychotherapy. It is the subject of affect. This is a first proposition.

Secondly, s/he is not the subject of certainty. On the contrary, s/he is someone who doubts. That is to say, s/he doesn't know what is happening to him or her. S/he suffers, but doesn't know why; s/he doesn't know the cause, and s/he doesn't even know if s/he is implicated in his or her own suffering. S/he is a subject of doubt and s/he is not indifferent to truth. On the contrary, s/he perhaps wants to know the true cause of his or her troubles. Thus there is a complete opposition between the Cartesian subject and the psychoanalytic patient.

The Freudian patient is not just any old patient, but what we call an analysand, and an analysand is someone who accepts to submit to Freudian technique. And what does Freudian technique do? First it transforms the subject of suffering into a subject of thought. It is what we call free association. When Freud or any other psychoanalyst demands free association of the patient, s/he demands that the patient speak as s/he thinks. Free association involves saying what you silently think. Free association thus demands something unusual of the subject, who has to articulate a series of thoughts without reflection or control. That is to say, s/he has to become a producer of thoughts. Here you see that Lacan has but a small step to take in order to translate thought into signifiers. Free association transforms the subject of suffering into a subject of thought, and it is a step closer to the subject of the cogito.

But here we see that a distinction arises between the patient and the psychoanalyst, because the analysand as a subject of thought is not a subject of certainty. On the contrary, the analysand speaks his or her own thoughts, comments on them negatively, denies their importance, and considers it all stupid. Thus the analysand doubts the truth of his or her thoughts, and here we encounter the Freudian hypothesis as a Cartesian hypothesis. The Freudian hypothesis is, "where thought is, the subject is, even if the person who speaks doesn't know it." Where thought is, in a dream for example (a dream consists of thoughts when the patient tells it), and especially when the patient does not assume responsibility for the dream thoughts or doubts them, Freud is certain that the subject of the unconscious is there too. It is a Freudian hypothesis.

In the chapter, "Of the Subject of Certainty," Lacan says:

> Freud, when he doubts [. . .], is assured that a thought is there, which is unconscious, which means that it is revealed as absent. When he deals with others, it is to this place that he summons the "I am thinking" through which the subject will be revealed. In short, he is sure that the thought is there with all of its "I am," so to speak, provided, and herein lies the leap, someone is thinking in his stead. (36)

Here we encounter the dissymmetry between Freud, or psychoanalysts in general, and Descartes. There is a dissymmetry regarding certainty. In psychoanalysis certainty is not found in the subject of thought, i.e., in the analysand. Certainty is situated in the Other or analyst. That is why Lacan says in another text, "Position of the Unconscious" (*Écrits* 1966), that the psychoanalyst is responsible for the presence of the unconscious.

The dissymmetry between Freud and Descartes consists of their different positions on certainty. Lacan says, "we know, thanks to Freud, that the subject of the unconscious manifests itself or thinks before it attains certainty." (37) Freud's position obviously implies a little more. Freud's position, which consists in supposing a subject behind the patient's thought, implies what Lacan calls "the subversion of the subject." (48)

I started out by saying that Freud was Cartesian; now I have to add that Freud nevertheless subverted Descartes' subject, because the Cartesian subject, as subject of thought, means self-consciousness and mastery. The subject of thought, as unconscious thought, means the subject as slave, not master: the subject submitted to the effect of language. It is a subject subverted by the system of signifiers.

Thus I must say something about the essence of the Freudian subject as a subverted Cartesian subject. What is this subject? This is Descartes' second question in the *Meditations*. The cogito ensures the existence of the subject and later Descartes asks what this subject is; in the same way we have to ask what the subject submitted to the system of signifiers is. If I wanted to provide an immediate answer, I could say that the subject is nothing: he is a signifier. That is the answer given by Lacan in this seminar.

I want to emphasize that this subject is primarily an effect, not an agent. The subject initially begins in the locus of the Other—the locus of the Other as the locus of signifiers and speech, as Lacan says. (198) Then he provides the answer to the question, 'what is the subject?':

> The subject is born insofar as the signifier emerges in the field of the Other. But, by this very fact, this subject—which was previously nothing if not a subject coming into being—solidifies into a signifier. (199)

Shortly thereafter Lacan repeats the same thing:

> ... by being born with the signifier, the subject is born divided. The subject is an emergence which, just before, as subject, was nothing, but which, having scarcely appeared, solidifies into a signifier. (199)

This is not so easy to understand. Perhaps I should stress the fact that the Other precedes the subject. The Other as the locus of language—the Other who speaks—precedes the subject and speaks about the subject before his birth. Thus the Other is the first cause of the subject. The subject is not a substance; the subject is an effect of the signifier. The subject is represented by a signifier, and before the appearance of the signifier, there is no subject. But the fact that there is no subject does not mean that there is nothing, because you can have a living being, but that living being becomes a subject only when a signifier represents him. Thus prior to the appearance of the signifier, the subject is nothing.

You have to understand the difference, hiatus, or split between a living being and a subject, or if you prefer, between a person and a subject. A friend of mine told me something funny, which will perhaps allow me to illustrate this difference. He is an Englishman, and you know that Margaret Thatcher recently invented a poll tax which every person—every living being—will pay. My friend said that the subject doesn't pay the poll tax. A living being or person pays it, but a subject does not, and the proof is that an autistic subject who does not speak must pay the same poll tax. Perhaps that will give you a more concrete idea of the difference between subject and person.

The subject is an effect, not a substance. So what is the problem? What is at stake for Lacan in Seminar XI? The definition of the subject as a subverted Cartesian subject is not invented in Seminar XI; it is merely summarized here. The problem in Seminar XI is to show how the subject, as an effect of language and speech, is related to the living being. That is to say, the problem is to understand how the asubstantial subject of speech is linked with the only substance at stake in psychoanalysis, i.e., with what Lacan calls jouissance. The major development in this seminar is the elaboration of the libido. Here Lacan starts to rethink what Freud calls the dynamic level of experience.

While the subject is not substantial, his or her symptom is. In the symptom, there is suffering, that is to say, jouissance. The body is involved, but not only the body: all real behavior. When we say that the subject is asubstantial, we shouldn't forget that psychoanalysis claims to cure or to change something at the level of the symptom, which is a substantial level, by operating on the asubstantial subject. The ambition of psychoanalysis is . . . vast.

THE SUBJECT AND THE OTHER (II)

Colette Soler

Today I will speak about what happens to the subject in the field of the Other, and thus I will have to speak about alienation and separation. I know that Éric Laurent is also speaking about those two concepts, but I suspect I will not repeat the same material. What is at stake? With alienation and separation, Lacan takes his first and main thesis, that the unconscious is structured like a language, a step further. When he elaborates separation, he takes that step.

What is at stake in my lecture? I have an intention when I speak to you. What is at stake for me is that I intend to show you that what we call the clinical level is at the same time a logical level. I want to show you, with alienation and separation, that the clinic is structured logically.

Thirdly, what is at stake for the subject of the unconscious in his or her link with the Other? What is at stake for the subject is to answer the question of his or her own being.

I mentioned last time that the subject of the unconscious, as a Cartesian subject, is an unknown subject—a subject about whom we know only that s/he exists. What s/he is remains unknown, undetermined. And s/he is not only unknown, but lacking, having lost his or her being. What is at stake is thus very simple. For every analysand (because the subject about whom we are speaking is the analysand, in particular), what is at stake is to answer the question of his or her own being.

In 1964, Lacan discussed two operations by which the subject realizes him or herself in the Other. He says, "through the effect of speech, the subject realizes himself ever more in the Other, yet he is already pursuing

45

there but half of himself." (188) (There is an error in the English translation, because in French Lacan says, *"il ne poursuit déjà plus là qu'une
moitié de lui-même,"* and the translation should read "but half," not "more
than half.") In the logical structure of alienation and separation, Lacan
refers to the operations known as "union" and "intersection" in set theory.
When you have two sets with a common part, the union of the two sets is
different from their intersection.

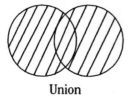
Union

Intersection

Intersection isolates that which belongs to both sets. I didn't say "the
element" which belongs; I said "that which belongs," without saying whether
it is an element or a part.

Lacan uses the logical definition of union, which is a *vel*. There are two
classic *vels* and Lacan creates a third. The first *vel* he calls the *vel* of
exclusion.

x	y	vel of exclusion	
T	T	F	line 1
T	F	T	line 2
F	T	T	line 3
F	F	F	line 4

It is a *vel* in which you have two elements, x and y for example. In the
exclusive *vel*, if you have x, you can't have y. When x is true, y must be false
(line 1) for the *vel* to be satisfied. And when x is false, y must be true (line
3) for the *vel* to be satisfied. However, both x and y cannot be false (line 4),
for in that case the *vel* is not satisfied (it is false). Likewise, x and y cannot
both be true (line 1), because then the *vel* is false. The *vel* accepts either
one or the other as true or false, but not both at the same time.

The *vel* of union is a modified *vel*, because it adds something to the *vel*
of exclusion.

x	y	vel of exclusion	vel of union
T	T	F	T
T	F	T	T
F	T	T	T
F	F	F	F

In this *vel*, x and y can be the same. That is to say, while like the previous *vel*, the *vel* of union is satisfied or true when x is true and y is false, and when x is false and y is true, it is also true when both x and y are true. Thus this *vel* is not exclusive. It allows *either* x or y to be true or *both* x and y. It "adds" x and y. It is false only when both x and y are false.

The third *vel* Lacan discusses is a rather unusual one, and Lacan associates it with his expression "forced choice." It is a *vel* in which, in reality, you have very little choice, because one of the two terms is always excluded. We can understand this *vel* better with the example of the expression "your money or your life."

Money	Life	Vel of "a forced choice"
T	T	F
T	F	F
F	T	T (our only choice)
F	F	T

When you are confronted by someone who says to you "your money or your life," you can't choose money, because if you choose money (true), life becomes false—you lose your life. You can't have both your money and your life, and your money without your life is also false. So when someone says to you "your money or your life," you have only one real choice: you obviously choose life. And in that case, your money is lost (false) and the *vel* is true. There is only one other possibility, the last one on the table: you have the possibility of losing both. But the main possibility for you is the choice of life; you thereby lose your money, and in that case your life is but half a life, a life in which something (money) is lacking. This *vel* always excludes one and the same term—money—and is a very precise, logical *vel*.

Lacan also modifies the operation known as intersection in set theory, which isolates that which belongs to both sets, to define separation. What changes at the level of intersection in Lacan's definition? Lacan's separation is an intersection defined by what is lacking in both sets, not by what belongs to both of them.[1]

Now we have to see how this logical structure is incarnated in subjective problems. In the subject's predicament, the two terms Lacan considers to be at stake at the level of alienation are: meaning and non-meaning (nonsense).

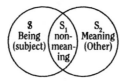

At the level of alienation, we have the set of the Other and the set of being (that being transformed into a subject by the Other, which is why Lacan adds "subject" to the left-hand side). It is not simple being; it is being transformed by language. In the middle he places non-meaning and to the right meaning. (211)

Lacan made it clear that the two terms from which non-meaning and meaning derive are the two terms of the signifying chain: S_1 and S_2. They are the terms with which we symbolize the signifying chain. The only choice the subject has is either to become petrified in a signifier or to slide into meaning, because when you have a link between the signifiers (S_1 and S_2), you have meaning.

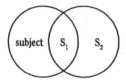

Thus there is either petrification or meaning, meaning implying the sliding of the subject into meaning, the infinite slide into meaning.

What Lacan calls a subject petrified by the signifier is a subject who doesn't ask any questions. The simplest definition of a petrified subject is one who has no questions about himself. S/he lives and acts, but doesn't think about him or herself. S/he even refuses to think about what s/he is. That is the norm, and it is the exact opposite of the analysand. An analysand is a subject who has chosen meaning. By entering into transference and by addressing a psychoanalyst, an analysand fights for him or herself. S/he fights for the cause of his or her own symptoms.

The subject of alienation in Seminar XI is not a new subject: it is the same subject about whom Lacan had been speaking for ten years. It is the subject included in Lacan's graph of desire on the lower level. If you look at that graph, you will see that the subject included on the lower level is the subject of alienation who has to choose between identification fixed by a signifier and meaning.

What then is the destiny of this subject of the signifier? His or her destiny is vacillation between petrification and indeterminacy, petrification by the signifier and indeterminacy within the slippage of meaning. That's what we might call the impasse of the subject of the signifier. It is the result of Lacan's ten year return to Freud—ten years in which Lacan constructed the subject of speech and language, ending up with an alienated subject, i.e., a subject who lost his or her being and is divided.

What is truly new in Seminar XI is the introduction of separation. The introduction of alienation is new at the logical level only, because Lacan manages here to formulate the logical structure of the subject of the signifier. But the subject of the signifier is not new in Seminar XI. What is new is what is introduced with separation.

Alienation is destiny. No speaking subject can avoid alienation. It is a destiny tied to speech. But separation is not destiny. Separation is something which may or may not be present, and here Lacan evokes a *velle*, in French *vouloir*, and in English "a want." It is very similar to an action by the subject.

Separation requires that the subject "want" to separate from the signifying chain. The term *velle* is not in this seminar, but there is something similar, simpler, and more striking. Having said that "the subject realizes himself ever more in the Other," Lacan goes on,

> That is why he must get out, get himself out, and in the *getting-himself-out*, in the end, he will know that the real Other has, just as much as himself, to get himself out or pull himself free. (188)

I want to stress the word "free" and the evocation of liberty here. Separation supposes a want to get out, a want to know what one is beyond what the Other can say, beyond what is inscribed in the Other.

There is a condition in the Other which makes separation possible, and that is the dimension of desire. Lacan says, in "Position of the Unconscious," "the subject experiences in this interval [of speech] something that motivates him Other [*Autre chose*] than the effects of meaning" (*Écrits* 1966, 843). Allow me to stress the word "experiences" here, which could also be translated "encounters," because the word also appears in Seminar XI.

The Other implied in separation is not the same as the Other implied in alienation. It is another aspect of the Other, not the Other full of signifiers, but on the contrary, the Other in which something is lacking. While we can write the Other full of signifiers as A, the Other as lacking is written with a bar through it: A̸

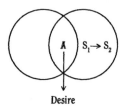

Desire

In the intersection between subject and Other is a lack, a void. What is this void in the Other? It is what Lacan called desire. But why does desire necessarily appear in speech? It is because there is an impossibility in speech: the impossibility to say what you want. For example, you speak with your lover, and the person who listens to you understands your words and sentences, and you can repeat them. You can even explain them. When you speak, you can develop meaning insofar as meaning is always produced between two signifiers. You can communicate that meaning and you can explain meaning, but the constant question for the listener is, what is he getting at? What is he after? (*"Où veut-il en venir?"*)

In speech there are always two dimensions: that of the statement (or utterance) and that of enunciation (or uttering). In every statement, there is always a problem of knowing what speech is after. Beyond what the other says, there is always the question, "What does he or she want?"

The presence of desire in itself is the presence of something lacking in speech. It is the presence of something which haunts speech, but which is not always translated into a precise demand. That is why Lacan says that desire is metonymy, something which slides in speech but is impossible to grasp. Lacan stresses that this is clearly present in clinical work with small children, in the link with the mother and father's speech.

Separation has a condition: the encounter with desire's lack. This lack is obviously present, but perhaps not so clearly present in this seminar as elsewhere in Lacan's work. We can designate this desire with our symbol for lack: $-\phi$ (minus phi).

The subject is lack, for s/he has lost his or her being. In this intersection, what is present and what is superimposed is desire's lack (the Other's lack) and the subject's lost being. A quote from "Position of the Unconscious" summarizes the whole development of separation: "The subject finds anew in the Other's desire the equivalent of what he is *qua* subject of the unconscious" (*Écrits* 1966, 843). What does that mean? We can write the Other with a hole, and the subject with a hole as well, and the sentence then becomes "the subject encounters in the Other's lack [the Other's desire is a lack] the equivalent of what he is as unconscious subject or subject of the signifier."

The subject's strategy in separation is very simple in reality. The subject, unknown and lacking in being, is a subject who wants to be. The subject is searching for being. You need lack if you want to understand the will as a search. For example, the subject who very clearly shows us the search for being is the hysterical subject. The dramatic position of the hysterical subject stems from the fact that s/he feels his or her own lack and suffers from it. Not every subject suffers from his or her own lack, but the hysterical subject has a strong feeling of being a void or nothing, and nothing but a void or envelope. In clinical work we find that the hysterical subject is searching for a sense or feeling of being—desperately, in general.

What is a simpler strategy? To have some feeling of being is to be loved or, more precisely, to be desired: to think there is someone who can't live without you or misses you. In that case you have a feeling of being. A great many people, above all those with hysterical structures and especially women hysterics, go into analysis because of a failure in a love relationship or the loss of a loved one. It is quite evident that this occurs because a hysterical subject is always positioned at the level of separation, i.e., at the level of questioning the Other's desire.

The greatest source of anxiety for the hysterical subject is, perhaps, that there is no place for him or her in the Other. This is why the hysterical subject always tries to make the Other incomplete. The obsessive subject is also positioned at the level of separation, but his or her strategy is different. The hysterical subject searches for the Other's lack, while the obsessive subject is afraid and flees the Other's desire because the Other's lack makes him or her anxious. The obsessive subject is very different from the hysterical subject in a certain sense, but the two subjects, as neurotic subjects, nevertheless share the same point of reference: the lack in the Other.

Thus, finally, the question which brings the subject to the point of separation is: What am I in the Other's desire? Psychoanalysis is the process of answering that question. In the end, Lacan says the subject can know what s/he is in the Other's desire without forgetting that the Other's desire is his or her own desire. I illustrated the problem with the desire for a partner, but this example shows that, when we speak of the Other's desire, it is the subject's desire as well.

Thus we have isolated the question; now we need to find the answer. The main problem of psychoanalysis is to provide the answer to this question. A neurosis is a question, and psychoanalysis claims to be able to provide the answer, or to permit the subject to obtain the answer.

Who can answer this question? The Other cannot, because all you can grasp in the Other are signifiers which don't allow you to answer the question due to alienation; the other part that can be grasped in the Other is a void. (Signifiers are elements of the set of the Other and desire is another part of the set of the Other. Thus you have to distinguish in the set of the Other between "elements" and "parts." When Lacan speaks about separation, he speaks about parts, and that is why desire is part of the Other without being an element of the Other.) It is not the Other who provides the answer, because in the Other you encounter only signifiers and the void—what Lacan called the interval between signifiers. The interval is a void.

Is it the subject who can answer the question? The subject of speech cannot, because the subject of speech is an alienated subject, i.e., a subject in whom one finds only signifiers and the void. Thus you need someone else. Who? Being. The being that answers is libido.

Libido is linked with the subject of speech, but is nevertheless something else altogether. If you prefer, "jouissance" can serve as a Lacanian translation of the Freudian term "libido." The answer to the question "what is the subject beyond the signifier?" is the drive. Thus the interval, intersection, or void between subject and Other is not as empty as all that, but it is an emptiness into which something comes. It is object *a*, insofar as object *a* is not always a logical, but also a bodily consistency, and also insofar as object *a* is a *plus de jouir*, as Lacan says—surplus jouissance.

It is only at the level of the drives that you find the answer to the subject's ineffable question. In speech, the subject beyond meaning is always ineffable, but in reality s/he is not always so ineffable, because s/he is also the subject of jouissance. Lacan articulates both speech and jouissance at the level of separation.

Thus the drives answer the question because the drives are silent. The drives don't speak because they satisfy themselves silently in action. For example, when a subject is a voyeur (I don't mean a pervert, but an ordinary neurotic subject with a scopic drive), the satisfaction of the drive is silent, and it is not in time. The temporal structure of the drive's satisfaction is the instant. It is a glimpse. In a glimpse the subject wants something that allows him or her to obtain a specific satisfaction. Here I can only provide an indication. It is important to understand the problem of time in psychoanalysis, i.e., the short session.

There are a lot of things one could say about time in the psychoanalytic session, but what I want to emphasize here is that there are two times in psychoanalysis, two times of the subject. There is the time of the signifier, that is, the time organized between anticipation and retroaction. That is the time of speech, if we symbolize speech, which develops as the speaker speaks. You are waiting for the last word of the sentence, which implies anticipation. And when somebody is giving a lecture, as for example now, you are necessarily waiting for the end because it is only at the end that you can ask yourself, "What has she said?" That implies retroaction. Together they constitute the time of the signifier. The time of the drive is very different. It is a time of encounter, structured like an instant, which operates as a cut in the continuity of signifying time. Thus it is not at the level of the signifier that the time of the psychoanalytic session is to be understood.

My last point today is that a subject is divided by the drive. We can say that it is in the drive that we find the true will of the subject, but it is not a conscious will. It is a will of which the subject is sometimes unaware at the beginning of analysis. The drive is something the subject can't help or stop in him or herself. It is not chosen or assumed in most cases.

Thus the subject is divided not only by the signifier, but by the drive as well. Analysis, in this sense, gives the analysand knowledge—the ability to learn something about him or herself. In his "Introductory Talk at Sainte-Anne Hospital,"[2] Jacques-Alain Miller spoke about discovery, which is not the same as what I am talking about here. He spoke about the discovery of unconscious knowledge. Something written with a signifier, a constant factor inscribed in the unconscious, is discovered. But there is also something learned, which is not completely inscribed or written, and that is the specific form of satisfaction the subject encounters in the drive. S/he can discover something about his or her unconscious as knowledge, but can also learn something about him or herself as a libidinal subject.

Notes

1. For a detailed discussion of Lacan's modification of set theory's classical operators, see "Alienation and Separation: Logical Moments of Lacan's Dialectic of Desire," *Newsletter of the Freudian Field,* 4, 1990.

2. Included in this volume.

SCIENCE AND PSYCHOANALYSIS

Bruce Fink

Lacan's seminars seem to me to be of perennial interest, and Seminar XI in particular. That is partly due to the fact that few people have paid any attention to what he said. In other words, we find ourselves in a situation where we must fight the very same battles Lacan was fighting some 27 years ago. What happened to Lacan in 1963? After a long series of meetings and arguments and back-stabbing and mudslinging, Lacan was more or less forced to leave the *Société française de psychanalyse* (SFP) because the International Psychoanalytical Association (IPA) refused to allow Lacan to be involved in the training of analysts. According to Lacan, the SFP was forced to promise to never ever let Lacan have anything to do with training analysts officially certified by the SFP. Lacan would either have to change his way of practicing psychoanalysis, agree to no longer train any analysts, or leave.

The projected unification of the European market looms ever more ominously on the horizon in Europe—not so ominously for international capital, but ominously for psychoanalysis—as certain forces within the IPA (Jean Laplanche for one) are trying to convince the various European governments that some sort of *standardized* certification is necessary to *regulate* the practice of psychoanalysis. In other words, those forces are pushing to make it illegal for non-state-certified analysts to practice. They are wittingly or unwittingly hoping to instate the American model whereby all analytic practitioners have to prove that they have been trained by an *accredited* institute that requires a specific number of hours of analysis, a specific number of hours of course work, and a specific number of hours of supervision. Otherwise they will not be allowed to practice, and will run serious legal risks if they see patients on the black market that is bound to spring up. State accreditation or certification of an institute or individual practitioner is necessarily based on a certain number of relatively fixed criteria, which are most easily implemented when quantifiable—452 hours of psychoanalysis, 326 hours of supervision, etc.—and who is going to establish those criteria, and on what basis? The answer in the case of Europe seems clear: IPA politicking analysts who are deliberately lobbying against the Lacanian institutes. Can you imagine what would happen if all of the French analysts who will be speaking to you in the course of the next two and a half weeks and all of their colleagues were suddenly forced to either give up practicing, practice in secret, or try to start their training all over again in IPA-accredited institutes?! Bedlam, sheer bedlam. From what I hear it seems unlikely to happen, but an attempt to impose such a system upon them is clearly being made.

In the name of what? In the name of bureaucracy? I hardly think so. In the name of public safety, i.e., of protecting the public from charlatans? That particular issue is no doubt being mentioned. But it seems more likely that it is in the name of science. The motives are surely political, but will no doubt be couched in the form of concerns about protecting the seriousness and scientificity of psychoanalysis as a theory and a practice. Whenever you want to throw someone out of your field—assuming it's a so-called social science or a so-called hard science—you claim that his or her work is unscientific, i.e., that it cannot withstand serious theoretical scrutiny or is scientifically irresponsible. In other words, you appeal to Science with a capital S.

The very first question Lacan raises in Seminar XI is: what is it that *authorizes* him to be speaking to his audience. (7) His question seems to be intended to apply more generally: what is it that authorizes him to be speaking in front of such a large public, a public unlike any he had prior to that time, no longer restricted primarily to psychoanalysts, but including all kinds of students in more strictly academic disciplines? What authorizes him to have any kind of a following at all now that he's been excommunicated from the association that was the seat of his most seemingly appropriate audience? The answer to that question seems to hinge on answers to further questions he raises: "What is psychoanalysis?" (9) and "Is psychoanalysis a science?" (12)

In this seminar and in several of the seminars that follow, Lacan is concerned with situating the status of psychoanalysis as either inside or outside of science, and that inevitably leads him to elaborate a theory of what science is, of what constitutes science, of how a scientific field is constructed, of its object, and so on. Lacan is preoccupied here with determining the nature and status of psychoanalytic "knowledge" and of the kind of truth at stake in psychoanalytic praxis. There are two articles in the *Écrits* in which these themes are taken up in some detail: "Position of the Unconscious," which Lacan wrote up in March of 1964 in the midst of *The Four Fundamental Concepts of Psychoanalysis*, and "Science and Truth," written as the first class of his seminar on *The Object of Psychoanalysis* in the fall of 1965. Lacan begins the seminar we have before us, Seminar XI, with some interesting reflections on the status of psychoanalysis and the nature of science.

Right from the outset, Lacan sets up a dichotomy: it seems that psychoanalysis can be classified either as a science or a religion. But while he rarely comes right out with his position anywhere in any of his texts, he hints at his true position here right from the outset:

> Psychoanalysis, whether or not it is worthy of being included in one of these two registers [science or religion], may even enlighten us as to what we should understand by a science, and even by a religion. (7)

In other words, he immediately situates psychoanalysis in the privileged position of being able to help us figure out what a science or a religion is, from outside, as it were, from some other position.

Lacan brings up the point, which was no doubt often made to him, that psychoanalysis is a form of research. He mentions that he is suspicious of the term research, and that he has never viewed himself as a researcher who goes out in search of truth. He quotes Picasso in saying "I do not seek, I find," and goes on to suggest that seeking and finding are in a sense activities that separate non-science from science. He characterizes religion by the famous line: "you would not seek me if you had not already found me," pointing out that the essential activity here is the seeking, as the having already found is in some way forgotten.

The very same activity characterizes the so-called human sciences in that they search for and research meaning wherever they look, meaning in its infinite, inexhaustible movement, where there is no inherent stopping point or term. Social scientists feel threatened by whomever is in the business of finding. Lacan sums up decades of barking up the wrong tree with the expression "hermeneutic revindication," designating thereby the demand on the part of hermeneutically oriented philosophers, psychologists, and social scientists that meaning be subject to endless elaboration, that social acts, human behaviors, and texts be open to unlimited, unbounded glossing and interpretation: the implication being that *there is no truth at hand*.

Many people believe that that is implicitly true of the process of psychoanalytic interpretation as well: Paul Ricoeur championed that view in France, and his work was read the world over. In Ricoeur's work, there is no ultimate stopping point, no final reference to truth, and interpretation is an infinite, unbounded project. To Lacan's mind, the very term "research" evokes that whole hermeneutic perspective.

Lacan clearly states here that psychoanalytic interpretation has nothing to do with this hermeneutical view. Interpretation aims at truth in psychoanalytic praxis, and one could even go so far as to say that it creates truth. That is a property it shares with true science as Lacan understands it: it creates something new, it introduces a new symbol or symbolism into the world, touching the real to the quick. That is thus one level at which we can distinguish religion and hermeneutically-inspired "human sciences" from psychoanalysis and from what Lacan calls science.

It seems to me that psychoanalysis cannot, according to Lacanian criteria, be considered to constitute a science. Like Freud, Lacan at times tried to bring psychoanalytic considerations under the aegis of science. In his doctoral dissertation in 1931, he claimed that psychological phenomena could be considered to be simple facts analyzable by scientific methods, as in the "hard sciences." Just as in the early days of physics, when certain phenomena were observed and taken to be simple facts which have since been found to be macro-phenomena that can be broken down and studied in a far more refined manner, in psychoanalysis, Lacan wrote, we are justified in studying the simplest mental events we can currently identify, knowing full well that in time our objects of study as well as our methods will be further refined. While never a biological determinist like Freud, in the early 1930s Lacan nevertheless believed in a sort of psychological determinism permitting of scientific treatment. His views on science evolved, however, and by 1964, in an article in the *Écrits* entitled "Position of the Unconscious," Lacan considers psychoanalysis to be what he refers to as a "conjectural science," with a status akin to that of game theory. In game theory, probabilities can be very precisely calculated, and abstraction can be made of the subject except insofar as the subject occupies a particular position in a game whose aim is given at the outset. In other words, game theory strips the individual of all of his or her characteristics, reducing subjectivity to a purely positional notion.

By "Science and Truth," written in 1965, Lacan's position has already changed again slightly: Lacan is no longer seeking to rally psychoanalysts around the banner of science—whether it be a "pure science" (like physics), or a human science like anthropology or linguistics. Lacan's claim at this stage is that psychoanalytic theory and praxis would never have been possible before the advent of modern science. I will try to explain why he makes out such a claim in a moment, but lest there be any misunderstanding on this point—and the point is a rather important one in an American empiricist context—let me make it clear that Lacan takes modern science to have been a necessary precondition for the development of psychoanalysis, and that while psychoanalysis is thus in a sense a by-product of scientific discourse, it does not in and of itself constitute a science.

A debate over the epistemological foundations of science began, in a sense, with the logical positivists of the Vienna school (Carnap), reached a serious turning point with Kuhn's work on *The Structure of Scientific Revolutions*, and continued with Lakatos, Feyerabend, and many other above all continental thinkers. Lacan, having attended Koyré's lectures for many years in Paris, and having kept abreast of work in the history of science of his time (Canguilhem, etc.), never seems to have cherished the naive notion that true science is 100% empirical—a notion that turns up time and again in American discussions on the scientific or unscientific status of psychoanalysis and of social sciences like sociology and anthropology. Freud himself was well aware of the importance of concepts in the foundation of any science, and realized that the concepts that go into the construction of any theoretical system are not derived exclusively from empirical considerations. In other words, any theoretical system must be at least in part built up on the basis of concepts that already exist in the researcher's mind, society, or culture. A science begins with a thinker's intuitive ideas, and those intuitive ideas come from his or her culture and language. Lacan had the advantage over Freud of three or four additional decades of research into the history of science: into the history of the true mechanisms driving scientific work, paradigm changes, and theory construction. He was also very excited about the possibilities being opened up by the "newer sciences" like structural linguistics and structural anthropology. In Seminar XI, Lacan explicitly refers to linguistics as a newly forming science which accounts for the scientific status of the unconscious (and which must be rigorously distinguished from social psychology). (20) He seems to have felt for a while that these newer sciences could constitute model types of sciences which could account for the status of a structural form of psychoanalysis as well.

But in "Science and Truth," Lacan indicates his disenchantment with such an approach. By 1965, his point of view is that psychoanalysis is radically different from any of these other disciplines, and that its epistemological status is not identical to that of linguistics, anthropology, or astronomy. Rather, psychoanalysis, instead of asking to be judged in terms of these other already established fields, is itself, according to Lacan, in a position to comment upon the structure of these recognizably scientific disciplines and pass judgment on their shortcomings.

Where does Lacan draw the line between science and psychoanalysis?

At the level of their divergent relationships to truth. Let's take the term "truth" in an ordinary, intuitive way for the time being. In describing what he takes science's relation to truth to be, Lacan brings up Descartes. According to Lacan, Descartes set out to find certainty, to find something which he could not throw into doubt. Descartes went so far as to throw the simplest truths of arithmetic into doubt: how can we be sure, he asked himself, 2 and 2 really add up to 4? Unlike Kant, Descartes ultimately concluded that while he could not be truly sure of the time-worn truths of mathematics, he could with full confidence state "I am thinking, therefore I am." What happens to those time-worn truths in Descartes' system? 2 plus 2 is 4 because God wants it to be that way. Responsibility for the truth is passed off to God—God guarantees such truths, while man becomes free to seek certainty as he can.

According to Lacan, Descartes set modern man free of the burden of truth—for most thinkers prior to Descartes truth was more or less co-extensive with Scripture—and allowed him to go on to develop knowledge that referred to nothing outside of itself. A post-Cartesian could at long last forego quoting the Bible at every step of the way, and begin to spin a web of ideas that stood on its own two feet, so to speak. Truth was set aside; it became a secondary consideration compared to that of applying to reality a symbolic grid, expressible in numeric terms, and developing the endless set of relations among the elements constituting that symbolic grid.

Thus to Lacan's mind, Descartes helped usher out the concern with transcendent truth, a concern clearly expressed in Plato's metaphor of the cave wherein man is likened to a poor creature trapped in a cave with but the faintest light by which to make out the world around him. Plato's concern with discerning the world by that infinitely brighter light outside of the cave, like that expressed in Christianity in the mysterious ways in which God is supposed to work, was at last cast aside by a number of philosophers—and most scientific inquiry was being carried out at that time by philosophers. That casting aside lent a new independence to the development of the sciences: relations were drawn between scientific notions in one field and scientific notions in another, and the mathematization of observable phenomena that had been so effective in physics was applied to other domains as well. Scientific discourse acquired a momentum of its own, obeying its own rules and developing its own internal structure. The theory or system of symbols that best *accounted for* the phenomena observable using the available scientific equipment was retained, while truth was relegated to the philosophers and considered a matter of sheer speculation. The development of sciences was obviously still tied to economic and political conditions, but a certain number of restrictions—epistemological strictures, so to speak—were lifted.

The Burden of Truth

The first distinction Lacan makes between science and psychoanalysis is that whereas science excludes considerations of truth, psychoanalysis takes truth as its fundamental point of reference.

Science and mathematics go so far as to reduce truth to a kind of value. In truth tables in logic, the letters T and F are assigned to various possible combinations of propositions.

A	B	A and B	
T	T	T	line 1
T	F	F	line 2
F	T	F	line 3
F	F	F	line 4

If I assert that Lacan was French (that's proposition A) and that he never set foot outside of France (that's proposition B), both A and B must be true individually in order for my statement as a whole to be true. The four lines in the truth table represent all four possible combinations taken into account by this kind of propositional logic. A can be either true or false, B can be either true or false, and thus any combination of their *truth values* is theoretically possible. If only one of them is true, my statement as a whole is false. It is only when both of them are true that my statement as a whole is true (line 1).

Logic thus relies on the designations "true" and "false," but these terms take on meaning only within propositional logic: they are values understandable within the axiomatic field defined by that logic. They make no claims to independent validity. They in no sense concern transcendental truth as understood by Plato or Kant.

"True" and "false" are thus simple values in scientific discourse, like plus and minus, 0 and 1: they are binary opposites that play a role in a specific context. Truth, on the other hand, is relegated to other disciplines in the world of modern science, be they poetry and literature, or religion and philosophy. In a word, Descartes marks the historical moment at which science breaks away from philosophy.

Thus while all the sciences—from anthropology to zoology—eject truth from their respective fields, psychoanalysis takes upon itself the burden of truth. Whatever truth's exact nature is, psychoanalysis assumes responsibility for it.

Psychologization of the Subject

In "Science and Truth," Lacan criticizes Lévy-Bruhl, a French sociologist who spent his time trying to get into the heads of the so-called "primitive" peoples he studied, and who came up with the glorious distinction between rational, objective thought—that of modern Western man—and primitive, pre-logical thought—that of his aborigines. Lévy-Bruhl tried to explain the behavior of such peoples on the basis of their feelings and belief systems—something Freud himself would have frowned upon, and which Lacan considered altogether misguided, neglecting as it does the importance of the unconscious and of the symbolic order itself. Lévi-Strauss offers up a prototype of true scientific anthropology in that he does not so much try to explain tribal behavior on the basis of the feelings expressed by his informers as on the linguistic distinctions made in the tribe between what is sacred and what is profane and as to which moitiés can marry with which others. As complimentary as Lacan often is about Lévi-Strauss' brand of structural anthropology, he is still critical thereof insofar as it does not take truth into account.

The term Lacan uses here is "psychologization of the subject." Whenever people try to explain the violence of British soccer fans by saying that the British feel badly over the loss of their former empire, or to account for Nazism by saying that the Germans believe in the fatherland, their explanations are based on the supposed conscious beliefs and feelings of the individuals in question. Freud teaches us that human motivation is not that simple, given the tremendous role of the unconscious in the determination of human action, and Lacan teaches us to seek explanations in the symbolic order itself: the unconscious, he says, is the discourse of the Other, i.e., the unconscious consists of linguistic elements, phrases, expressions, commands, social and religious laws and conventions that are part of the culture at large as well as being part and parcel of every household. The unconscious is composed of the speech of a child's parents and family members, itself largely determined by the social/linguistic world around them. Explanations are thus, to Lacan's mind, to be sought in the symbolic order insofar as it has become the basis for an individual's unconscious.

"Psychologization of the subject" means that one takes an individual at face value, polling his or her conscious attitudes and beliefs, and using them in constructing one's theory. Lacan takes Lévy-Bruhl to task for doing precisely that, and accuses Piaget of finding nothing more, in his studies of the logic employed by children, than the logic Piaget himself used in designing the tests he administered to children. Both of them fall into the trap of the "archaic illusion." To Lévy-Bruhl the primitive is a lesser version of a modern person, and like a child is stuck at an earlier stage of development; to Piaget a child does not have a specific logic all his or her own, but is rather gropingly acquiring one adult moral notion after another. Neither thinker ever seems to attempt to understand the particular workings of the primitive or child's system as it stands, to understand the complex series of synchronic relationships among terms, or the substitutions and displacements that take place in the diachronic unfolding of the system. What Lévi-Strauss dubbed the "archaic illusion," this tendency to view tribe members as childlike in their development or rather underdevelopment (with adult modern Western man as the norm of full development), is generalized by Lacan with the expression "psychologization of the subject." A truly scientific anthropology is one which is able to avoid that pitfall.

The Conjectural Sciences

In considering examples of scientific disciplines, Lacan also takes up game theory. According to Lacan, in game theory "one takes advantage of the thoroughly calculable character of a subject strictly reduced to the formula for a matrix of signifying combinations." In other words, a player in game theory is a positional notion (A is the attacker, B the defender or opponent), and each position is defined by a strictly defined number of possible moves. The rules of the game define what moves are licit, and the goal of the game determines why a player chooses one move instead of another. In game theory, all of the possibilities available to a particular player can be listed in a matrix of symbolically or numerically defined moves. Game theory thus provides a formalization of game situations wherein the probability of a player making a particular move can be precisely calculated, as can the best possible move or moves.

According to Lacan, when a so-called conjectural science like game theory can offer such precise calculation, the distinction between the exact sciences and the conjectural sciences breaks down. In quantum physics, an electron's position in a particular orbital around a nucleus is given by a simple probability curve: there is a 50% chance, say, of finding the electron within 1 micron of the nucleus, a 20% chance of finding it 1 to 2 microns from the nucleus, and so on (these distances are by no means exact!). Quantum mechanics' extensive reliance on probability brings it closer and closer in structure to conjectural sciences like game theory. (Though Lacan refers in Seminar XI to linguistics as a "human science," he rather disliked that term and adopted that of "conjectural sciences.")

Subject and Cause

While attempting to formalize psychoanalysis in many ways, Lacan certainly never finally categorizes psychoanalysis as a conjectural science in which the subject can be reduced to a simple position characterized by a simple aim. And he parts ways with structuralism, as the latter implies an attempt to explain everything in terms of a more or less mathematically determinate combinatory which plays itself out without any reference whatsoever to subjects or objects. While structure plays a very important role in Lacan's work, it is not the whole story, nor was it ever at any point in Lacan's development.

In Seminar X, *Anxiety*, Lacan associates the supposed progress of science with our increasing inability to think the category "cause." Continually filling in the "gap" between cause and effect, science progressively eliminates the content of the concept "cause"—events leading smoothly, in accordance with well-known "laws," to other events. Lacan understands cause in a more radical sense, as that which disrupts the smooth functioning of lawlike interactions. Causality in science is absorbed into what we might call structure—cause leading to effect within an ever more exhaustive set of laws. A cause as something that seems not to obey laws, remaining inexplicable from the standpoint of scientific knowledge, has become unthinkable—our general tendency being to think that it will just be a matter of time before science can explain it.

What distinguishes psychoanalysis from the other sciences is that whereas linguistics, for example, takes into account the subject only insofar as he or she is determined by the symbolic order, i.e., by the signifier, psychoanalysis also takes into account the cause, and the subject in his or her libidinal relation to the cause. The two faces of the subject: 1) the "pure subject" of the combinatory or matrix—the subject without a cause, as it were, and 2) the "saturated subject," as Lacan calls it—i.e., the subject in relation to an object of jouissance (a libidinal object), the subject as a stance adopted with respect to jouissance.

That relation between a subject and an object is present in Lacan's formula for fantasy ($ ◊ a$), and that is what Lacan means when he talks about the saturated subject. It's not your typical French person who eats gobs of "saturated fats" such as butter and *crème fraîche*; it's a subject characterized by the dialectical relations of alienation and separation.[1]

The project of psychoanalysis is, in part, to maintain and further explore these two primordial concepts—cause and subject—however paradoxical they may seem. Lacan even goes so far as to say that, were object a as cause to be introduced into science, science itself would be fundamentally transformed.

Note

1. See Seminars XI, XIV, and XV, "Position of the Unconscious" in the *Écrits*, my article "Alienation and Separation: Logical Moments of Lacan's Dialectic of Desire" in *Newsletter of the Freudian Field*, 4, 1990, and Éric Laurent's papers included in this volume on those logical operations.

THE NAME-OF-THE-FATHER

François Regnault

The Name-of-the-Father may easily be considered a major concept of Lacanian psychoanalysis. People are sometimes inclined to take it for granted because of Freud's considerations about the murder of the father in *Totem and Taboo*, but I prefer not to consider it obvious and instead, to express surprise. The father, fine, but why his name?

The Name-of-the-Father is a Lacanian concept, not a Freudian concept. It becomes more and more important to Lacan as his work advances, although it cannot be considered a "fundamental" concept, because there are only four fundamental concepts of psychoanalysis to his mind: the unconscious, repetition, the drive, and transference.

Even so, it is of crucial importance, so much so that Lacan intended to devote a whole year-long seminar to it in 1963, but was forced to leave Sainte-Anne Hospital before he could give more than one lecture. He never came back to that topic as such, though he very often discussed it briefly. He even called one of his later seminars, that given in 1973–1974, *Les non-dupes errent*, which is a play on *Les Noms-du-Père* (the two syntagms are pronounced the same way in French), and means "those who are not duped err"—the people who always pretend not to be mistaken are the most mistaken. But the pun also means that instead of *"les Noms du Père,"* which Lacan refused to take up again as such, a substitution is made: non-dupes take the place of the father, and their errancy takes the place of his name.

It is more than just a question of institution or status. It also means that it is of the nature of a name to be substituted: it is substitution itself!

65

Indeed, the name *as* father is as important in Lacan's theory as the father as name (*Ornicar?* **5**, 54). I shall therefore try to define this concept and trace its evolution in Lacan's thought.

The Father

If we refer to the Rome discourse, "Function and Field of Speech and Language in Psychoanalysis," it is clear that the father functions, first of all, to support the symbol, i.e., to prop up the symbolic order. Man is constituted by that order: "Man speaks, then, but it is because the symbol has made him man" (*Écrits*, 65).

Following Lévi-Strauss, who provides Lacan with the formal, structural laws of relationships—a symbolic order constituted around a sort of void, which is the prohibition of incest—Lacan remarks:

> It is in the Name-of-the-Father that we must recognize the support of the symbolic function which, from the dawn of history, has identified his person with the figure of the law. This conception enables us to distinguish clearly, in the analysis of a case, the unconscious effects of that function from the narcissistic or even real relations the subject sustains with the image and actions of the person who embodies that function (*Écrits*, 67).

This means that we have to distinguish the symbolic function of the father, which can be found in the signifier as such (i.e., in the signifying chain), from the imaginary relationship between the father and child. It also means that one of the most fundamental principles in psychoanalysis is that the father is first of all a name—a signifier—and only secondarily a person (a man, in most cases). Thus fathers cannot be found in nature, because the animal that has begotten you is only a contingent medium for the name you give him. Stated otherwise, animals, strictly speaking, have no fathers. (Nor mothers, and certainly not uncles or aunts, nephews, cousins, etc. Except of course if you tame and breed them, and bring them into your symbolic order: then you give them a pedigree.)

From the clinical standpoint, it is clear that a young child encounters its mother's desire, and that beyond that desire, it comes up against something which it feels its mother is obeying: the law of the father. It encounters its father as a signifier through that law, not necessarily the man it may love or hate, and with whom it identifies. Thus a separation takes place, not between the child and its mother and father, but, Lacan says, between the breast as cause of desire, and the mother who represents the father's law at that moment.

At that moment too, the idea or rather the experience of a symbolic debt to its father takes root. That debt means that there is too much of something in one place and not enough of it elsewhere, allowing objects, goods, and women to circulate and move along the signifying chain in a primitive tribe's social relations.

The Name-of-the-Father poses a twofold problem: that of the father and that of the name, or indeed, that of the symbolic father—the father as a name—and that of the proper name. In one sense, "father" is not at all a proper name (from a logical or Russellian point of view), and in another sense, it is *the* proper name. We receive his name; we get our name from him, through him, because of him, and so on.

Lacan begins with Freud's view of the father as the tyrant of the primal horde who is murdered and becomes a symbolic totem; he arrives at a view of the father as a proper name, a pure signifier, a sort of mathematical or formal property.

Freud also considers the father to be a name. For instance in *Totem and Taboo*, he remarks that, in some Australian tribes, "a man uses the term 'father' not only for his actual procreator, but also for all the other men his mother might have married according to tribal law and who therefore might have procreated him." (6) The same is true for the term "mother."

But it is also true that Freud considered the father to be essentially the dead father. And in his reference to Australian tribes, it is not the father who names, but rather the son. In one of the last articles of the *Écrits*, Lacan asks: what is a father? His answer is very clear: " 'It is the dead father,' Freud replies, but no one listens, and, concerning the aspect Lacan takes up again with the term 'Name-of-the-Father' it is regrettable that so unscientific a situation should still deprive him of his normal audience" (*Écrits*, 310). It is as if neither Freud nor Lacan could be believed when they spoke of the symbolic father.

Let me bring out another difference between Freud and Lacan regarding this concept. Whereas Freud, in *Totem and Taboo*, essentially refers to ethnological data, representing mankind's past, Lacan refers to religion representing mankind's present as well: "if the symbolic context requires it, paternity will nonetheless be attributed to the fact that the woman met a spirit at some fountain or rock in which he is supposed to live." So much for ethnology. But Lacan continues:

> It is certainly this that demonstrates that the attribution of procreation to the father can only be the effect of a pure signifier—the effect of recognition, not of a real father, but of what religion has taught us to refer to as the Name-of-the-Father (*Écrits*, 199).

So much for religion—even one of the most important and recent ones, the Christian religion, in which the Name-of-the-Father is the first name to be invoked, before being associated with those of the Son and the Holy Ghost.

Lacan does not postulate that psychoanalysis is a science (cf. Popper and others). Rather he asks: "What would a science that includes psychoanalysis look like?" (Seminar XI, chapter 4). That is why he asserts that the subject of psychoanalysis is the same as the subject of science. He even goes so far as to defend Freud's scientism. But it is important to point out that the concept of the Name-of-the-Father comes from religion, not science. While there are many religions, and they can never belong to the same category nor have a common essence, constituting an inconsistent class, religion in the singular could nevertheless be defined in a Lacanian manner as that which teaches us the Name-of-the-Father. Religion not only teaches it, but respects it. Which may lead to a catastrophe—offering up sacrifices to obscure gods, as for instance in Nazism (where father and *Führer* are linked).

It is because religion situates the symbol at so high a level that one can say that. This leads Lacan to be truly interested in theology, much more so than Freud, and essentially in Christian theology. Let us not forget that the Koran, for instance, refuses to refer to God as a father, and scoffs at the family of the Holy Trinity.

This is also why Lacan often quotes the passage in the Bible in which Adam names the animals and plants. When you say "the Name-of-the-Father," you can consider the "of" as either a subjective genitive—the names God goes by, the names you call God (the "divine names" are a well-known problem in theology)—or an objective genitive—the names a father gives his children. The "Name-of-the-Father" can thus refer either to the father's name or the name the father gives his sons or daughters, the name by which we refer to our God or the names God gives his creatures. This is a precious ambiguity.

By way of conclusion on this point, let me quote another passage from "On a Question Preliminary to Any Possible Treatment of Psychosis" concerning the relationship between fatherhood and death:

> How, indeed, could Freud fail to recognize such an affinity, when the necessity of his reflection led him to link the appearance of the signifier of the Father, as author of the Law, with death, and even with the murder of the Father—thus showing that, while this murder is the fruitful moment of debt through which the subject binds himself for life to the Law, the symbolic Father is the dead Father insofar as he signifies this Law (*Écrits*, 199).

Naming

We shall now consider three problems of names and naming in relation to the father. I shall not discuss Lacan's considerations about proper names in the seminars that preceded his undelivered seminar on the Names-of-the-Father. But I shall say that the problem gets more and more complicated from 1963 on. In the end, the Name-of-the-Father is the Borromean knot itself.

First of all, the essence of naming, with regard to the father, is substitution: it is as if, as soon as you know your father's name (which is also your name), you are led to suppose another name, and yet another, and so on *ad infinitum*. That is why Lacan prefers saying the Name*s*-of-the Father. Thus there are only metaphorical names, which is why the Name-of-the-Father (in the singular) is in fact a metaphor. One signifier is substituted for another. But the main signifier to be substituted is the phallus, which represents something missing, such that, as Lacan says, for the subject's imaginary, "the signification of the phallus . . . is evoked by the paternal metaphor."

The formula for metaphor Lacan provides (*Écrits*, 200) is as follows:

$$\frac{S}{S'} \cdot \frac{S'}{x} \longrightarrow S\left(\frac{1}{s}\right)$$

Where:
   S = signifier
   x = unknown signification
   s = signified produced

If you apply that formula to the paternal metaphor, you get a metaphor which puts a name in the place where the mother is absent (recall here the *fort-da* game Freud discusses in *Beyond the Pleasure Principle*):

$$\frac{\text{Name-of-the-Father}}{\text{Desire of the Mother}} \cdot \frac{\text{Desire of the Mother}}{\text{Signified to the subject}} \longrightarrow \text{Name-of-the-Father}\left(\frac{O}{\text{phallus}}\right)$$

   Where O = Other

It is when such a name or signifier proves to be missing that something is "out of joint," to borrow Hamlet's expression. This is why Lacan asserts that the very structure of psychosis is what he calls a foreclosure (an exclusion or elimination) of the Name-of-the-Father. Something does not fit.

The Name-of-the-Father, which is substitution as such, is an unusual signifier. Its signification is that of a signifier which is missing from the battery of signifiers, that is, from the field of the Other. Thus Lacan writes O/phallus instead of 1/s in his formula for the paternal metaphor.

Lacan applies that to Schreber, whose whole psychosis begins when, not being able to have children, that is, to become *a* father, he becomes a woman—God's wife.

By way of conclusion on this point, we can guess the function and usefulness of the Name-of-the-Father by considering what Lacan says in "Position of the Unconscious":

> On the side of the Other, the locus in which speech is verified as it en-
> counters the exchange of signifiers, the ideals they prop up, the elemen-
> tary structures of kinship, the paternal metaphor considered *qua* principle
> of separation, and the ever reopened division in the subject owing to his
> primal alienation—on this side alone and by the pathways I have just
> enumerated, order and norms must be instituted which tell the subject
> what a man or a woman must do. (*Écrits*, 1966, 849)

Let us now refer to one of the first graphs Lacan uses to represent, among other things, the link between the paternal function and his trilogy: real, imaginary, and symbolic. He considers the subject to be structured by three relations: the symbolic order, as we have seen, the imaginary (beginning with the constitution of his ego, especially when he considers himself as a whole in the mirror, and falls into the illusion of believing himself autonomous), and thirdly the object or "real thing" (cf. the beautiful title of a short story by Henry James) which causes desire. Lacan constructs a square which represents the structure of the subject, both from a static point of view and from a dynamic (or historical) point of view.

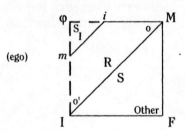

Schema R

It is constituted by the association of two triangles: that of the symbolic order and that of the imaginary, which are linked together by the quadrangle of the real.

S: subject under the signifier of the phallus
i, m: imaginary terms of the narcissistic relationship
I: ego ideal
M: mother, primal object
F in O: position in the Other of the Name-of-the-Father

From a static point of view we have:
Triangle I: dual relation of the ego in the Other (i=o), φ, m, i.
Triangle S: I, signifier of the object M (=a), Name-of-the-Father F in the field of the Other.
Triangle R: considered as the effect of the symbolic on the imaginary (the real as a remainder).
From i to M: aggressive and erotic relationships.
From m to I: the ego, from its Urbild to paternal identification.

From an historical point of view we have:
The relationship with the Mother (real Other)—*das Ding.*
The different images which form the ego.

In 1966, Lacan explains that this square, which in 1958 he considered from a geometrical or algebraic point of view, must also be reinterpreted topologically as unilateral surfaces (cf. the Möbius strip). You have to join *i* to I and *m* to M (cf. Vappereau, *Etoffe,* 240-1).

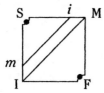 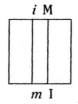 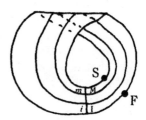

Schema R Topologically Transformed

In such a strip, *m* and M first, and *i* and I secondly, are identical (*mi* = MI). If you cut the strip from *i* to *m* (= from I to M), you once again obtain the flat surface of Schema R. The subject is that cut itself, and what falls away through the action of cutting is the object. In Lacan's view, the subject is structured like an edge, and the object is structured like a fallen remnant. But you cannot see either the subject or the object on the strip (*mM/i*I). It is interpretation that cuts the strip and produces both subject and object.

In such a schema, you see that the Name-of-the-Father is a firm, fixed point which orients the subject's relationships. On the strip, on the contrary, F and S are borders constituting only one side, but a hole as well.

It is possible to refer to the Name-of-the-Father as that hole. At one time, Lacan might have thought that the subject was equally determined by the symbolic, imaginary, and real—equally oppressed or strangled by them. Later he came to believe that a certain topological structure, the Borromean knot, was the perfect structure for sorting out the threefold relationship between them and the subject. (Freud was not far from thinking of such a structure when analyzing how inhibitions, symptoms, and anxiety are linked together. Freud also says that the *ego* is equally opposed to three terms: the *superego*, the external world, and the *id*. If you want to link them to Lacan's registers, you might suppose that the external world or reality is the imaginary, the superego is the symbolic, and the id is the real.)

This knot has at least one property: each one of the three terms is linked with each of the others by the third (cf. *Ornicar?* **5**, 92).

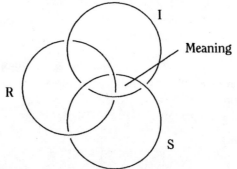

One of the obvious reasons for introducing such a thing into the Freudian field is that the real allows the analyst "to unknot what the symptom consists in, that is, a knot of signifiers" (*Television*). Knotting and unknotting are not metaphors, but the real structure of the signifying chain. Elsewhere Lacan says that these three elements chained together constitute a metaphor. Not a metaphor of the unconscious, but of the chain itself. A metaphor of number (*Ornicar?* **10**, 5).

I shall not discuss the very complicated properties of the Borromean knot, when, instead of three circles, you have more than three—innumerable rings, or even an infinite number—or when instead of rings you have lines, chains, and so on. Several books have been written on the subject. Instead, I shall take the Borromean knot as the "joint" out of which everything separates and falls to pieces. The "joint" is the Name-of-the-Father. But, when Lacan develops the idea of the Name-of-the-Father as this knot, he asserts the following:

- The Name-of-the-Father is the knot itself. And what is a knot? It is a hole and a knotting around that hole. The proper name is a hole (as the thing has no name, you put a name upon the absence of the thing). The Jews, Lacan says, "are very clear about what they call the Father. They shove him into some part of a hole we cannot even imagine: 'I am that I am'—that's a hole, isn't it? A hole [...] swallows things up, and sometimes spits them out again. What does it spit out? The name, the Father as a name" (*Ornicar?* **5**, 54).

- But since the Name-of-the-Father is a metaphor, you slide from one ring to the next. There are only Names-of-the-Father. "The Names-of-the-Father are the symbolic, the imaginary, and the real. They are the first names insofar as they name something" (*Ornicar?* **5**, 17).

- Yet the Name-of-the-Father is added to the knot as something more, something added. Because it *is* a name. "Of three consistencies, one never knows which is the real one. That is why there have to be four. The Four is what, with a double loop, supports the symbolic in what it is mad for: the Name-of-the-Father" (*Ornicar?* **5**, 55). The Name-of-the-Father is another name for the symbolic as such, as we saw at the beginning.

By Way of Conclusion

To conclude, there is a symbolic naming but also an imaginary naming (i.e., the Platonic supposition that names fit things [ειδοσ]), and there is what Lacan calls a naming of the real as anxiety (from a "clinical" point of view), but also the real as supposed by the referent (from a logical point of view—Kripke rather than Russell) (*Ornicar?* **5**, 64). That is why Lacan speaks of the names of the stars.

With these three kinds of naming you can grasp the whole circulation and structure of the Name-of-the-Father, which becomes imbued with ever more meaning in Lacan's theory, and in the end becomes, in one sense, *structure* itself.

There are, from one or the other of these points of view (symbolic, imaginary, real) many names of the father—Woman, for instance, or the masked man. "The Father has so very many [Names] that there is no one which suits him, except the Name of the Name of the Name.[1] There is no Name which could be his proper name, except the Name as an ex-sistence" (*Ornicar?* **6–7**, 7).

We are now in a position to understand why Lacan provided, in "Science and Truth," a very strange definition of psychoanalysis: "psychoanalysis is essentially what brings the Name-of-the-Father back into scientific examination" (*Newsletter of the Freudian Field*, **3**, 22).

Note

1. The words *"nom de"* figure in many French curses: *"nom de Dieu,"* *"nom d'un chien," "nom d'un nom,"* etc.

PART III

TRANSFERENCE AND THE DRIVES

TRANSFERENCE AS DECEPTION

Pierre-Gilles Gueguen

I have picked transference, instead of the many other topics that could be chosen from Seminar XI, for several reasons, some of which are obscure to me, but certainly because I think it's a very "practical" topic. It has to do with the way we practice analysis today, and that is what I am most interested in. I am also interested in what psychoanalysis is currently, and that is probably one of the reasons I have chosen the topic of transference as deception.

I'd like to start with Freud's first perspective on transference, which involved transferences instead of transference in the singular. If you take transference as a daily life phenomenon, it is an insult to reason. It is a nuisance in everyday relationships between human beings who are, as Lacan said, beings of speech (*parlêtres*). When you observe transference in daily life, it appears in the guise of the most contradictory feelings: love, hate, real or feigned indifference, confidence, defiance, anxiety, and so on. In short, transparent and rational communication is blocked at all times by various processes that can be classified under the general heading of affects since they keep affecting the message which can only be transmitted at the cost of numerous distortions.

Freud and other analysts, including Melanie Klein, noticed this clinical phenomenon, but transference is not found in the clinical realm alone. Politicians, educators, leaders, and all types of people have had to take problems of transference into account in their daily lives. They have had to take into account the unpredictable nature of the reactions of the electorate, pupils, patients, and so on. Some of them are quite cynical about the transferential problems that arise in human relationships. Some try to act in accordance with psychoanalytic suggestions on the subject. Others simply give up, and try to pass on the transferential burden to the supposed specialists—which is probably why there are psychoanalysts. Finally, there is a category of people, including analysts, who dedicate themselves to studying such seemingly erratic behavior. Many theories have been constructed regarding the doctor/patient relationship. Some educators have tried to understand transference as well. Tons of literature has been produced regarding the improvement of pedagogy. Politicians keep an obsessive eye on the polls, as attentive as aging stars looking at themselves in their mirrors.

Now all these techniques belong to the realm of imaginary mastery. Everyone acts as if some sort of pure transmission could surmount the obstacles of affect and transference. But the more the media spreads information and the networks expand, the more misunderstanding grows. In that respect, transference can be looked upon as an interference of the three passions Lacan considers worth mentioning—love, hate, and ignorance—with the transmission of knowledge. Transference as such can be envisioned as an obstacle to the progress of reason inasmuch as it claims to be scientific. For example, Descartes, in his *The Passions of the Soul*, carefully distinguished between passions and thoughts. To his mind, there are thoughts on the one hand and passions on the other together with the body and soul; the body is added to thought to make affect. In that paradigm, transference is deceptive because it stands in the way of truth.

Another aspect of transference relates to subjects who are given false confidence—members of the electorate, pupils, and patients, all of whom are dupes of transference. This question has always been at the core of current affairs, and it was a crucial issue at the beginning of psychoanalysis. It was also a crucial issue at the beginning of modern medical treatment and in past and present circumstances of political choice. Today one might ask the following questions: "Is my choice a good one? Did I pick a good analyst? Is my decision devoid of blind passion? Why have I chosen this particular psychoanalyst? Is it because s/he's brilliant; is it because s/he's mean; is it because s/he's good looking; or is it because s/he knows how to speak in a gentle tone?" All of us have such questions when we undertake psychoanalytic treatment. "Is my choice devoid of blind passion? Is it reasonable?" Any choice has its risks. Any choice is a way of betting on the Other.

Politics, education, medical practice, and psychoanalysis all require some kind of adherence or belief, some kind of risk-taking at the beginning and throughout, since the choice has to be renewed everyday. Every time you go to your session, you have to ask yourself these questions again because such risks can be taken, not in the name of reason or science, but only in the name of love. Some of us may try to deny the fact that love interferes in our choices. Some may place choice under the cover of a philosophical tradition of utility, but there is no choice without belief, no choice without transference in the broadest sense of the term, as long as transference is always a question of believing in the knowledge of its legitimate representative, whether politician, professor, doctor, or psychoanalyst.

Can we then accept the fact that transference always deceives whoever believes in it, or at least suspends whoever believes in it in a revelation that will eventually be verified in the aftermath of the decision? I think this is a very critical question for whoever addresses a politician, professor, doctor, or psychoanalyst: "How can I be protected against myself? How can I be protected against the possible negative effects of my blind love, hate, or ignorance?"

Transference is thus a deception from the scientific standpoint, but must also be considered a mistake if it is merely a belief in the righteousness of the other as counterpart. There is more to it, however, and we will try to examine what is added to the simple belief in the righteousness of the other as counterpart. If we want to know more about it, first we must notice that transference introduces intersubjectivity between the subject and object of transference.

This point has been developed philosophically by Descartes, Kant, and Wittgenstein. Kant, for example, asks, "What can I know?" Wittgenstein poses the problem of certainty anew, but adds to it a supplementary dimension, that of language. In his *Investigations*, for example, he analyzes philosophical discourse as a pure language game which bears no relation to reality. He questions the seductive power philosophy has over philosophers: "Why does it seduce philosophers? Why does it captivate them?" Wittgenstein tries to capture and stabilize the value of words, encapsulate them within their patterns, to describe their arrangements through the use of a metalanguage. In so doing, Wittgenstein refuses the world of essences. He also gets lost in an infinite dispersion of meaning, which, when he tries to get rid of it, leads him to the conclusion that silence is the only solution left. That is not where psychoanalysis leads. Psychoanalysis gives its own answers to the same problem, and they are different from Wittgenstein's.

I propose to examine today, first, Freud's solutions to the problem of transference, and then the solutions proposed by ego psychology, Klein, and Lacan. I don't mean to suggest by this ordering principle that Lacan's solutions are definitive, but certainly that they are different from the others. In my opinion, they explain more than the others.

First of all, let us examine Freud's solutions. In the case of Dora, Freud presented a developed theory of transference. "Dora" was written in 1900 and published in 1905. By then Freud had already laid the foundations of the theory he maintained until his death. This theory can be summed up in the following way: transference is a new version of ancient impulses and their consequent fantasies. When Freud talks about transference, it is a facsimile obtained with the help of a displacement of infantile reactions onto persons in the patient's environment, in particular, onto his or her parents. The core of Freud's thesis, to my mind, is that transference is a facsimile. Secondarily, it involves a displacement onto the analyst of infantile reactions to others. That is our basic conception of transference.

This theory of transference, as Freud said, is a false connection theory. It involves true knowledge that is displaced by a false attribution. Lacan emphasizes in "The Agency of the Letter in the Unconscious" (*Écrits*) that this false connection contains a displacement involving the combination and substitution of signifiers in language. In short, transference, according to both Lacan and Freud, is transference from one signifier to another signifier, from one signification to another signification. Here Lacan aligns himself with the way Freud used the concept even before transference was conceptualized as the motor force of the intersubjective link between analysand and analyst. Lacan develops this intersubjective link more extensively in his "Seminar on 'The Purloined Letter' " (*Yale French Studies*, 48, 1972). The question of intersubjectivity is recast by Lacan in "The Direction of the Treatment" (*Écrits*). To Lacan it is obvious that the analyst, as Freud had already noticed, is highly dependent on the patient's transference. Now this reverses the first question I asked, "How can I have confidence in this person?" In the "Seminar on 'The Purloined Letter,' " Lacan demonstrates how the analyst is dependent on the patient's transference, and this is very Freudian.

In his 27th introductory lecture on psychoanalysis, Freud emphasizes the analyst's dependence on his patient. He qualifies such transference as the greatest menace to and yet the most useful tool for treatment. Thus you see that I am not forcing things; in a way we can say that Freud was Lacanian. The key here is found in Freud's article "On the Question of Lay Analysis." There transference is no longer looked upon as an obstacle but, Freud says, as "the true object of psychoanalysis." Yes, the patient is deceived—the patient deceives him or herself. Yes, the analyst is lured by the traps and lies of transference. But this very illusion is essential since illusion itself is what the analyst interprets. Within treatment, this illusion can be reduced to that which has altered the patient's judgment in relation to parental figures.

Transference is not, if we read Freud in a Lacanian manner, a question of displaced affects. It is a question of why one's judgment is so distorted. That is what Lacan is most interested in, and Freud can also be read in this way. The patient, Freud says, tells us the most intimate story of his or her life, reproducing it in a very tangible way, as if it were happening, instead of merely being remembered. It's not a matter of remembering things from the past; it's a matter of eliciting distortions of judgment during the analytic session. In this respect, transference puts the analysand and the analyst in the same boat.

The analysand's false belief is really what is most intimate and authentic, to use an expression of Lacan's. The analyst's job in Freud's day was to link the false connection with the patient's past as s/he really lived it or as s/he portrayed it in his or her imagination. The analyst had to locate the false connection and determine what it had to do with the patient's history. Lacan stresses this aspect of Freud's practice in his commentary on Dora in the *Écrits*. Dora complains bitterly that her father betrayed her by sending her against her will into the arms of a man she did not love; the result, she complains, was that she was traumatized. Lacan, interested in how Freud handles Dora at the beginning of her treatment, notes that Freud doesn't tell her, "Dora, you're wrong; you're misinterpreting your father's intentions." Freud doesn't say anything of the kind. Rather, he says, "You may be right, but that's not the point. The question is why you allowed yourself to participate in a situation you denounce." Freud, in dealing with this false connection, does not attempt to reestablish the truth, but only to guide Dora in finding out the why and wherefore of this false dimension.

In 1951, Lacan joins forces with the Freud of 1900. Lacan speaks of "subjective rectification." That's the word he uses in alliance with Freud who thinks that transference should be integrated. We can agree with this act of integration, but we have to ask ourselves what Freud really meant when he said that transference should be integrated. Lacan states that transference is an act of interpretation, a way of involving the subject in the search for the why and wherefore of such a false connection. It's not that Lacan believed that "now you're taking me for your father or mother." That is not what Lacan seeks in Freud's writing. For Freud it is also possible that the subject is lying. Maybe Dora is lying, maybe she isn't; that is not what is of interest to us. The way in which the imagined past is reenacted and/or constructed in the present transference relationship is more interesting.

Now we can focus on the intersubjective dependence of the analyst and the analysand in the transference situation. Who depends on whom? One solution Lacan suggested was that there is truth only with the help of a lie, or, in other words, truth can only be half said. In Dora's case, for instance, maybe she was wrong, maybe she was right, but there was some truth in the lie that she supposed, in the lie of her articulated transference to Freud. And that's really what we have to deal with; that's really what psychoanalysis is all about—manifesting truth effects even if we lie in transference.

Who doesn't lie in transference? We always lie in the transference situation, and that's what Lacan tries to take into account.

In Seminar XI, Lacan speaks of transference as a path of deceptiveness, and he warns psychoanalysts against the temptation to speak the truth in order to counter deception. Lacan very strongly emphasizes that psychoanalysts should not be the champions of truth. That would be the hysteric's discourse, not analytic discourse. But perhaps this warning should be approached with a little caution. The complete quotation is, "in the path of deception where the subject errs, the analyst is in a position to formulate 'You are telling the truth,' and interpretation never takes on meaning if it is not in this dimension." That's interesting, for interpretation is really what happens in psychoanalysis.

If an interpretation is made in the mode of negation, there tends to be more denial; this is not an accurate conception of reality since the unconscious doesn't know negation. Here we could introduce the distinction between the subject of enunciation and the subject of the enunciated. In other words, to someone who thinks s/he is deceiving the analyst, the analyst does not respond, "I agree to be deceived" or "I refuse to be deceived." The analyst answers with some phrase like, "Yes, you're telling the truth," which is ambiguous because it contains a certain deceptiveness: "you're telling the truth of the deceptiveness that is at stake between us."

There is always some deceptiveness. "I thought I could deceive the Other, but in fact, I am the one who is deceived." The divided subject tries to instate deceit in the place of truth, putting false words in the Other's mouth because it is only when uttered by the Other that a message can be welcomed as truth. Let me provide an example. A patient in a session tries to show his analyst what a good guy he is. In this way the patient places the burden of division on the analyst: his message is "believe me, I'm a good person; you know I'm bad in some ways, but deep down I'm good." The patient attempts to put this message in the Other's mouth (in this instance, in the analyst's), but the analyst refrains from playing the game. In this way the message comes back to the patient: "now you see what you're doing: you're trying to persuade me that you're a good person when you know perfectly well that you're not such a good person." It comes back to the patient, and the division first transposed onto the analyst returns to the patient.

This, of course, assumes that the analyst maintains a specific position. It assumes that there is no transferential interplay, no proclamations like "in doing that, you think I am your father" or "you think I am your mother." Silence is probably the best solution in the trivial example I have chosen. Freud gives us some explanation for this analytic position at the end of his life. It can be found in *An Outline of Psychoanalysis*, which was written in

1938. In that text Freud says that, in spite of everything, a patient is willing to continue in the path of deception while looking for the truth because of love. That is why the patient continues to move toward recovery, abandoning the jouissance he derives from his symptom.

Freud's explanation of transference at the end of his life reads like this: "the patient recovers to please the analyst, and hopes, in so doing, to gain his applause and love." Here Freud demonstrates how cautious he is regarding transference. He believes that transference can be the motor force of analysis, but also the source of every analytic danger. In clinical practice, love can change very rapidly into hatred, and there is nothing worse than deceived love. Thus, Freud shifts slowly during his lifetime from interpreting transference to handling it at the end of analysis.

Since transference is helpful in providing an indication of the patient's actual past, it must be treated with caution. Analysts should not let transference reach the heights of love, not only because it is overtly dangerous, but because the consequences of letting the patient reach such transferential heights would allow for an immersion in ecstasy that could imaginarily overwhelm the patient while reinforcing antiquated patterns of jouissance. There would be no work, but rather a state of enchantment. Some people, at a certain point in their analysis, become really taken with their analysts. They dream for their analysts, or do other things to become good analysands. They are very happy, but do no work. Consequently, they learn very little about their unconscious processes.

Freud warns us not to let transference go too far. On the other hand, he warns us not to let transference reach the heights of hatred because, if it does, the patient will probably break off his or her analysis. Freud's position, best described as paradoxical, is still new to us. The more the analysand loves the analyst, the more s/he is alienated by signifiers of transferential desire. Conversely, the more the analyst handles transference, that is to say, the more s/he counters it, the more counter-transference is introduced into the cure, which is problematic from a Lacanian perspective.

Here I would like to quote Colette Soler, a very well known member of the *École de la Cause freudienne*, who says, "there is no such thing as counter-transference; rather, the problem is to counter transference." That is what Freud proposes: to handle transference. Handling transference means countering transference—not letting it become too strong because, if an analyst, immersed in the patient's belief about transference, tries to respond to the patient's transference with his or her own transference, then the situation reaches a standstill about which nothing can be done. Colette Soler has labeled this situation that of the "pyromaniac fireman": if transference is not strong enough, you have to fan it; if it is too strong, you have to pour some water on it.

Freud indicates that transference places the subject in a new dependent position, and it is the analyst's responsibility to understand this new dependency and to deal with it properly in the analytic situation. That is why, for example, Lacan contends that not everyone should be taken into analysis because the analyst takes responsibility for handling transference. I do not mean that a patient simply picks an analyst and is then freed of all responsibility; s/he is still responsible, and the analyst, as Lacan emphasized in Dora's case, must try to implicate the patient in his or her own responsibility. But in the final analysis, it is still the analyst who is responsible for handling transference; there is no way, once an analysis has begun, for the analyst to say, "let's stop now; I don't want to play this game any more."

That is why Freud advised analysts to be very cautious in handling transference, and especially not to use it as a means of frustrating the patient. If the analyst does that, Freud notes in *An Outline of Psychoanalysis*, s/he assumes the position of the superego; Freud states that you have to be careful not to put yourself in that position. You must attempt to handle transference, but not use it to push the patient too far. In the *Écrits*, Lacan explains that transference gives the analyst responsibility and power. He says that this power gives the analyst a way out of the problem only on condition that s/he not use it (*Écrits*, 236). Only then does transference take on its own development. You see that, in this respect, Lacan is very faithful to Freud. The handling of transference is central to the very notion of transference. Transference is only to be handled and analyzed. But on the other hand, with the transferential situation comes a power that is granted to the analyst, which must not be used so that the entire transference can develop.

Transference is repetition, but it is more than that, and this is one of Lacan's main points in Seminar XI; repetition is only a very small part of transference. If we use transference as Freud and Lacan advise us to in analytic treatment, we emphasize the handling and not the interpreting of the transferential relationship. In this way the analyst deceives the patient. S/he knows something that might be relevant to the standard of truth, if we can speak of such a thing, but s/he does not communicate it to the patient because it is not appropriate in the analytic situation. In that sense there is some deceptiveness, and Lacan suggests a reason for that in Seminar XI. I'll paraphrase his point here. Something is always being avoided; this is not an excuse, but the reason for transference, namely, that nothing can be obtained in absentia. This means that transference is not a shadow of something that was once alive. On the contrary, the subject, insofar as s/he is subjected to the analyst's desire, wants to betray the analyst for this subjection by making him or her love the analysand when offering up the duplicity that is love. Transference produces an effect of deception insofar as it is represented in the here and now. It is repetition of that which possesses the same form from another scene. It is not the shadow of the former deception of love.

These are Lacan's essential ideas from this passage. I'd like to stress that whether or not the enacted transferential relationship really existed in the patient's infancy is less important than what appears in transference. This is precisely what the psychoanalyst has to confront. Although the analyst is a person and therefore not indifferent to the analysand's pain, in a way you can say that the analyst's position as analyst is to be indifferent to suffering. For example, s/he will not say to the patient recovering from a trauma of this kind, "How unfortunate you are! Have we found the guilty party?" This is not the recommended perspective of the psychoanalyst; the psychoanalyst accepts whatever is traumatic in the subject's experience, and tries to incite the subject to develop the signifiers that were fixed in the trauma.

Obviously this point of view is quite different from most other views regarding the tolerance of pain. And it is a relevant conception even if we think that transferential relations have to do with what really happened in the subject's past. Whether or not we think it true that what is said in transference is a reenactment of the actual past, the subject in the present will still try to elicit the analyst's love. Of course, I am using correlations developed by Lacan inasmuch as they are very much in tune with Freud's final perspective on transference. Freud remained very skeptical about whether a psychoanalyst works with ultimate truth. For example, in "Analysis Terminable and Interminable" Freud states that there is a point in analytic dynamics that we cannot traverse. When we reach the Oedipal triad or the castration complex, there is some point where no ultimate truth can be revealed. That is not Lacan's solution, and it is probably why he invented object *a*—in order to go a little bit further. But object *a* is not ultimate truth; it is a construction as such that has to do with the ultimate false connection between the patient's relationships and his or her object, not something that is delivered up from the past as some truth of origins.

Ego psychologists changed the spirit of Freud's research by isolating portions of his work and interpreting the ego as an autonomous agency of the personality. I would like to delve a little more into the solution ego psychology provides regarding transference. Here are some of the questions that we associate with this type of therapy: "How can I choose? How can I pick an analyst? How can I make a choice in my life?" Such questions lead me to the conclusion that ego psychology presents a solution of therapeutic lies. It entails an extensive analysis of transference which neglects the question of the therapeutic alliance. If we go back to classical Freudian psychoanalysis, we find that the working alliance—the therapeutic alliance—has to do with a contract, and this contract is made between one ego and another, between the patient's ego and the analyst's ego. In Lacan's model, there is no way to think of analysis as a contract between the patient and the analyst.

From Lacan's viewpoint, the question is how to think of a contract that does not involve the free will of both the analyst and the analysand. If he were to speak of contracts, Lacan would say that the analytic contract is made between the patient, the real, and his or her unconscious. Thus the analyst is just a semblance or counterpart of the contract. Thinking of psychoanalysis in terms of contracts means thinking of psychoanalysis as a process that occurs between counterparts. But, according to this paradigm, how can you isolate a place for the Other if you think treatment starts with a contract? Ego psychology defines what happens in the analytic situation as a contract. But to define a contract, we have to define an alliance that steers clear of neurotic games and works with the patient's "adult reactions."

In the solution provided by ego psychology, the patient is supposed to communicate with his or her words or feelings. But what does it mean to communicate with one's feelings when there is no such thing as a pure feeling? The patient is supposed to communicate with words, feelings, reflection, meditation, and self-observation to maintain contact with analytic reality. If the patient had such good contact with psychoanalytic reality, I don't see why s/he would need treatment in the first place! Ego psychology does accept the possibility of there being a bad fit in the patient/analyst relationship, and if you come across problems in this situation, then the solution is to be realistic and reasonable, whatever that means. I like to quote the former Vice-President of the International Psychoanalytical Association from an article written in the 1970s about the notion of reality. It is a very touching article. He is completely at a loss when asking whether or not we should adapt patients to a specific reality, because the question becomes to which reality they should adapt, that "before the Vietnam war or after the Vietnam war; because everything has changed so much, we don't know what values we can really stick to." This is not a trivial issue if you think you have to adapt people to reality. If you are a proponent of adaptation, then you have to ask yourself to which reality one should adapt, especially because reality is historically based and ever changing. You can have problems establishing transference if your advice is supposed to be realistic and reasonable.

There is something very difficult about this approach, especially if you believe that at the beginning of treatment you have to establish a reasonable, fair contract based on reality. Secondly, you are supposed to analyze the patient's transference, and we know that transference involves the projection of a plethora of false connections and untrue ideas onto the figure of the analyst. This certainly presents a problem for psychoanalysts: how can they relate the idea that they have an adult contract at the beginning of treatment with the idea that, in this relationship with the analyst, the patient repeats childish situations? As you probably know, the following interpretation predominates in analytic circles: "You're taking me for somebody else, and I'm not that person in reality." In this case, the analyst uses him or herself as the standard for reality.

But how many times can we ask the question, "What is reality?" If you are a psychoanalyst, you have a tradition, and such questions are part of it. But if you are a traditional ego psychologist, you have to answer such questions by privileging your answers as the correct ones. To the ego psychologist, external reality is not psychical reality, as Freud would put it, but an objective, external reality that is valid for both partners. My question in this context is, how then are we to handle transference? It is interesting to note that Freud warns that the handling of transference is secondary and that the main thing is its analysis. This is the exact opposite of ego psychology, where the handling of transference is more important than the analysis of transference, which becomes secondary. In ego psychology, the handling of transference is no more than a strategy adopted by the analyst to manipulate the patient to the point where the patient's transference reactions are amplified enough to become analyzable.

This is not the point of view Lacan adopts. He does not think that handling transference is a kind of manipulation, but rather that transference should be handled very carefully. According to Freud, it is not a matter of manipulating patients to elicit their reactions so that they can be analyzed but, on the contrary, of providing situations in which love and hate are not so strong that they prevent patients from developing the signifiers of their own transference.

In the classical way of explaining psychoanalytic treatment, the analysis of transference can be prevented by the analyst's counter-transference. This incorporates the idea that transference is a matter of feelings; you have to gauge analysis by the patient's feelings, and then you have to be careful about your own feelings revealed through counter-transference.

The Lacanian solution does not involve feelings, especially not the analyst's feelings. Lacanian analysts obviously have feelings, and hopefully they are sensitive enough not to reveal that they like one patient more than another, for example. But for Lacanians it is not a problem of liking or not liking this or that person or of being overwhelmed by one's own feelings; the problem is establishing situations in which the patient is able to recognize his or her own signifiers. This technique is very different from the methods adopted by ego psychology. In "The Direction of the Treatment,"

Lacan criticizes such procedures. He claims that, from this point of view, transference becomes the analyst's security blanket. In this way of behaving, Lacan says, "there is an insistence that opens the door to all kinds of pressures, conveniently dubbed 'strengthening of the ego.' "

I would now like to examine the Kleinian solution to the question of transference. There is an article by Melanie Klein, written in 1952, that is called "The Origin of Transference." Her thesis there is that transference is based on returning the subject to the constitution of his or her object relations, namely to the intense love and hate that characterize the first relations of the body. This explains why Melanie Klein placed so much emphasis on the analysis of negative transference, since to her it has to do with pre-Oedipal relationships based on the schizoid-paranoid position. In this article, Klein opposes the idea that the analyst's role is to receive unconscious projections of the subject's real father or mother. She also maintains that transference is not a literal representation of ancient reactions, for the primitive images of the father and mother have been distorted.

In the spiritual realm, Klein thinks every primitive internal experience is mingled with fantasies, and conversely, each fantasy contains elements of real experience; thus it is only by analyzing the deeper layers of transference that one can discover the past in both its realistic and phantasmatic aspects. Now Melanie Klein's position is obviously quite different from that of ego psychologists. Transference here can only be envisioned as a mix of reality and fantasy, not as a dynamic built upon actual relationships to actual persons. This is very interesting because it is a new conception of what psychoanalysis is all about.

Lacan's solution is different from Klein's because he does not let things mingle, as does Klein; she mixes the boundaries of the phantasmatic and reality. Lacan advances something else, and this invention is object *a*. His invention refers not to reality but to the real. To Melanie Klein, transference says nothing about the parent's imagoes since it refers only to what the real subject sees, conceives, and imagines. Thus the word "imaginary" is very well chosen to typify Klein's findings, since a subject imagines his or her relationship to mother and father figures.

Klein also insists on the necessity of taking into account the unconscious elements of transference. But for her, as for ego psychologists, it is mainly a question of analyzing rather than handling transference. Lacan calls her writings the axis of object relations theory, which he believes is built upon the fantasy of reparation: once the idolized object has fallen from its exalted status, the subject can repair this imaginary destruction by reinstituting a so-called relationship to the total object that is more realistic, more temperate than its previous one. In "The Direction of the Treatment," Lacan criticizes this pastoral vision of analytic treatment as a way to reform the subject. Ego psychology tries to reform the subject by adapting him or her to reality; the Kleinian movement tries to master the subject by perpetuating the ideal of restoration of the object. Ego psychology provides the equation "reality is objectivity." Klein provides the equation "the imaginary is objective."

Now I would like to say a few words about Lacan's solution. It takes its original form in Seminar XI in 1964, and is developed in October 1976 in "On the Discourse of the Psychoanalyst." To my mind, the basic idea is that psychoanalysis can in no way be a process of disillusionment. Lacan indicates as much in the *Écrits*: "The analyst who desires the subject's well-being repeats that by which he was formed, and sometimes even deformed. The most aberrant education has never allowed the analyst to say to his analysand 'Go out there. Now you're a very good child.' " (256) On the basis of this quotation, how can we pose the question of truth or certainty in Lacan's concept of transference?

First of all I would like to emphasize that to Lacan, the question of handling transference is *a* question of analysis, whereas for some analysts today it is *the* question of analysis. The analyst doesn't have to tell the truth; s/he doesn't have to be the Other of the Other. The analyst's only job is to ensure the conditions of possibility of the rectification of truth. The analysand can recount the different variations of his or her fantasies, that is, the way s/he has a grasp on the Other, in order to register it with the counterpart. The analyst doesn't have to analyze transference; the patient will do so. In analyzing transference, the patient will develop the different ways in which s/he tries to catch hold of the Other, namely the psychoanalyst, in order to reduce the analyst to a counterpart. The problem of what has to be analyzed by the patient is what ego psychology places at the beginning of transference.

When you introduce the idea that the analytic contract can be made between counterpart and counterpart, you present the patient with an enactment of a fantasy. The fantasy depicts how in our own lives we reduce other people to counterparts; that is a very simple definition of what fantasy roles are. According to this paradigm, the patient eventually finds out at the end of analysis how s/he uses transference to reduce the analyst to an object in the same way that the pervert reduces his or her partner to an object. It's not just a manner of speaking when Lacan says that the fundamental fantasies of all neurotics are perverted. The fundamental fantasy in each subject, even the neurotic, is a perverted fantasy. Which is not to say that Lacan believes all human beings are perverts. On the contrary, he thinks that very often the neurotic tries to persuade the analyst that s/he is a pervert for fear of really being one.

Now, in developing transference, the patient can gain some insight
into what s/he is doing. The patient is able to construct his or her own
fundamental fantasy, and grasp the ways in which it fixes that object s/he is
for the Other. This is what Lacan calls the crossing over of fantasy. Interpretation is to be understood not so much as the delivering up of knowledge to
the patient, for there is no symbolism to discover; the analyst is not the
repository of truth, since truth is verified by its effects.

The second idea I would like to develop briefly is that, in the analytic
situation, transference is a particular kind of love addressed to knowledge.
If the analysand loves the analyst, it is merely because the analysand supposes that the analyst has the key to his or her own unconscious knowledge. This display of emotional thinking could very well lead the patient to
a psychologist or a psychoanalyst who promises the illusion of happiness.
This knowledge promises to turn suffering into signification. But transference from a Lacanian point of view allows the subject to enter the path of
deception because, at the beginning of treatment, the analysand thinks that
there is a subject who knows, a subject who knows the truth about truth.
That is why the subject is engaged in such "research": because s/he loves
the signification of the symptom.

But Lacan does not consider this knowledge, even unconscious knowledge, where a subject finds such certainty. Lacan suggests that the subject
must put an end to transference, which doesn't rest on pure knowledge. It
is an idea that depends on the apperception of the subject in relation to
object a. And this is probably what differentiates classical psychoanalysis
from Lacanian psychoanalysis. The aim of analysis is not the same in the
two approaches. For Kleinians and ego psychologists, it is a matter of restoring access to reality; for Lacanians it is a matter of enabling the subject
to catch a glimpse of the real.

THE PASSIONATE DIMENSION OF TRANSFERENCE

Jean-Pierre Klotz

Today I would like to introduce the problem of transference from a Lacanian perspective. I will talk about passion because passion is one way to introduce the dimension of transference. The definition of transference in the field of psychoanalysis is very well known: transference is a form of love. That was the definition Lacan once provided in a videotaped talk he gave in Louvain, Belgium. But it is also the classical definition of transference, i.e. Freud's definition. Images of transference are impossible to ignore in the psychoanalytic encounter, an encounter which provides a means of emergence. Transference is encountered, as is anything in analytic practice, as an obstacle.

Transference love is encountered as an obstacle, but it is an inescapable obstacle. Analysis confronts obstacles. The appearance or emergence of love, a passionate phenomenon produced by analysis, is a gauge indicating what is going on in an analysis. Transference is love, but if we try to question transference love and the transference of love, we are faced with another question. What is the cause of this love effect in analysis? Love is a way to encounter the phenomenal. For if we try to comprehend transference, we are left with the passionate dimension of love which emerges as its effect, an effect which obliges us to question the causes of this love.

To use transference in directing treatment, we have to ask what causes the effect that is love. It is necessary to distinguish transference as a concept from this emergence of love as transference love. It is not love as passion that we use to construct the *concept* of transference; rather the emergence of the passionate dimension is used in treatment to construct the conceptual framework of analysis. To use transference in analytic treatment enables the analyst and analysand to confront the problem of the direction of the treatment itself. In Seminar XI transference is encountered by Lacan as a theoretical trajectory different from that encountered by IPA analysts. Lacan believes that the usual ways of conceptualizing transference are misleading. He even believes that the notion that love is related to the unconscious, in the subjective dimension of experience, is misleading.

Lacan emphasizes the dimension of love that lies or misleads, suggesting that this misleading belongs, as such, to the dimension of truth. Lacan develops the idea that it is impossible to encounter the dimension of truth without being misled. Love is the point of encounter, i.e., transference is the point of encounter which introduces the dimension of truth into analytic practice itself.

Feelings of passion are often expressed regarding analysis. A colleague of mine was once telling me about psychoanalytic relations when he suddenly said, "I am passionately fond of psychoanalysis." This formulation was unexpected, and I was quite surprised by it. Then I felt astonished at being so surprised, for, I reasoned, isn't it possible for somebody who devotes so much of his time to a field to speak of his relation to it as passionate? Nevertheless, at that time I found it curious.

Here is another example. In the course of analysis, an analysand may occasionally or repeatedly say, "I am bored and fed up with analysis." This is a much less surprising declaration of love, but it usually does not prevent the treatment from continuing. It presents a discontinuity in analysis, something which should not automatically be considered to belong to the chain of free association.

A more typical feeling expressed in psychoanalysis is: "I don't know what psychoanalysis is; I understand nothing about it." We are familiar with these words coming from an analysand during treatment, but it may be less usual to associate them with a psychoanalyst. In these three quotes, psychoanalysis is present in both the statement and the enunciation. They are discontinuities that stand out and that may have the effect of an awakening for the subject. Psychoanalysis provides no automatic approach to handling such discontinuities, but rather a set of choices or considerations that help the analyst interact with the analysand.

I believe that these three sentences have something in common: the emergence of discontinuities at a moment of passion. They all signal the emerging presence of passion inside and out. This may strike you as surprising—not so much the initial examples, which concern love and hate, but the third one in which knowledge is at issue, or more precisely, ignorance. In Lacan's teaching, ignorance is a passion which occupies a central place in analysis. Transference is bound up with knowledge—knowledge as a dimension.

Freud's scientific ambition neglected the dimension of passion. Science does not include passion. Which does not mean that scientists are not passionate. That is precisely a way of tackling the question. There may be passion in the suffering which pushes somebody to become an analyst. As an emotional dimension of the patient's symptom, passion is an imaginary phenomenon. In this instance, interpreting the symptom, which aims at overcoming repression, also aims at suppressing such imaginary effects.

Freud emphasizes sex rather than passion. Freud is not preoccupied with love when he interprets unconscious formations, even if he says here and there that trust in the analyst improves the effectiveness of this kind of work. But for the analyst, the scenery changes when, in analysis, so-called transference love emerges. It does not appear right away, but it is encountered. It is a particular phenomenon which arises at certain moments during treatment. In his observations on transference love, Freud shows that it is an obstacle; he places it in the register of resistance. Free association is impeded, and the analyst, as the object of such passion, has to be careful how he or she responds.

The goal of love is not the same as the goal of analytic work. But transference is produced by the analytic work itself. It does not simply fuel the patient's demand; it functions as an impediment to the analytic situation itself. The status of that passion is not canceled out by the symbolic interpretation of imaginary effects, characteristic of Lacan's interpretations in the early years of his teaching. At that stage he views transference as a passion situated in a psychoanalytic context rather than a purely scientific one.

Allow me to justify my choice of the word "passion" here. Why should we approach the problem of the discontinuity constituted by transference as an experience of passion? Why use this word? Lacan is falsely reputed not to consider the affective dimension of transference. Lacan merely states that this dimension has to be considered in relation to the signifier's function. Passion takes its place around this function. Passion is a little more than love. There is a supplemental strength or intensity that characterizes what we commonly call passion's object. And passion is essentially oriented by an object.

Now the origin of the word "passion" is religious. In Christian theology it designates the suffering unto death sustained by Christ. But his suffering and death were followed by a positive effect: the Resurrection. And this Resurrection acts to redeem with love's effect. Thus, first, passion is something suffered, a state endured. There is a passionate subject who suffers, and who is marked by his suffering. Second, this subject becomes active, as passionate—he is stirred by passion. The first instance is negative, while the second is positive and appears to cancel out the first with a strength proportional to the suffering endured. This is a sign of the subject being marked by passion. Lacan makes use of the term "passion" when he speaks of the signifier's passion. That is especially useful here, since it binds together the symbolic and the affective dimensions.

(The problem of transference in analysis is revealed when transference is seen in relation to the symbolic dimension of the signifying chain. We see that the real as such, as the ground of analytic experience, is sex. What allows us to link the symbolic and the real is desire. The problem has to do with the place of desire, the object of desire, and the signifier of desire. The way desire is dealt with in analysis directly impacts any conception of transference.)

The distinction between signifier and signified is bound up with the signifier's passion. To give that opposition its full scope, the signifier actively determines the effect of the signified, of what appears to endure its mark, becoming through that passion the signified. In other words, the signifier has an active function, while the signifiable—that which can be signified—endures its mark. The signified is caused by the signifier. It bears the mark of the signifier. In "The Signification of the Phallus" (*Écrits*), Lacan introduces the signifier as passion.

The patient is someone who suffers, someone who has been marked by the signifier. In this stroke of subjectification, the subject is marked as both patient and passionate, but passion does not appear as a contingent characteristic of the subject. There are no more passionate subjects; only a signifier can be passionate. This is a structural reference for the analyst or analysand encountering the passionate dimension of analysis in the form, for instance, of transference love, or more generally speaking, transference passion. Signifiers can appear in analysis as an obstacle, gap, or lack which resists. There would be no possibility of analytic treatment without that, because such a gap characterizes the subject in his or her relationship to the symbolic dimension which causes him or her.

Thus far I have approached passion from the standpoint of the signifier, that is to say, from a structural perspective. In practice, the grammar of passion indicates that the subject confronts the real (which is impossible to symbolize) in relation to sexual intercourse. It is no accident that the first term of the signifier's passion is the phallus. It is with regard to the phallus that the signifier's passion was introduced by Lacan, who later said that love—and why don't we say passion here?—acts as a substitute for sexual relationships which do not exist. Passion has to be encountered in the particularity of every clinical case. The signifier's passion, on the one hand, and the relationship with sex, on the other, must be present when we assess the impact and status of passion in the cure.

Any signifier is potentially passionate since passion belongs to its dimension of lack. The English translation Lacan proposed for *manque-à-être*, "want to be," indicates rather well the subject's passionate dimension, his activity tied to passivity, and his submission to language. Passion manifests itself in demand, and it is through demand that the signifier's passion operates.

To illustrate passion's role in analysis, I will discuss a case of hysteria. It is the case of a young woman whose initial symptom was a classic, but no less disabling, animal phobia. It was all the more limiting for her since this sophisticated city dweller, who had an unrelenting passion for different fields of knowledge and was an eternal student, was living in the country at that time, a suitable place for encountering creatures large and small. At the beginning of the treatment she manifested in various ways the problem of the subject's relation to knowledge. She challenged her analysts on the grounds that they were men and therefore not beneficial to a woman like herself because they could not provide her with the answers she nonetheless never stopped hoping for. Here we can already grasp the notion of woman as a question.

Her father figured in her disappointment as far back as she could remember. Her father had ruined her life, and when she spoke about him, he was usually associated with animals, often with big dogs, and once with a donkey. But she was no more fond of women, even if she wanted to sympathize with them. She considered the fact that she was a woman to be a curse. With her mother, she had nurtured a relationship that could be described as one of hateful complicity. In fact, the entire family atmosphere produced the same revulsion as the animals that intruded upon her world.

For a while it was difficult to get treatment underway. She continued to study and work, and in order to preserve her freedom, she refused to keep a permanent job. In fact, her analysis began when she gave up a stable and serious job that did not interest her. The expressions "it interests me" and "it does not interest me" always signaled her passionate dimension. She claimed that entering analysis was a choice of freedom for her, and that her phobia was her last restricting bond. After several crises in the transference, including an interruption of a few months, she resumed her analytic work. She obtained a stable job, a managerial position for which she was eminently qualified, but had no interest in it. Though her phobia was absent from her discourse for long periods, whenever she mentioned it, the phobia appeared firmly rooted.

The analysis slowly changed, however, and little by little she developed a conviction that had already suggested itself here and there. A figure of a woman emerged, but this figure became associated with a witch, a frightening phantasmatic figure, and she started to reveal her anxiety about harming people, especially men with whom she had dealings. Her anxiety came to a climax at her place of work when a man offered her a promotion which would increase her professional responsibilities. Far from delighting her, this recognition of her abilities proved insufferable, because she had absolutely no idea what abilities she had that might have led to her promotion. The fact that she was involved in another type of work, that of transference, sparked another development; she started speaking of her transparency, of her envy, and of being afraid to find herself, which indicated that her anxiety was related to what was opaque in her seeming transparency to the world, to what could be defined as the Other's gaze.

Above all, she recounted an experience she had during this time when she encountered a spider, formerly a particularly phobogenic creature for her. In this instance, the spider caused only a normal fear. In a way, one could say that the anxiety had the effect on her of what she produced in the Other, and this cured her of the phobia. But it was a cure that suggested a passage from one dilemma to another. The phobia appeared to be founded on a generalized anxiety, localized at the outset and displaced onto an animal. Her question became a sort of impossible alternative—she had to either experience her phobia or regard herself as a filthy animal that placed the Other in danger. It had all the characteristics of a forced choice over which she had no control. Moreover, she felt that the place which marked her gaping phobia was a void. But despite the horror that confronted her, she still wanted to know more.

What I have described here is the first year of treatment, which is still in progress. Passionate topics, such as her fear of animals, are much less prevalent now. But what I call her passion to know still remains, as it has never stopped being a major part of the treatment. Because of the promise of a cure, it is knowledge about psychoanalysis that interests her; she has become more and more passionate about psychoanalytic knowledge, as an hysterical subject often does. Yet a moment of intellectual curiosity is often followed by a moment when she stops and stares at what seems to be a hole. Then she starts again, saying that she hopes to extricate herself from everything that does not interest her. But her passion remains oriented towards what she cannot handle.

Psychoanalysis for her has become more and more a point of ignorance because she has begun to understand herself in relation to that gap. More precisely, she has recently begun to understand that the phobia was a way to extricate herself from that gap, and that the transformation from phobia to generalized anguish, which was worse in one way, actually helped her by providing her with a relation to knowledge.

This case helps illustrate the relationship between knowledge and love in Lacan's view of transference as love and ignorance as passion. The patient's movements of love and hate around the gap in knowledge were numerous. For the neurotic subject, the gap in knowledge and resulting discontinuity induce symbolic castration, since this passion covers over a fundamental separation between the subject and the Other. There wouldn't be a subject without the Other, which allows us to say that the subject is a consequence of the signifying order, i.e., the subject must submit to this order. But the hysterical subject allows for better analytic operation because of his or her active orientation towards the Other. The obsessive subject remains more within his or her confines, avoiding the Other. The obsessive's major passion is closer to hate. That is why Lacan speaks of the "hystericization" of the subject which is necessary to put the patient to work. But it is fundamentally ignorance as passion which best defines the neurotic's passion: ignorance as the name of one's relationship with knowledge.

I began my paper with the analyst who told me of his passion for psychoanalysis. It seems that, at the end of analysis, the neurotic subject's passion should disappear. And yet Lacan speaks of an increase in passion— as a solution to the neurotic's passion—which is to recreate the subject in relation to symbolic castration. Passion enters at the place of the subject, between the subject and the Other. But when an analysand becomes an analyst, what happens to that passion?

THE DRIVE (I)

Marie-Hélène Brousse

I want to begin with chapter 1 of Seminar XI, entitled, "Excommunication," where Lacan asks two questions: What are the fundamentals of psychoanalysis? And what grounds it as a practice? I find that a useful way to introduce the drives because the question that arises from this text is why Lacan begins precisely with the four concepts he chooses and not others. For example, why the drives and not desire? What is more fundamental about the drives than about desire?

I shall try to answer that question. There are many possible responses, but I think the first one is related to Lacan's problem at that time in his teaching, which is indicated in the very title of the chapter, "Excommunication." I am referring to his situation in the psychoanalytic movement in 1964, because he links the problem of what is fundamental in psychoanalysis with the problem of training analysts. In a sense, if he works on the four fundamental concepts, it is from the perspective of training analysts: what is to be taught in a training analysis and what is fundamental for the transmission of psychoanalysis?

When Lacan speaks of the training of analysts in this first chapter, he emphasizes the question of its aims, limits, and effects. That made me associate it with another text written the same year, a very important text for us today and for psychoanalysis in general, the founding text of his school of psychoanalysis, the *École freudienne*. In June of 1964, he brought out what he called the "Founding Act"[1] of his school. The same problem exists, in a way, in the seminar on the four fundamental concepts and in his psychoanalytic trajectory concerning the future of psychoanalysis, because it is the future of psychoanalysis with which he is concerned.

We can associate these two texts, and I think it is important to situate the drive as a fundamental concept in terms of this main orientation and in terms of Lacan's concern with the future of psychoanalysis. In a way, the "Founding Act" of June 1964 is an answer to the future of psychoanalysis. Some of us in Paris have been thinking about it recently because the *École de la Cause freudienne* is ten years old. It is a moment of looking forward, but backwards as well. We are thinking about what we have done with the school Lacan left us and what we want to do with it in the future. It is the same kind of problem Lacan is emphasizing. In referring to the "Founding Act" we can see that it is exactly the same type of questioning, because it is a way of getting one's bearings.

What is an institution, a psychoanalytic institution, knowing that Lacan's counter-model was what had become of the International Psychoanalytical Association (IPA)? What kind of institution of psychoanalysis do we want? What are the aims and limits of a psychoanalytic institution? Lacan proposed a "school" as opposed to, as an answer to, the psychoanalytic institution. Not an institute, a school. Why?

Secondly, the term, "training." How is one to situate the training of the analyst in his training analysis as opposed to an ordinary analysis? What is the difference between the two? What makes the end result of an analysis the production of an analyst? How is it that an analysis produces an analyst, knowing that people generally enter analysis, even if they say it is to become an analyst, for other reasons?

The third term is the "teaching" or "transmission" of psychoanalysis. In the "Founding Act," Lacan speaks of the school, work, and training, and then introduces another term, *contrôle*. He introduces something new with the term.[2] The main obligation of a school is *contrôle*. There is internal and external *contrôle*. Lacan says, "the work involves reconquering the Freudian field." The school is to provide training and *contrôle*. But training analysis occurs outside the purview of the school. What does that mean? It means you can choose training analysis or non-training analysis, and it is the *end* of your analysis that decides which it was. If your analysis produces an analyst, as confirmed by your *contrôle* at the school, then it was a training analysis. But you only know that after the fact. That is why Lacan emphasizes the fact that there can be no analyst without a training analysis, but nevertheless, training analysis is not *directly* controlled by the school. It is both external and internal, internal from the point of view of its result but external from the institutional point of view.

What is teaching? It is defined very precisely in the "Founding Act." It is not equivalent to the teaching dispensed in schools or universities. It is not the teaching of the university discourse or the master's discourse. It is a peculiar form of teaching which is at the same time inventing. We have

Freud's inventions, Lacan's inventions, and x's inventions. X's invention are possible if we can rely on Freud and on Lacan's teachings, as it seems we can. Lacan was very self-conscious of the importance of his teaching in 1964 for many reasons. The IPA's rejection of his teaching merely emphasized its importance. And as many people were using his concepts (often without acknowledgement), he knew that what he was teaching was having an impact in the psychoanalytic community.

Lacan also proposed the "pass." It is a process he proposed to the analytical school he was creating for producing new knowledge about psychoanalysis. Just as Freud produced a new field of knowledge called psychoanalysis, Lacan intended to produce something new, not simply to repeat what Freud said. We cannot imagine the future of psychoanalysis without new creation. If there is no creation in psychoanalysis, psychoanalysis will die. Thus teaching is to be taken in a very strong sense to mean invention, which differentiates it from the university discourse, which has its values but which is more concerned with erudition, repetition, and the master discourse—oriented towards the power of the master signifiers.

I think we can read Seminar XI as the link between Freud's teaching and Lacan's teaching, that is, as the guarantee of a school, an analytic institution. That is exactly what Lacan says in chapter 1 when he speaks about how Freud's teaching grounds psychoanalysis as a praxis:

> Without this trunk, mast, or post, where can our practice be moored? Can we say that what we are dealing with are concepts in the strict sense? Are they concepts in the process of formation? Are they concepts in the process of development, in movement, to be revised at a later date? (10–11)

The question is also: why was Freud the one who gave us those four fundamental concepts and how did he find them? The question concerns the search for a guarantee regarding the main problem of psychoanalysis: how to train analysts.

Lacan is looking for a link between the analyst's desire and the analyst's training. The problem in psychoanalysis is that you cannot view training as you do in academic disciplines, for you cannot produce an analyst without a process of purification of desire. Lacan sets out:

> to put in question the origin, to discover by what privilege Freud's desire was able to find the entrance into the field of experience he designates as the unconscious. (12)

We can ask the same question of Lacan's desire: what allowed it to produce this tremendous quest to impose psychoanalysis upon civilization and its discontents?

That takes me to another question: if the main problem is desire, why doesn't he consider desire to be a fundamental concept of psychoanalysis? That is the question we are going to deal with here. Why the drive and not desire? Because desire is Lacan's invention, and he knows it at that time. Lacan's invention is the notion of the analyst's desire—that is not found in Freud's work. It is implicit in Freud and defined as a search for truth. Freud is searching for truth in his cases, but we cannot say that Lacan is in the same position. Let us assume that Lacan speaks of drives here instead of desire in order to produce a new signification. We have to find it. And that is what I am going to try to do with you.

I want to start with chapter 12, "Sexuality in the Defiles of the Signifier." I shall comment mainly on that chapter today, and next Monday I shall comment on the next two chapters, "The Deconstruction of the Drive" and "The Partial Drive and its Circuit." The introduction of the drive, as you might have noticed from the table of contents, does not occur directly, but rather through transference. The section title is "Transference and the Drive." Hence, the question is: how do we get from transference to the drive? And why is it necessary to examine transference to reach the drive?

Chapter 12 provides a definition of transference, which is exactly the same as the definition Lacan provides in another fundamental text, "The October 9, 1967 Proposition Regarding the Psychoanalyst of the School."[3] The definition is: "transference is the enactment of the reality of the unconscious." (149) In French it is, *"le transfert est la mise en acte de la réalité de l'inconscient."* Transference is produced by the enactment of the reality of the unconscious. This definition refers to the category of the act, and opposes any attempt to define transference as imaginary. Transference is not imaginary; it is an act (*une mise en acte*). The drive is to be derived from this definition of transference and from another term, "sexuality." Transference introduces the reality of the unconscious; through transference we have access to the reality of the unconscious. Transference is a process of producing the unconscious in the analytic relationship. When the reality of the unconscious is produced, you can define the type of reality the unconscious has: sexual reality.

"The reality of the unconscious is sexual reality" (150), and from that definition, you can introduce the drive by means of a few definitions. In the above-mentioned "Proposition," the definition is, "At the beginning of psychoanalysis is transference," and in the chapter "Sexuality in the Defiles of the Signifier," you have a reference to the idea that there is no psychoanalysis without transference. You can understand it historically: psychoanalysis began with Freud's treatment of hysteria. You can also understand it clinically: there is no way of establishing an analytic relationship without producing transference. The importance given to transference emphasizes the organic link between transference and the unconscious. In a way, they are almost the same. There is no such thing as the unconscious without transference.

There can be transference without psychoanalysis, but the opposite is not true. You can say that because many other social institutions rely on transference as a possibility, but do not ground their action on transference. Transference is present in teaching, for example. It is present in medicine. It is present in many facets of social life, and in politics too. But it is not taken as the reality of the unconscious. The difference is that, starting with Freud, transference appears as the reality of the unconscious. Freud does not invent transference—he simply runs up against it. Freud invents the unconscious, but it is the unconscious produced through the use of transference.

There are two main axes in transference. There is the axis of knowledge, linked to signifiers and repetition, and there is the axis of love, linked to being. Freud runs up against the fact that, although you cannot produce the reality of the unconscious without transference, at the same time you cannot touch the unconscious using transference. Nor can you define psychoanalysis by transference as signifying repetition. The second axis of transference runs counter to the first. There is a facilitating orientation of transference as the arrangement that produces the reality of the unconscious. But in another way, there is transference as love; and love, as Lacan says in Seminar XI, is an effect of transference. Thus love runs counter to the reality of the unconscious and its use.

This is very clear in clinical circumstances. A patient comes to see you. Transference is manifest in the choice s/he makes, first of psychoanalysis, as opposed to other existing therapies, and second of you as analyst—s/he chooses you without knowing why, because of your name, age, sex, etc. S/he chooses you in a transferential movement and, with that, what happens? S/he comes with grief or suffering, and the effect of transference is to transform this suffering into a symptom, that is, a formation which has meaning. S/he thinks that because you are an analyst, you know the meaning of his or her symptoms.

That is the facilitating orientation of transference. It is linked to the analytic situation. This is the facilitating orientation of transference I was presenting as one axis of knowledge—unconscious knowledge.

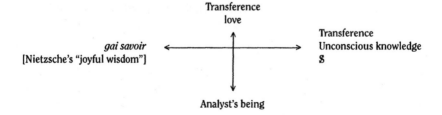

That is what Lacan means when he says "at the beginning of psycho-analysis is transference." Knowledge is another term for the unconscious. Of course, as the treatment goes on, this knowledge produces what Lacan calls the "want-to-be" or lack of being, because the unconscious is defined by subjective division ($). In the same movement in which you present your suffering as a symptom, you present it as something with which you live and which you do not know. Its meaning escapes you just as the meaning of dreams escapes you. Therefore, as you propose the unconscious, at the same time, you propose subjective division, because the unconscious is lack of being (*manque-à-être*).

The other axis, transference as love, is the mere result of the emer-gence of subjective division, produced by free association, in the psychoana-lytic situation. The only fundamental rule in psychoanalysis is free association. You have to say whatever comes to mind without any censoring of your thoughts. This fundamental rule produces both transference and the unconscious as such. Free association produces subjective division, which is another name for the unconscious. Why? Once this is produced, your being escapes you when, for example, you tell a dream or you make a slip. If you consider the analytic situation, it appears that the signifier with which you thought you could define your being escapes you. This is how transference produces a lack of being.

Lacan speaks of want-to-be, which implies lack. Want-to-be is, per-haps, better in English, because it explains why the other side of transfer-ence is love. What does love give? Love gives being. The object you love gives you some being; your love gives you being. Thus, as the psychoana-lytic dynamic affirms subjective division again and again, in the same move-ment, it gives rise to love, which is the intent. That is why Lacan speaks of transference love as an *effect* of the production of the unconscious. Love gives being where the psychoanalytic relationship engenders a want-to-be. Of course, unconscious knowledge changes during analysis in the same way that transference love changes during the analytic process.

There is a crossing of these axes which allows us to see that they are opposed, while at the same time they cannot be separated from one an-other. Now in this chapter, Lacan says that the reality of the unconscious is sexual. That was Freud's position, and it was the cause of the quarrel be-tween Jung and Freud. Jung did not believe in the sexual reality of the unconscious. He asserted the existence of a desexualized libido, while Freud always stuck to the idea that the reality of the unconscious is sexual.

What Lacan does in chapter 12 is, in a way, define the meaning of the reality of the unconscious as sexual. He draws an obvious distinction be-tween biological sexuality and what he calls social sexuality. In this opposi-tion, biological sexuality is oriented towards reproduction, whereas social sexuality is oriented towards seeking affiliation or alliance, that is to say a combinatory of signifiers. Lacan writes:

> Existence, thanks to sexual division, rests upon copulation, accentuated in two poles that time-honored tradition has tried to characterize as the male pole and the female pole. [...] Around this fundamental reality, other characteristics have always been grouped and harmonized that are more or less bound up with the finality of reproduction. (150)

There is a definition of sexuality as reproduction, which is biological and based on the difference between the two sexes, male and female, and there is a social definition of sexuality as affiliation or alliance. Lacan quotes Lévi-Strauss two or three times in this context.

In his clinical work (not in this seminar), Lacan speaks of a Jungian analyst who is in supervision with him, and interprets the dreams she reports as all centered around the question of affiliation—the transmission of a name. Affiliation is the transmission of a name or signifier, not of life. In the biological realm, you have the transmission of life or of the species, through the lives of individuals. In the social realm, you have the transmission of a name, that is to say, the passage of a signifier from one individual to another. Lacan introduces the drive on the basis of that opposition.

He does not emphasize the difference between drive and need here, but we can situate need and the living being on the left, and the subject and the drive on the right.

Biological	Social
reproduction	alliance/affiliation
transmission of life	transmission of a name
need	drive
living being	subject

Now what is the relationship between drive and need? Drive is defined in terms of the signifier or combinatory of signifiers. It has nothing to do with biological sexual difference. Nothing at all. What is the main signifier in that construction? What is the main sexual signifier? The phallus. And there is no link between the phallus and the male sexual organ. One of the consequences of this distinction is that while there are two organs and two sexes, there is only one signifier. How do you produce two sexes with one signifier?

Freud centers everything on the Oedipus complex, a confusion being possible between the organ and the signifier. Lacan rereads Freud using linguistics and separates the organ and the signifier. He reduces the phallus to a pure signifier of difference, or what he calls the loss of jouissance.

At that period of his teaching, Lacan thinks that there is one privileged process of metaphorization, which is the Name-of-the-Father. You can imaginarize the Name-of-the-Father in different ways, Oedipally as Freud does, or logically as Lacan does in *Encore*, without any mythical significa- tion, reducing the phallic signifier to a sacrifice of jouissance, related to the mere fact that you have to speak. You have to say something about your jouissance, and when you say it, you lose a part of it. It is true that, clinically speaking, the occurrence of this principle is related to the father. The agent of that sacrifice is the Name-of-the-Father. At that time, Lacan is still Freudian, even if his work is informed by linguistics and structuralism. At the end of his teaching, mainly after his work on James Joyce, he says that there is no privilege, except for the factual privilege—the fact that more people use the Name-of-the-Father. There are more neurotics than psychotics.

In psychosis the Name-of-the-Father is foreclosed. It does not direct the process of signification. In neurosis everything has a phallic significa- tion. Let's go back to what Lacan says here. He says that the question of the sexual reality of the unconscious is a question of the relation between human sexuality and the combinatory of signifiers. What he proposes is, I think, that to start with, you have need and nothing else.

The signifier bars need and produces the drive. The drive is the result of the operation of the signifier on need, which produces a remainder. Something escapes, and that is desire. The drive is defined by Lacan as the result of the functioning of the signifier, that is, of demand: the Other's demand.

A baby has a need that is biologically defined and that has an object biologically related to that need. Milk is related to hunger. What happens? As a little human being, it is situated in a linguistic environment. Its mother talks, before it is born and from the moment it is born too. She talks all the time, even when giving the baby the objects its need requires. Her use of the signifier or language has consequences on the feeding of the need. For example, she gives the baby milk at times in a specific way. For need to be satisfied, a little human being has to deal with the Other's demand. To be satisfied it has to take the Other's demand into account. Hence the drive is a consequence of the articulation in language of the Other's demand. Of course, the Other's demand does not absolutely correspond to the need. Something escapes the correlation between need and demand which is central for understanding the drive. It is desire. As Lacan says, "The nodal point by which the pulsation of the unconscious is linked to sexual reality must be revealed. This nodal point is called desire. . . . " (154)

Thus the pulsation of the unconscious is the Other's demand, and social reality is linked to the Other's demand, the result being desire. In a way, Lacan provides a new articulation here between need, drive, and desire, drive being defined in terms of the Other's demand. In "Subversion of the Subject and Dialectic of Desire," he also emphasizes this articulation between drive, need, and desire. There is no such thing as a drive without the Other's demand. And when you introduce the Other's demand, you introduce the Other as combinatory of signifiers. You also introduce the principle of the sacrifice of jouissance, introducing desire thereby, because desire originates not in what you have, but in what you lack. That is why Lacan says, at that time, that a "drive is never anything but a partial drive" (*Écrits* 1966, 849).

We shall see why he says that in the next chapter, and why he says that "every drive is virtually a death drive" (*Écrits* 1966, 848). That is not particularly Freudian. Freud always refers to the opposition between the life drives and the death drive, while Lacan says there is no other drive than the death drive. Why? We'll go into that next time.

Notes

1. In *Television,* Norton, New York, 1990, 97–106.

2. The French term *"contrôle"* has many meanings in French implying verification, monitoring, supervision, control, checking, etc.

3. *"Proposition du 9 octobre 1967 sur le psychanalyste de l'École,"* *Scilicet* 1, 1968.

THE DRIVE (II)

Marie-Hélène Brousse

Last time I tried to sketch out the distinction between need, drive, and desire. I tried to present it to you in a way that concerns living beings, whether human or not. Then there is the Other's demand—as long as the Other speaks, it demands. All speech constitutes a demand, but Lacan speaks of the Other's demand, the demand of an other that is not barred: a real Other.

In the *Écrits*, Lacan deals with the drive and desire when he presents the mother as the real Other. Thus he describes the real Other, but also the Other of language. Now when the real Other is demanding, when it is in the field of speech, then in a way it is in the field of language without being barred. It is real, but you could also say that it is brought into the symbolic. Need is barred here, and the drive is a result of that process—the barring of need by the Other's demand. The conjunction between the Other's demand in speech and need produces the drive plus a remainder which remains implicit, that is, desire. You can write that as the subject, because the drive is related to the subject as barred; the baby taken in the field of language is barred, marked by the signifier.

In a way, S_1–S_2 is a representation of the Other's demand. The consequence is the effectuation of the subject as a result of the signifying process, as a signification of the Other's demand. The subject is defined through the signifier of the Other's demand. Let us take a clinical example. I have a patient who is grappling with her mother's desire because she can't decide whether or not to have a baby. In reference to her mother's desire she can only remember one sentence. It's a memory of her mother being furious with her children, running after them saying, "I'm going to kill you." The signifier of her mother's desire is "I'm going to kill you." In a sense, my patient was constituted on the basis of those signifiers, to kill a child. It's her interpretation of the Other's demand. The Other's demand is "die!"

Here dying is related to the effectuation of the subject, and what is related to desire is the object as what is left over from the subjective operation or constitution. That is what we are going to see here because, in chapters 13 and 14, that is what Lacan is considering. What is the correlation between the drive and the object? It's an immense problem. Lacan provides the formula of the drive in the *Écrits*: ($\$ \lozenge D$). (321) Now the neurotic, whether hysteric or phobic, identifies the Other's lack with the Other's demand (D). As a result, the Other's demand assumes the role of the object in fantasy, that is to say, fantasy ($\$ \lozenge a$) is reduced to the drive ($\$ \lozenge D$).

In the case of neurosis, the object is defined by the drive. In a way, the object in neurosis is defined as, or by, the Other's demand. There is quite a fusion in neurosis between the object of desire, the object which causes desire, and the object the subject thinks the Other is demanding of him or her.

In the case of my patient and her mother, the Other's demand is quite simple: the definitive silence of the children. She demands that they be quiet, and that is the ultimate consequence. In that case, the mother's demand, "be quiet," can be understood as "be dead"—the object of the patient's fantasy. In her fantasy she always appears as disappearing. What is her object? Her own disappearance as an object. It's not the only sign in her life because she's placed in the phallic position. But in her relationships with men, this is the way she sees herself. When she has a love affair with a man, it is important for her to see herself as a bad object, a scrap, something scorned.

Making jam for no one to eat, she sits at home, lonely and abandoned. In the aforementioned passage from the *Écrits*, you see the connection in neurosis between object *a* in fantasy and the Other's demand. It means that in a neurotic fantasy, the object of desire or the object which causes desire is the object evoked in the Other's demand. That is why, in psychoanalytic literature, objects are very often taken as the objects of demand, objects demanded by the Other or mother. That is what Lacan states when he makes a distinction between object *a* and the object as understood in object relations theory; there the object is clearly the object of the Other's demand, although that is not said in so many words.

Referring back to what I said last week, there is an operation of the drive which involves the replacing of need by the drive with the effect of producing desire. We must remember that the Other's demand, the mother's

demand, does not suffice in and of itself to produce the object which causes
desire. Why not? Because if you can imagine a child and its mother, the
mother being the Other of demand, it is not sufficient to think of a process
of separation between mother and child. One can think of pathological
actions between mother and child where the child is defined strictly as the
object of demand. Lacan indicates as much in *Écrits* (1966, 852) where he
clearly indicates the consequences of this position. He says the problem is
that the child would remain devoted to sexually serving its mother, which is
another way of saying that the child cannot function as a subject if it
remains in the position of the object of the mother's demand, devoted to
her sexual satisfaction. To produce a drive, we need only the Other's demand, the real Other being the mother; but to produce the connection with
desire, and the object that causes desire, we need to bring about a separation between the child and the mother's demand.

Let me mention the case of a little girl who had all the symptoms of
psychosis in her relationship with her mother. Their relationship was extraordinary—it was a real link offering no possibility of separation. It even
manifested itself bodily. The mother repeatedly touched her little girl. Although this habit was longstanding, she said she was going to stop when
her daughter turned fifteen. The habit was reinforced by the fact that the
little girl was unable to walk. It was like a dynamic that attached her to the
little girl all the more since the girl couldn't do without her. But every time
the daughter achieved some degree of independence, her mother clung to
her, manifesting great anxiety.

"Sexual service" is a term Lacan uses. It's not genital but libidinal. In
psychoanalysis there is a problem: perversion is not a feminine solution,
but a masculine solution to desire. Why is that? It's masculine because, in a
way, the relationship of man to woman involves only the object. It's always
a fictitious kind of relationship. But why not vice-versa? I think it is perhaps because the perverse attitude is easily realized in maternity. Maternity
is, in a way, structured in the same way as perversion. And as it is socially
encouraged and even necessary, women have no need for perversion. (I'm
referring to the table in Seminar XX, *Encore*.)

There are three points that I want to develop today. First, I'd like to
take up the paradox of drive satisfaction. Drive satisfaction is paradoxical
from the perspective of the pleasure principle as well as from the perspective of biology. Second, we should see what Lacan calls "montage," which
has clinical consequences that can be drawn from information concerning
the paradox of satisfaction. All of Lacan's argumentation in chapter 13
emphasizes that the drive is not organized by sexual polarity.

The notion that the drive is not organized by sexual polarity means
that there is no relation between the drive, drive satisfaction, and the oppo-

sition between male and female. Nor is the drive organized by another opposition Freud substituted for this first one, passive and active—Lacan is very clear about that. Is some other polarity organizing the drive? First let me show that it is not organized by a sexual polarity. Its meaning, I think, can be determined by the way Lacan analyzes the four components of the drive.

First, the source, the impetus, the object, and the aim. All of Lacan's work emphasizes the fact that there is no common ground between instincts and drives. An instinct is a momentous birth; a drive is constant because the consumption of an object cannot lower the force or impetus of the drive. Satisfaction does not imply that the drive's force changes; it stays constant, which is rather paradoxical. Second, there is no natural object linked to any impetus. Yet there is an object that corresponds to each need or instinct. To the hunger of a little baby corresponds the mother's milk. But there is no object that corresponds to the oral drive. Thus any object can be adopted as the drive object, though the drive object is not just any old object. The Other's demand determines which object is adopted. That is the meaning of the dissociation between aim and object. Lacan says that you might think you could compare the drive to a wild animal emerging from its hole to seek its prey and devour it, but that is not the aim of the drive. (165) The same problem arises as concerns the source. The drive does not originate in a biological source.

For these four reasons, there is no sexual or active/passive polarity which organizes the drive. That's why Lacan says it is a montage. It is a montage precisely because it is not determined by a momentous force, an innate object, an aim in its finality, or consumption. In a way instinct is not a montage; it's more like a program. It's an organized program of correspondence between the outside world and the internalized program. For the drive there is no such coherence between the outside world and the inside program, thus montage must be opposed to program. It is a montage because it links together two things which are heterogeneous: the Other and sexuality as defined by the need for reproduction. That implies that the drive should be partial and that there shouldn't be any genital drive. This may be rather difficult to accept, but it's in Freud's work.

Sexuality is never determined by reproduction, but you cannot ignore the fact that you are a living organism. As real, you are a sexual organism. Once in the field of language, a part of you escapes that field, remaining in the field of biology. That is in no way a psychoanalytic definition of sexuality. It is like any exigency of the real: you cannot pretend it does not exist. For example, if you consider the case of transsexualism, the subject, in his confrontation with the real, wants to change it. A contradiction has to be dealt with: the subject is convinced, for example, that he is a woman, but finds himself saddled with a male organism. He is forced to find a way to adapt the real to his imaginary and symbolic conviction. Although this is not in any way a definition of sexuality in the field of the unconscious, it appears to be the frontier of this field as real. The drive is thus, as Lacan says, an apparatus by which to bring some sexuality as real into the field of the imaginary and the symbolic.

That is what Lacan is getting at when he says that the drive tricks the real because, as you revolve around the object, you make it your prisoner, that is, you bring a little bit of it inside the symbolic structure. (168) That's what the drive is made for, and this is the kind of link it makes with sexuality as defined in terms of the real. The real is not reality. The real is made up of both the symbolic and the imaginary. When someone walks in the door for the first time, you think you know the sex of that person, but you are wrong. You can never immediately know whether that person is a woman or a man in the unconscious sphere. You can determine the sex of the subject in the social sphere and, in most cases, in the biological sphere. But you cannot say one way or the other in the unconscious sphere, because there is no drive possible to define genital sexuality.

That's why Lacan says that the drive is always partial, meaning that it involves the erogenous zones which are never linked with objects, and are always partial. But as he says in "Position of the Unconscious" (*Écrits* 1966), these partial objects are not to be considered as a set or totality. You can never construct a whole with those parts. You are always involved in a new fantasy, a new bit or piece of desire, which is precisely the definition of object *a*. And that piece is defined by an image, because as Lacan clearly emphasizes here, the object itself is lack. The drive revolves around a hole, which is veiled by images that your history provides. For example, in the case Jacques-Alain Miller spoke about in his "Introductory Talk at Sainte-Anne Hospital,"[1] the image that yielded the object in that case was death, and images were developed to emphasize that signifier: whiteness, rigidity, etc. The drive revolved around this object which manifested itself in the form of an image related to a master signifier. Those little bits are at stake in your fantasy and in your object choice, in a Freudian sense.

In "Position of the Unconscious," Lacan speaks about libido, saying that libido is connected to death. In that text he says that every drive is a death drive—there is no drive other than the death drive. In a way, then, libido is an aspect of the death drive too. There is a film based on that realization: *Aliens.*

In Seminar XI, Lacan says:

> The lamella is something extra-flat, which moves like an amoeba. It just happens to be a little more complicated. But it can go anywhere. And as it

is related—I will tell you why shortly—to what the sexed being loses in
sexuality, it is, like the amoeba compared to sexed beings, immortal. It
survives any division, and any scissiparous operation. And it can run around.

Which is anything but reassuring! Suppose it comes and covers up your
face while you are sleeping peacefully. . . .

I can't see how we could avoid doing battle with a being with such properties. But it would not be a very easy battle to fight. This lamella or organ,
whose characteristic is not to exist, but which is nevertheless an organ—
I could give you more details as to its zoological status—is the libido.
(197–8)

Biological life is limited; it begins and ends. Libido, on the other hand,
is a representation of life as indestructible. The fact that life is represented
as indestructible is related by Lacan to the fact that it has been freed from
the cycle of sexual reproduction. As long as you define the life drives in
terms of reproduction, you cannot refer to libido. Libido results from the
separation between biological sexuality and human sexuality as organized
by the signifying process. Once you get this type of construction, it can be
linked to the symbolic order because it is only by applying the symbolic
order to living beings that you can produce this abstraction: "libido." The
symbolic order is organized through a basic reference to death. As Lacan
states in "Position of the Unconscious," the symbolic order is organized by
representation, and representation implies the death of the thing.

Death is always connected to the symbolic order. That is why the drive
defined by this order is the death drive; for Lacan, libido is a name for the
death drive. It's a paradox. Once you've produced libido as a representation
of indestructible life, you can only define it as correlated with death precisely because it is a pure representation.

When Freud opposed the death drive and the life drives, he was
already proposing a sphere that exists beyond the pleasure principle. Lacan
is, in that sense, Freudian because he too proposes a dimension that
exists beyond the pleasure principle. But what changes in Lacan's work
after Seminar XI is the definition of the drive, which is purely symbolic
here. The barred subject and demand are purely symbolic. Thus there is
no room for the real in this presentation. There is no connection with
object *a*, because in the neurotic's fantasy, object *a* is defined as the
Other's demand. With object *a* Lacan introduces the real—that is,
jouissance. In the formula of the drive ($ \cancel{S} \lozenge D $), there is no real barred
subject, but as you move from the Other's demand to the object, which is
what happens in analysis, the more you work on your fantasy, the more
you disconnect from the Other's demand. In the end, the object appears
without the veil of the Other's demand. For that reason the real is rein-

troduced in the construction of fantasy, and the real reveals itself as a pure hole, pure nothingness.

In analysis one works on the Other's demand because it is an aspect of speech. Even the analyst's silence can be taken as an injunction to "speak" or "shut up." I once said to a patient, "have a good vacation," and it spoiled his vacation because he thought I was mocking him, demanding that he not go on vacation. Whatever you say or don't say in analysis, it will always be taken as the Other's demand. The problem is to confront the Other's desire, to abandon all identifications linked to the object of the Other's demand. In the end it appears that the Other was demanding absolutely nothing, which Lacan writes A. The Other's demand is but a construction, for the Other does not exist. In analysis you go from A to A, and from the imaginarization of the object to the bare emptiness of the object. Although it always escapes you, you become familiar with your favorite veil, and it always manifests itself in connection with anxiety. The more anxious you get, the closer you are to your object.

We have seen that there is no reason to replace the supposed sexual polarity, male-female, by the active-passive polarity, and Lacan provides the expression *se faire* as the emblematic formula of the drive. This *se faire* indicates that we have something done to us by someone else. *Bouffer* means to eat, and the expression *se faire bouffer* implies that someone is going to accomplish it for you because you cannot do it yourself. You need an other. You need the Other's demand.

That's not the same as *être bouffé*, to be eaten. That's why it is a solution to the active-passive opposition Lacan is trying to go beyond.

The example Lacan provides is making oneself understood. *You* make yourself understood, but you depend upon the other in order to be able to do that. There are many common sexual expressions in French using *se faire*. *Se faire* implies both the Other's demand and your utilization of the Other's demand to obtain satisfaction. It implies that your satisfaction depends on the use you make of the Other's demand. To be satisfied you need to construct the Other's demand as such. In every fantasy there is an opposition between you in place of the object and the subject as well: there is subjective division in the place of the object of the Other's enjoyment.

Se faire is the montage I mentioned earlier. It's a way of connecting your sexual satisfaction with the Other's demand, and of introducing your sexual satisfaction, in a clandestine manner, into the field of the Other, to complete the Other.

There is something very important from the clinical point of view in this chapter which details the sequence between symptom and interpretation—symptom being defined by the process of metaphor. Lacan says here that if there were only those two things, psychoanalysis would be a pure theory of interpretation. There would be no problems; psychoanalysis would be a "hard" science. The problem is that between those two things is the partial drive as the subject's sexuality. That is the question of the object. Since the drive introduces the object as satisfaction, it is real because of its connection to loss. We need to take into account the fact that there is an element of heterogeneity in the combinatory of signifiers. Interpretation alone cannot deal with symptoms. To reach the symptom, you've got to deal with the formula for fantasy, for it provides the key to the symptom. You cannot understand someone's symptom by referring to his or her signifiers alone. You've got to take into account that person's favorite mode of jouissance. Since the symptom is linked to fantasy, it has consequences: what you interpret on the basis of fantasy is not defense against the drive; it's the drive itself. Lacan specifically illustrates this distinction when he discusses one of Kris' clinical cases.

It's the case of a man who complains that whenever he writes, he thinks he is plagiarizing someone. What does Kris do? He asks the man to bring him some of his work. After reading it, he tells the man that it's clear that he is not a plagiarist, that he says he is a plagiarist to defend against the fact that he can write, and that he can have new ideas not found in other people's writings. In the following session, the patient says, "something has happened to me; I don't know why, but when I leave your office I have to go to a restaurant and eat fresh brains." That is what is known as "acting out."

Lacan says that acting out is an interpretation, as interpretation has to do with desire. It's a way of forcing the patient's desire against the analyst's interpretation concerning defense and the ego. Lacan says that what we have to interpret is not ego defenses but the drive. But what is a drive? Here the drive presents itself in the form of what Lacan calls "mental anorexia." Anorexia as related to ideas is to have no ideas. Lacan mentions the connection with the patient's father and the grandfather who were great idea producers. He says what you've got to interpret is not the defense against the drive, but the drive itself and the Other's demand present in the drive.

The object here is an idea. But it provides us with the form of a new idea, the nothingness of ideas. To interpret the drive you should emphasize this nothingness, exactly as is done in anorexia. In anorexia, you defend against your own greediness, or against your love of food. Thus the analyst must try to work on the nothingness you want to eat. You want to eat nothing. In the case of Kris' patient, he wants to have no ideas, a nothingness of ideas. Interpretation should be more oriented towards what that nothingness represents in relation to his subjective position, in relation to his combinatory of signifiers.

In analysis, you go from the object as demand, the Other's demand, to the object as loss. In the end, you've got object *a* as the lost breast. A new object can be put in that empty place. Once the subject's relation to object *a* is established, you can find no other definition of the drive than that related to the fundamental fantasy. The drive is connected to the fundamental fantasy, not as object of the Other's demand but as object *a*. In analytic work on the fundamental fantasy, you can bring about a change in the subject's position of jouissance or at least hope to do so.

Note

1. Included in this volume.

THE *DÉMONTAGE* OF THE DRIVE[1]

Maire Jaanus

> . . . desire remains essentially determined by things and related to them.
>
> —Hegel

In Lacan's Schema L, the body was sketched in as a distinction between the body image and the fragmented body. In Seminar XI, Lacan, with a new cut, creates two new "bodies," the body of the instincts and the body of the drives. The division separates the previously nondelineated, incoherent pre-mirror body into two distinct topological levels of surface and depth. The act orders a storm of inchoate, disjointed movements into a stratified and more intelligible carnal cosmos of different kinds of objects, aims, sources, and thrusts.

Behind the visible mirror form emerges the invisible and complex life of flesh. Merleau-Ponty called flesh the "brute" or "wild logos." For him this oxymoronic "wild being" served to indicate that the body was merely the other side of the mind, its *Gegenseite* or reverse side.[2] For Lacan, however, flesh is "wild" because wordless, but a logos in that it has an unalterable life and death logic of its own. What Merleau-Ponty called the chiasm of mind and body is, in Lacan, the crossing over of two entirely different "substances." Language and libido are not the same, or simply reversible opposites. "Moterialism" *(motérialisme)* is not part of the order of the libidinal real as bodies are.[3] Still, the relocation of ourselves and the world in this oxymoronic "wild logos" and the unanswered questions concerning our

119

emergence from this corporeal locus are at the heart of chapter 13. As Lacan said, "the Freudian project has caused the whole world to reenter us, has definitely put it back in its place, that is to say, in our body, and nowhere else."[4]

The body of the instincts is a body of need *(Not)*, and the body of the drives is a body of want, lack, or requirement *(Bedürfnis)*.[5] *Not* refers to necessity, to that which is indispensable for self-preservation. We need to eat and breathe to survive. *Bedürfnis* on the other hand refers to a strong, or even overwhelming want or requirement that feels like a necessity, but that is in fact not a matter of survival. In German one can say, *Ich habe ein Bedürfnis ins Kino zu gehen,* i.e., I have a want to go to the movies, but obviously, doing so is not a matter of self-preservation.

Both the body of need and the body of drive are real insofar as their source *(Quelle)* is in the body, but whereas need involves the inside of the body, the inner organs (the stomach, intestines, and other vital organs), drive involves the surface zones of the body and the erogenous openings. (The eye is a special case in terms of source in that it is an organ which is half inside and half outside, rather than a hole as the mouth and ears are.) The openings are vanishing points where the inside meets the outside. The two bodily zones, though distinct, interface. They are superimposed and connected via the figure of the interior 8 (155–6). The continuity and connection of the zones makes transgression possible. The interior 8 writes or draws one body upon the other as in a palimpsest or pentimento.

> Old paint on canvas, as it ages, sometimes becomes transparent. When that happens it is possible in some pictures, to see the original lines: a tree will show through a woman's dress, a child makes way for a dog. . . . That is called pentimento because the painter "repented" or changed his mind. Perhaps it would be well to say that the old conception, replaced by a later choice, is a way of seeing and then seeing again.[6]

The "original lines" are instinct, over which is drawn drive, and then desire. Sometimes it is possible to see through the levels, each of which is a new and different reading of pleasures and losses. "Its source in the body is what gives the drive its distinct and essential character, yet in mental life we know it merely by its aims," said Freud.[7] Given the common aim *(Ziel)* of pleasure, how then is drive pleasure distinguishable from instinctual pleasure?

Without pleasure, as Wordsworth once put it, we would not be, for pleasure is the "grand elementary principle" by which man "knows, and feels, and lives, and moves."[8] Pleasure has to do with wanting to be, to persist. The pleasure principle, said Lacan, is "the rule of the deepest instinct."[9] But archaic pleasure is without eroticism, or as Lacan put it, it is "the pleasure principle unforced by the drive."

> ... the neutral real is the desexualized real. ... There can be no doubt that there is a real. ... [T]he subject has a constructive relation with this real only within the narrow confines of the pleasure principle, of *the pleasure principle unforced by the drive*. ... (186) [my ital.]

The body of the instincts is a desexualized body. Instinct is real, but it is only real. The real is the desexualized. That, however, does not mean that the real is without pleasure, only that the pleasure principle, in its unaltered and unforced state, is homeostatic rather than erotic. There is a real ("there can be no doubt that there is a real"), and our bodies come from it, but whereas instinct is desexualized, drive is erotic. Thus to eat because one is hungry is one thing, but to eat in a dream requires drive with its hallucinatory eroticism. (155) For greater satisfaction there has to be erotization.

> The wild animal emerges from its hole *querens quem devoret,* and when he has found what he has to eat, he is satisfied, he digests it (165).

The desexualized zone of need, lodged in the motor organism, or in what Lacan calls the *moratorium,* is capable of concrete action and movement. It seizes its prey and consumes it. But, asks Lacan, how satisfying is instinctual satisfaction? Patients go to analysts because they are not satisfied, yet they cannot be relieved by being given instinctual satisfaction. Because the pleasure principle is satisfying but not *that* satisfying, the analyst must uncover what drives the patients are subject to. Since patients give satisfaction to something, they are submitting themselves to some other, obscure "law of pleasure," (166) which operates differently from the pleasure principle.

The stomach is empty and needs to be filled, or the bladder is full and needs to be emptied. We feel this *must* be done. It is a matter of dire necessity. The instinctual act provides a shock-pleasure in that an excess pressure recedes or is suddenly eliminated. But drive is not the absolute pressure of need that *Drang* (impetus) is. "Drive is not *Drang,*" says Lacan (162). Drive is not regulated like the bladder and stomach are by a momentary, strong, kinetic energy, and by thrusts. With drive, it is also not a matter of the graphic, physical movements of the moratorium or of the actual discharge of substances. Drive follows "the law of pleasure," (166) but transgresses it or "forces pleasure" (184). We *constantly* force pleasure because the thrust of the drive is *"eine **konstante** Kraft,"* a constant force, steady and continual, rather than shocking as the impetus of instinct can be. Drive "has no day or night, no spring or autumn, no rise and fall. It is a constant force" (165). What we psychically know of drive is pleasure, and our constant need for it. Thus, these two levels of our being, instinct and drive, move, fundamentally, in two different ways. The instinctual level, with its organic rhythms of sleep and wakefulness, of hunger and satiety, occasionally comes to rest; drive is as if unrest itself. Its steady forcing of pleasure alters the homeostatically programmed flow of the instincts.

In *The Will to Power,* Neitzsche wrote: "The force one expends in artistic conception is the same as that expended in the sexual act: there is only *one* kind of force."[10] Lacan says, no, there are two kinds of forces: there is instinctual shock-force and there is the stationary tension of the drive. The jubilatory conception of "one force" is a fiction just as the jubilatory greeting of the unified body image in the mirror is. One "grand elementary principle of pleasure" pleases the grandeur of the imaginary, but hides the fact that pleasure is split and heterogeneous. The notion of a single pleasure-principle or will, common in the psychological-philosophical tradition of the nineteenth century, is just another example of our desire for fusionary unity and simplification, in this instance of the partialized pleasures of the drive.

Instinctual is the reaction of the hen which will "run to ground if you place within a few yards of her the cardboard outline of a falcon" (169). Instinct yields a rationally correlated image of reactions, with a source, an object, a momentum, and an end, but drive produces what looks more like a surrealist collage, without a head or a tail, a beginning or an end, a source or a goal. The lack of beginnings and endings, of causations and objectives, leaves us without a fixed path or defined reality. The paradoxical image resulting from drive is a montage that might show "the working of a dynamo connected up to a gas-tap, a peacock's feather emerges, and tickles the belly of a pretty woman, who is lying there looking beautiful." In reversed form: "one unrolls its wires, it is they that become the peacock's feather, the gas-tap goes into the lady's mouth, and the bird's rump emerges in the middle" (169).

Drive seems peculiarly unqualified and undetermined. It is as radical an alteration of instinct as a montage is of the pieces of reality of which it is composed. Within the drive, the component elements of the instinct no longer make immediate sense. The reconstruction is discontinuous and disjointed (163), inmixing the natural with the unnatural, the mechanical with the sexual, and illogic with mere intimations of intention. The whole, preposterous and eclectic, is somewhat like the *tableau changeant* or anamorphosis described in *Nadja,* which delighted Breton because it lacked any kind of rational correlation between the different figures (a tiger, a vase, and an angel) that appeared in the engraving when viewed from different angels.[11] Drive compared to instinct is more artistic, inventive, freer, or precisely, surreal.[12]

It is the surreal drive, and not instinct, that shows up the brokenness between us and nature, Lacan's constant theme. Instincts can, of course, also be interfered with. Even animals that are given access, for example, to unlimited amounts of food begin to overeat. They begin to respond to outside cues, whereas animals in the wild respond only to internal cues. Still, because it lacks language, an animal never develops fully either drive or desire. The Pavlovian dog can never be made to desire (228–9, 237). It has never lost anything, the fundamental requirement of both drive and desire. And, therefore, it has no conception of radical otherness. It is out of losses that the various forms of the Other develop.

It is self-evident that humans are actually never in the wild state or in a state of pure instinct. We respond to outside cues, to the other and to language, from the beginning. The instinctual program immediately encounters the pressure of the larger fixed programs of a specific socio-historical culture and the demands of language with its inbuilt signifier to signifier interplay. We have the opportunity, therefore, to extend our pleasure either by connecting it to another or to a signifier. The crucial connecting point and, therefore, the decisive point of *human* emergence (and, ultimately, of sublimation) is drive, not need, although philosophy and psychology have, in the past, more commonly assumed the contrary. The reason for this is that language hooks fundamentally into drive, as we shall see, and not into instinct.

Drive is also what makes the Aristotelian ethics of moderation in all things useless for us or not much better than an ethics derived from the stomach.[13] Keeping stimulation at a certain point, not too little and not too much, is the ethics of the pleasure principle, but drive forces pleasure, rejecting moderation. Thus, there is a moderate pleasure principle and an immoderate one. Our *psychic* core, insofar as it is sourced in something not wholly psychic, but something real, is drive. We as humans are and in a sense begin at drive, not instinct. We spend our lives being driven, not in instinctual homeostasis. We want more pleasure. How can we try to prolong and extend it? From where or how shall we get it?

When the drive transgresses, immoderately, in the direction of instinct, it enters an excluded, desexualized zone (172). Within this desexualized fallout zone, which is on the side of the real, the sexualized object can once again become merely the parcel of meat, which is there to be consumed. In such instances, the sexual partner is reduced to a function of the real and the reaction may be disgust, hysterical vomiting, or cannibalistic desire. Whenever you go back inside the organism, you get the *real* reactions and the shock-force, not the erotic reactions. For the same reasons, when a drive object is approached in an instinctual way, as in anorexia, something merely psychic and absent is "eaten" as if it were present and filling. Conversely, in perversion, an uneatable, instinctual object may literally be consumed, with erotic pleasure, as if it were the object *a* of the drive:

> My husband's whim is to have himself sucked, and . . . as a corollary to that one: while, as I bend over him, my buttocks squarely over his face and cheerily pumping the fuck from his balls, I must shit in his mouth! . . . He swallows it down![14]

Coprophagy is a drastic example of the transgression of drive back into instinct. As a radical instance of perversion, this moment of re-instinctualization in Sade's *Philosophy in the Bedroom* reveals the extreme of autoerotic love: love as a type of auto-cannibalism. Sade's pervert, rather than accepting the fundamental objectlessness of the drive, seeks to fill in the lack, uncovered in the erogenous zone of the mouth, with a real object. One way to be sure one has the lost feces back again is to ingest them. Instincts should not operate like drives or drives like instincts, but they can, even though erotic pleasure as such is not real and drive in itself is not perverted (181).

Instinct or the desexualized real has to do with a pure self-preservation that neither knows nor recognizes any otherness. Instinct, uninfluenced by language, produces no relationships. Consumption is not a relationship. If an object is consumed, there can be no relationship to it. Whenever we move from eroticism back to consumption and mere self-preservation, we have moved from drive back into need or instinct. Once you consume something it is not there for you to have a relationship with it. For there to be relationships, something has to be left over, something must *not* be consumed.

What is not consumed? The placenta, "the most profound lost object," says Lacan (198), the afterbirth, the breast, feces, urine, all the waste products and discharge that fall from the body. "The *a*, the object, falls. That fall is primal."[15] It is with these lost and fallen raw materials that we, unlike the animals, can have the deepest of narcissistic relationships. These lost substances are things that point us ultimately to the Thing (*das Ding*), as we shall see. But loss is the indispensable requirement in relations of drive and desire. With language, everything is lost. So the constancy of desire in language is easily explained. Lacan now formulates a new question that can perhaps be stated like this: Is there an equivalent material loss in the body that might explain the constancy of drive?

Already Freud had suggested that the object of the drive "may be a part of the subject's own body."[16] Lacan says initially the subject "is no more than such on object."[17] At stake in drive are lost, objective fragments of our own body. And even instinctual self-preservation (on which drive leans) dictates that we ought first to preserve what is ours. "The object *petit a* is what falls from the subject in anxiety."[18] The anxiety is a sign of the radical autoerotic investment. The first loss, therefore, given our narcissism, that begets our attention is the loss of a part of our own bodily substance.

> I propose that the interest the subject takes in his own split is bound up with that which determines it—namely, a privileged object, which emerges from some primal separation, from some self-mutilation induced by the very approach of the real, whose name, in my algebra, is object *a* (83).

The speaking subject is the consequence of a double castration, linguistic and bodily. Physical castration is, as Lacan says, an inescapable and inexorable "self-mutilation" (83) which forces him to develop a new fundamental hypothesis about the genesis of psychic objects from what are seemingly parts of our own flesh and to conjecture the relationship of these objects to a theoretically enlarged concept of the real.

This unavoidable self-castration or intrabodily division tears us apart and scatters our substantial fragments about, throughout the universe, somewhat as were the body parts of the mythic Osiris. Subsequently, drive becomes a fetishistic search for what was once ourselves but is now an extra-bodily, alienated otherness that can "appear" almost anywhere, and in anyone or anything. For this reason, our fundamental being, ever dispersed into parts, can also never become a conscious "Hegelian synthesis" (221). Desire *does* remain "essentially determined by things and related to them," but not in the literal and immediate way Hegel thought.[19] First of all, it is drive, not desire, that is related to things, and second, the Lacanian "things" are psychic or mere traces of a real thing. The objects *a* are only the *psychic objects* of the drive and merely the *psychic cause* of desire.

Physical castration, which occurs within the body of drive, is as necessary as castration by language. This "primal separation" effects something real, a death, which has to occur, in order that something exist outside the structure so that the symbolization of substances becomes possible. It is a trauma not of meaning and meaninglessness as language is, but a trauma of being and non-being, ultimately of immortality and mortality, and hence proximate to the greatest possible states of anxiety and bliss. Reality is structured on the rejected object *a*, the something (a piece of our own being) relegated to non-being. That loss (in separation) produces simultaneously the object *a* (the real) and reality. The psychic object, once a real other, can no longer be seen or heard. Invisible and inaudible, it nonetheless gazes at us or speaks inside us from the outside, arousing anxiety. It is the archaic object, annihilating or enticing us from the outside of our being with imminent non-being or the promise of fulfillment.

Unlike the imaginary body, the bodies of instinct and drive are "object-ive" and ultimately related to the real, not the merely virtual as the body image is. Compared to the weightlessness of images and words, they have weight and substance. Compared to the speaking subject for whom signifiers anchor its meanings, the drive "subject" is an object anchored in the real by lost pieces of its own flesh. This piece of substance (the *objet petit a*), like the reel with which Freud's grandson played:

> is a small part of the subject that detaches itself from him while still remaining his, still retained. . . . [M]an thinks with his object. It is with his object that the child leaps the frontiers of his domain. . . . If it is true that the signifier is the first mark of the subject, how can we fail to recognize here . . . that it is in the object to which the opposition [the *fort-da*] is applied in act, the reel, that we must designate the subject. (62)

The subject is first a part object. It plays first with pieces of its own body. It learns its being from the divided parts of its own being. It "thinks" first its own substance. As a languageless, and therefore "headless subject" (181), it "leaps" beyond itself within itself, or within its own substance, or with pieces of its own substance. The phonemic soundings, *fort-da*, are initially treated as if they were bodily pieces. Language, emerging here as sound pieces, is born from the real, as these pieces of sound belonged once to the body of the child or more precisely to the erogenous openings of its ears. The first verbal sounds are superimposed over the most intimate physi-cal "things," with which one can *act*. The child wants back what it has thrown away from itself or has lost, e.g., its thumb or its soundings. The game is a type of headless or languageless "subjectification," or a subjectification without a subject since in drive one is merely an object, playing with psychic part-objects of oneself. Thus the basic game Freud's grandson played was a game of drive, but superimposed on it was the language game.

Instinctual pleasures give us back some sense of the physical weight of the real, but the unconscious as instinct, says Lacan, "has nothing to do with the Freudian unconscious, nothing at all" (126). The Freudian uncon-scious, structured like language, "gears into the body" at the point of drive.[20] It is the invocatory drive that is at the basis of our erotic relationship to language and the jubilatory babblings of *lalangue*. It is what initially makes sounds enticing. As is evident in the instance of the *fort-da* game, the signifiers that Lacan called the "moorings that anchor our being" hook into the pleasure of the invocatory drive.[21] Yet, the signifier also is, as memory was for Proust, "like a rope let down from heaven," which alone sustains our possibility for sublimation.[22]

Pleasure extends outwards in all directions from the interior of our bodies to others, language, and ultimately, to the lamella. With language we are furthest away from the depths, from the instincts and the drives, forced to a surface. Where shall we let ourselves be pleasured? Which pleasure shall we chose, the pleasure with objects (*Sachen*), with things (*Dinge*), with others, or with words?

The object *a*, separated from us by a prelusive "self-mutilation," is something we do not know as a formed, specular object. As this primal castration occurs before the institution of language and the imaginary proper, this unique object is pre-linguistic and pre-specular (neither symbolic nor imaginary). Of it we have neither images nor words. It remains the unobjectified object, the non-represented object, the pre-object, or the ab-ject (*abjet*)[23]—unseen, unheard, unsmelled. It is that part of jouissance that can never be spoken. It can only be lived. It has to happen. Thus drive is freedom from any visible, defined object. It is a movement or merely the re-enactment of a movement, guided by something unclear, fragmentary, and impossible. "The essence of drive" is "the trace of the act" (170). Objectlessly, drive merely retraces an unrecuperable act.

As a prelinguistic drive to be, to make one's bodily self exist, drive can attain its aim only partially. Oddly enough, it aims to make itself (*se faire*) be eaten, pissed, shitted, seen, or heard. Lacan's grammar or formula for drive which changes Freud's *werden* (to become) to *machen* (to make, *faire*) in order to show up the activity of the drive, is beyond the active-passive polarity (i.e., to eat and to be eaten) as the reflexive middle voice returns to the self (*se faire*, to make oneself be eaten) (195). Still, this *se faire*, this minimal way of making oneself exist, is a matter of perpetuating our being, even if only as a partial object, against what drives us towards non-being. Because this game of being and non-being goes on without and beneath language (with the self and the other placed as part-objects), there is, according to Lacan, no subject in the drive. The drive is "a radical structure—in which the subject is not yet placed" (181–2). The reflexive voice makes a montage of the self and the other but as partial *objects*. The self has actively to get itself to be eaten by the other without the aid of the signifier.

Thus, when the child Freud urinated in the parental bedroom, as Lacan mentions in Seminar II, it was not because he needed to urinate, but because he was making the turn in the drive: to urinate, to be urinated, to make oneself (*se faire*) be urinated. He was driven to attempt to be recognized as urinating or as a urinating being. His act was the jubilant performance of the instinct with the aim of demonstrating mastery rather than subjection. Micturition becomes a demonstration of a power of pleasure, of being, and of acting. It is the creative exploitation and modification of what we have of necessity. It is the instinct sublimated and put to another purpose, beyond instinctual need.

Compared to the instinctual, mindless need to urinate, one can perhaps call Freud's exhibitionary performance a free use of urination, or simply, "free urination" or "urination as free play," in the sense that Kant talked of the aesthetic experience as the "free play" of the mental faculties.[24] Drive, then, is the paradox of a "free instinct." Just as there is for us a free use of the imaginative-mental faculties in the act of judgment, so there is for us a free use of our instinctual potencies when these have been mastered. The comparison can be taken further as, both in drive and in the aesthetic judgment, there is no need for the presence of a real object, given that both evince a paradoxical "disinterested interest" in the existence of things and focus instead on the subjective feeling of pleasure. To the aesthetic subject in the animated state of pleasure, its judgment seems universal but this is merely a paradoxical "subjective universality." The "drive subject-object" similarly wants to compel the other, but has to master itself instead, masochistically, without ever attaining the mastery of the other's enjoyment.

Drive imitates the instinctual act without being identical to it, without being fulfilled within and by the act. The purpose is not the act, but something else, a more intense pleasure. Here urinating shifts from need to drive. It becomes an erotic act:

> It is because of the reality of the homeostatic system that sexuality comes into play only in the form of partial drives. The drive is precisely that *montage* by which sexuality participates in psychical life. . . (176)

Freud, the seven year old child, as a urethral being is taking steps towards asserting himself as a libidinal object, as a urethral object for another. Clearly, the act is one of seduction as Freud later claimed that of the Wolf Man's was: "His urinating on the floor was in reality an attempt at seduction, and the girl replied to it with a threat of castration, just as though she had understood what he meant."[25] The reaction of Freud's father was equally negative, as he reportedly said, "the boy will come to nothing."[26]

The instinct does not urinate *for* anybody or for the other. It simply does what it must. Instincts are autonomous. They can also not be transferred. The other cannot urinate for us. The drive, however, tries to transfer the urination. It puts it into circulation for the other. And it is in this transfer that the function of drive is realized, says Lacan (179). However, to effect the transfer, a special kind of "passivity" has, momentarily and paradoxically, to be introduced into what is at core a pure activity. For in the field of the drives, it is a question of "pure activity *durch seine eigene Triebe* [by means of one's own drives] for the subject," and not a matter of reciprocity (200). Hence, the passivity of drive is fundamentally active, since drive turns, resting neither in the movement of "to urinate," nor in the passive of "to be urinated," but only in the completed drive act of "making oneself be urinated." Drive is a matter of mastery and control, and establishes how one is an *active* partner in whatever is done to one.

Nonetheless, the passive phase, albeit momentary, introduces pain or the possibility of pain:

> *At what moment*, says Freud, *do we see the possibility of pain introduced into the sadomasochistic drive?* [. . .] It is . . . when the subject has taken himself as the end, the terminus of the drive. At this moment pain comes into play insofar as the subject experiences it from the other. He will become . . . a sadistic subject, insofar as the completed loop of the drive will have brought into play the action of the other. What is at issue in the drive is finally revealed here—the course of the drive is the only form of transgression that is permitted to the subject in relation to the pleasure principle. (183)

The pain is that of what one might call an "object-subject" which asks not, like the desiring subject, "what do you say or think of me?" but "what will you *do* to me?" Drive asks about action and the real: Will I get pleasure or pain? Am I your "reel?" In Freud's exhibitionistic urination, his member is in a sense "the reel" and the active stream of urine "the string." Lacan associates the flow of the word, trying to get through the images and the ego in the dream of Irma's injection, with Freud's urethral drive and erotism.[27] Although the question is *enacted* rather than asked, it is the first acknowledgement of another, even if only as a dim some*thing*, a body on which the somatic must also make mental demands in the way that it does on oneself.

> There are not two stages in these drives, but three. . . . [W]hat is new is the appearance of a subject. This subject, which is properly the other, appears insofar as the drive has been able to show its circular course. It is only with the appearance at the level of the other that what there is of the function of the drive may be realized. (178–9)

Drive satisfaction requires our reduction from whole object to part-object. Freud is replaced by his urinating phallus. There is a displacement and investment of the self into a part, offered to the other. This is the masochistic humiliation. But in order to be recognized, even if only as a libidinal partial being, an other partial being (the "new" . . . the "subject, which is properly the other") has also, in turn, to be recognized. One needs the other to do the act of recognizing. What the other does is decisive. Freud was haunted by his father's negative reaction for the rest of his life.

Drive is a type of active subjectification of the subject-object that occurs paradoxically without subjects. It is the result of a nonlinguistic pleasure-pain "dialogue," sadomasochistic in essence, conducted with erogenous bits and glances, between ourselves and others. Drive is Hegel's master-slave dialectic in bodily form. The other is drawn in but as a part object of pleasure or pain, not as he will be later, as a signifier for another signifier in the act of verbal communication.

Freud's 1932 essay on "The Acquisition of Power Over Fire" is yet another elaboration of the proximity of instinct, drive, and sexuality and of how the need to make distinctions is demonstratively operative in various mythological fragments and the key to their structure. The confusion begins in the male body, as primitive man "had to try to grasp the external world with the help of his own bodily sensations and states."[28] The phallus unites in a single organ, water (urination) and fire (sexual desire), and despite the segregation of functions, the unity suggests the fusion of instinct and drive and sexuality, as in fact occurs in the fantasy of children:

> Children still believe that they can combine these two functions; one of their ideas of the way babies are made is that the man urinates in the woman's body.[29]

Thus the very fact of the phallus immediately presents man with a dialectical opposition that requires resolution, namely the conjoined presence of synthesis and antithesis at the same site. (Freud's essay also, inadvertently, points to the physical and masculine origin of traditional dialectical thought.)

The hollow rod (the phallus) in which Prometheus brought fire to humankind is but one instance of how the drives arise out of the instincts in order thereafter to participate in the drama of the law as well as in homoerotic desire. The Mongolian law against "pissing upon ashes" suggests to Freud that this law, at its core, was a reference to "a pleasurable struggle with another phallus" (i.e., man extinguishing his own fire with his own urine also suggests a homoerotic situation of phalluses only).[30] The essay seems to be an avowal that Freud's ancient shame and guilt involved the working through of his own homoerotic desire for his father. The distinctions are as difficult to sustain in the body as they are in socio-cultural reality and law.

Drive is a psychic movement around an object (subsequently fallen away) that once surrounded our body and closed up our now open and empty erogenous orifices (such as the breast that filled our mouth or the sound that filled our ears). These fallen partial objects, however, were once themselves part of a totality that Lacan calls the lamella. The lamella is libido persisting without sexuality. It is immortal, self-subsisting life:

> It is the libido, *qua* pure life instinct, that is to say, immortal life, or irrepressible life, life that has need of no organ, simplified, indestructible life. It is precisely what is subtracted from the living being by virtue of the fact that it is subject to the cycle of sexed reproduction. (198)

The lamella or libido is the ultimate substance or real from which singular existences come (197). It is the immortal life that we lost at birth. It is us as libidinal, but pre-sexual *substance*, not as subject. It is the lost greater real of the subject as an immortal "object" or the capital Other of the biological body. But because it is an immortality to which we are only connected by death, it is fundamentally a negative immortality.

Lacan's myth of the lamella or of immortal life, the false instrument or organ, at the center of the field of the drives and its objects (196), is his effort to explain the attraction and pleasure of death (of suicide, for example) and the real of the death drive. The myth, by reversing normal ideas about life and death, shows sexed life up as a loss of immortal life so that sex becomes, paradoxically, the death of immortality, while death, on the other hand, becomes a desire for immortal life (196–8). In exchange for our lost real immortality, we have only sex:

> This lack [of the lamella] is real because it relates to something real, namely, the fact that the living being, by being subject to sex, has fallen under the blow of individual death. (205)

Sex is a gift of pleasure that comes concomitant with the surrender of immortal life. Real, eternal life and our wholeness are behind us and they can never be recuperated except through death. The love myth of Aristophanes obscures and represses this more fundamental loss of immortality. Lacan's myth of the lamella aims to correct the myth of Aristophanes, and thereby to lift this ancient repression. For nearly two thousand years we have used sex and love to hide the ever present death drive that the lamella, the greater libido, sustains and includes.

From the perspective of the immortal libido, sexual realization is a deception, urging us to an imaginary wholeness with another and tempting us to reproduce another unsatisfied being who will, like us, suffer from a lack of immortal fulfillment. From the perspective of the myth of the lamella, the myth of Aristophanes is a false lure or a merely partial pleasure. But from the perspective of the singular, mortal being, love, sexuality, and sublimation are all that we have. Because we are de-immortalized, we cannot afford also to be de-sexualized.

Existence as such depends fundamentally on the possibility of transference—onto others, language, and objects. We must be able to transfer, translate, and sublimate. When such transferences are blocked, we are endangered and exposed to the seductions of an immortality that is, for us, simultaneously death. As suicide shows, object *a*, unmoored from the features of the other and from the other as such, directs us to the lamella and death. Object *a* is the momentous psychic object within transference and, therefore, the position that Lacan as the analyst finally assumed in the four discourses.

All the forms of object *a* are ultimately representatives or figures for this lost libido, which is beyond biological life (198). The objects *a* are "the residues of the archaic forms of the libido."[31] Thus, the loss of the various particular objects *a* is not merely a "self-mutilation," but a repetition of our original fall from immortality into mortality. Each object *a* is a reminder or remnant of the greater totality of which we were once a part. The objects *a* are fundamentally connected to and centered on this great Other, which is opposed to the radical capital Other of language. This is a centeredness on life as such, which, without language, spells death.

It is obvious therefore why, as representatives of immortality, the objects *a*, centered on this lamella, are not susceptible to satisfaction within mortal sexuality, and why drive is also of necessity a death drive, unless one is deflected or diverted by the other or caught up in the signifier (the *fort-da*). Ultimately, the signifier (*fort-da*) is alone capable of taking us away not only from "the reel," the body pieces, others, the instincts and the drives, but from the lamella, to *lalangue* and communication. The radical Other of language is the absolutely necessary opponent to *das Ding*.

There is the immortal life of language that Lacan calls the radical Other and there is the absolute Other of libidinal matter: the immortal life of libido. We live between two immortalities (or two impossibilities). Both the Thing and language demand a type of castration. Yet castration is the operation that gives significance or meaning to what previously had no meaning. Both threaten our identity and make us anxious. Language always ends, and we do. And because our drive is fundamentally focused on immortality, the other can never completely reduce our anxiety:

> The most archaic aspirations of the child are both a point of departure and a nucleus that is never completely resolved under some primacy of genitality or a pure and simple *Vorstellung* of man in human form by androgynous fusion, however total one may imagine it. There always remain dreams of these primary, archaic forms of the libido.[32]

The primal scene is not primal. Beyond the image of our sexually fused parents are more primordial dreams of fusion with the lamella. As Lispector says "I am more what is not within me."[33] Intimations of this lost and distant libido occur via experiences that we have with the objects *a*. The most extreme conflicts that we, as originally immortal matter, can have within our biologic condition of mortality involve these objects. They are part of every extraordinary drive movement of transcendence.

In Lispector's *The Passion According to G.H.*, the heroine reingests the primordial matter from which she was once, immemorially, separated. And she experiences jubilation.

> I who had thought that the best proof of my internal metamorphosis would be to put the cockroach's white mass into my mouth. And in that way I would approach . . . the divine? the real? For me the divine is the real.[34]

She eats the innards of a cockroach in order to rediscover the other side of the human world, namely the world of pre-human material neutrality, non-human and awesome, and she does so with a desire that is beyond disgust. It is not true, as Kristeva has set forth in *The Power of Horror*, that the real as such is contrary to any sublimation and horrifies humanity. For Lispector, this contact with the non-human real makes the entire cultural human network, designed to hold it at bay, reverberate more forcefully and beautifully, turning the whole into an oratio of sounds.

> Contact with the thing must be a murmur, and to speak to God I must put together unconnected syllables. My lacking came from the fact that I had lost my inhuman side—I had been expelled from paradise when I became human. And true prayer is the silent oratorio of inhumanity.
>
> No I don't have to rise through prayer: I must, ingurgitated, make myself a resonant nothingness. What I speak to God about has to make no sense! If it makes sense it is because I err.[35]

Lispector leads into the dimension of the real, where nothing makes any sense.[36] Does she reach the most original enjoyment, that of the fusion of the human with the non-human, or even more primal, that of matter with matter itself? Matter enjoying itself with itself—is that what the ultimate immortal pleasure would be? Is that when "the divine is the real?"

Aristophanes' myth focuses on mortal pleasure, but is there also a senseless immortal pleasure, which we know nothing about, which we have not yet begun to explore because we have indeed become too human and because we have, since the advent of language and, far more recently, the scientific revolution, grown too distant from pre-human life? To even begin to make amends in a socio-historical culture so fixated on sexuality, the narcissistic imaginary, fame, money and success, one would have to relearn or begin a new jouissance with something beyond anthropologically fixated humanity—at the least, a jouissance with the air that we breathe, the sea, and the forest. And even that would only be the very beginning of a sublimation which Lacan defined as the elevation of object *a* "to the dignity of *das Ding*."[37]

Notes

1. The mistranslation of *démontage* as "deconstruction" in the title of chapter 13, "The Deconstruction of the Drive" (*Démontage de la Pulsion*), has been used by some critics as the basis for referring to Lacan as a deconstructionist.

The substitution of the word "instinct" for the German *Trieb* (when Freud also had *Instinkt* available to him had he wanted to use it, as the French has *l'instinct*) in "Instincts and Their Vicissitudes" is particularly unfortunate. *Trieb*, from the verb *treiben*, meaning to drive, push, force, set in motion, propel, impel, urge on, stimulate, promote, refine, raise (metals), put forth (leaves, branches), or carry on, practice, has many more powerful and wide-ranging meanings as well as cultural-historical ones attached to it than *Instinkt* does. *Treiben* is often used in German in connection with oneself and others, as well as nature. A mother will typically say to a child: *"Was treibst du da?"* meaning not only what are you doing there, but what are you pushing or driving, emphasizing the sense of activity. Similarly one says of nature: *"Die Sonne treibt die Blütten hervor,"* i.e., the sun is driving or pushing out the blossoms, which again puts emphasis on the idea of an active power and force. Or one says commonly: *"Er treibt es auf die Spitze,"* meaning to push to extremes or exaggerate, again suggesting force. Schiller used the word to describe his notion of the human subject as a composite of a play drive, material drive, and form drive. In Schiller's connection of matter and drive we see again the emphasis on becoming, development, and unrest, which then became the very definition of Absolute Spirit in Hegelian philosophy and the romantic conception of being as a driven, dynamic becoming.

2. Maurice Merleau-Ponty, *The Visible and the Invisible* (Evanston, Illinois: Northwestern University Press, 1968) 169, 211, 259 et passim.

3. Lacan's coinage joins the French words, *"mot"* and *"matérialisme."* "Geneva Lecture on the Symptom," trans. Russell Grigg, *Analysis* (No. 1, 1989) 14.

4. Jacques-Alain Miller, *The Seminar of Jacques Lacan VII: The Ethics of Psychoanalysis* 1959–60 (New York: W. W. Norton and Company Inc., 1992) 92.

5. Jacques Lacan, *The Four Fundamental Concepts of Psycho-Analysis*, ed. Jacques-Alain Miller, trans. Alan Sheridan (New York: W. W. Norton and Company Inc., 1978) 167. Future references in the text are to this edition.

6. Lillian Hellman, *Pentimento* (New York: Signet, 1974) 1.

7. Sigmund Freud, "Instincts and Their Vicissitudes," in *General Psychological Theory* (New York: The Macmillan Company, 1963) 88.

8. William Wordsworth, "Preface to the Lyrical Ballads" in *Selected Poems and Prefaces,* ed. Jack Stillinger (Boston: Houghton Mifflin Company, 1965) 455.

9. Lacan, *Ethics*, 96.

10. Friedrich Nietzsche, *The Will to Power*, trans. Walter Kaufmann & R.J. Hollingdale (New York: Random House, 1968) 432.

11. André Breton, *Nadja* (New York: Grove Press, 1960) 59.

12. The image Lacan invented might also well be a parody of one of Sade's multiple tableaux in *Philosophy in the Bedroom*:

> I am going to insert my prick in her ass; . . . you will frig her . . . by means of the position I place you in, she will be able to retaliate in kind. . . . After a few runs into this child's ass, we will vary the picture: I will have you, Madame, by the ass; Eugénie, on top of you, your head between her legs, will present her clitoris to me; . . . Next, I will lodge my prick . . . [The Marquis de Sade, *Three Complete Novels*, trans. Richard Seaver & Austryn Wainhouse (New York: Grove Press, 1965) 240.]

For Sade there was only a body of the instincts; for him there was no body of the drives. He understood the law of the pleasure principle and of discharge, but he knew nothing about the impossible and unobtainable psychic object of the drive. Instead he tried to realize and enact the various strata of sexuality within the confines of the flesh.

13. "Because what else is the famous lowering of tension with which Freud links pleasure, other than the ethics of Aristotle?", Jacques Lacan, *Television*, trans. Denis Hollier, Rosalind Krauss, Annette Michelson (New York: W.W. Norton & Company, 1990) 19. See also *Ethics*, 110.

14. Sade, *Philosophy in the Bedroom*, 227.

15. Lacan, *Television*, 85.

16. Freud, "Instincts and Their Vicissitudes," 88.

17. Lacan, *Écrits* (New York: W.W. Norton & Company, 1977) 315.

18. Lacan, *Television*, 82.

19. G. W. F. Hegel, *The Philosophy of Fine Art* (New York: Hacker Art Boos, 1975), 49.

20. Lacan, *Television*, 37.

21. Lacan, *Écrits*, 174.

22. Marcel Proust, *Remembrance of Things Past*, vol. I, trans. C.K. Scott Moncrieff & Terence Kilmartin (New York: Random House, 1982) 6.

23. Lacan, *Television*, 21.

24. Immanuel Kant, *Critique of Judgement* in *Philosophical Writings*, ed. Ernst Behler (New York: Continuum, 1986) 200 et passim.

25. Sigmund Freud, *From the History of an Infantile Neurosis* (1918) in *Three Case Histories*, ed. Philip Rieff (New York: Collier Books, 1970) 285.

26. Peter Gay, *Freud: A Life for Our Time* (New York: W.W. Norton & Company, 1988) 23, 112.
See also Leonard Shengold's commentary on Freud's urination in his *Halo in the Sky: Observations on Anality and Defense* (New York: The Guilford Press, 198) 168–171.

27. Jacques Lacan, *Seminar II, The Ego in Freud's Theory and in the Technique of Psychoanalysis 1954–1955*, ed. Jacques-Alain Miller, trans. Sylvana Tomaselli (New York: W.W. Norton & Company, 188) 159.

28. Sigmund Freud, "The Acquisition of Power over Fire," in *Character and Culture* (New York: Collier Books, 1963) 300.

29. Ibid., 299.

30. Ibid., 297.

31. Lacan, *Ethics*, 93.

32. Ibid., 93–4.

33. Clarice Lispector, *The Passion According to G.H.*, trans. Ronald W. Sousa (Minneapolis: University of Minnesota Press, 1988) 116.

34. Ibid., 161.

35. Ibid., 154.

36. *"Nous pouvons . . . être sûr que nous traitons quelque chose de réel seulement quand il n'a plus quelque sens que ce soit. Il n'a pas de sens parce que ce n'est pas avec des mots que nous écrivons le réel."* "Yale University, Kanzer Seminar," 24 novembre 1975, Le Séminaire de Jacques Lacan, XXIII Le Sinthome, Texte établi par Jacques-Alain Miller.

37. Lacan, *Ethics*, 112.

PART I V

THE GAZE AND OBJECT *a*

THE GAZE AS AN OBJECT

Antonio Quinet

Lacan states in Seminar XI that the gaze can function as an object, which at first seems rather strange. Most people familiar with Seminar XI know that Lacan's reference to the gaze as object *a* comes from *The Visible and the Invisible* by Maurice Merleau-Ponty. Merleau-Ponty points to something that becomes central in Lacan's work: there is a preexisting gaze, a kind of staring at us by the outside world. This is Merleau-Ponty's main thesis and, according to him, the visible depends on the eye of the seer. The introduction of a seer indicates that, in his work, there is a Platonic perspective with an absolute being that is all-seeing. For Merleau-Ponty there is an imaginary being behind the eternal gaze. Yet such a being doesn't exist. What exists is the split between what one sees and the gaze, a gaze which is neither apprehensible nor visible, a blind gaze which is erased from the world. It is exactly in this way that the drive manifests itself in the scopic order.

For Merleau-Ponty there is a universal all-seer whereas for Lacan there is the pre-existence of a given-to-be-seen. Lacan takes this expression to mean that, in the initial relationship to the world, something is given-to-be-seen to the seer. Before the seen there is a given-to-be-seen. This notion is primary for other themes developed by Lacan. The pre-existence of a gaze is correlated with the given-to-be-seen of the subject. In other words, the drive indicates that the subject is seen, that there is a gaze which aims at the subject, a gaze we cannot see because it is excluded from our field of vision. This gaze gives us the distinction between what belongs to the imaginary order and what belongs to the order of the real where the drive

139

manifests itself. The real can be defined as the register in which the drive manifests itself; what is shown to us and what we see belong to the imaginary order. Our visible world is one of images whose geometry is given by the mirror, and the mirror stage is, in fact, a prototype of the imaginary order in which the ego is constituted in relation to the *semblable*[1] or fellow being at the center of the ego's constitution. The *semblable* is the prototype of the mirror stage, and its specular order is marked like the scopic order, which is the register of the gaze.

The visible world of our perceptions is a world of images. In addition to the world of vision, there is the realm of the invisible that is the register of the gaze. The former is an imaginary perceptual order; the latter is real. In one we have images, in the other drives. And as we shall see, the manifestation of the drive predisposes the subject to a passive attitude. There are two grammatical attitudes: "I see," which is of the specular order, and "being seen," which indicates object *a* as a modality of the gaze in the scopic order. What corresponds to object *a* in the visible is the image of the other [i(a)]. The gaze is not seen because there is something which covers it over. What hides it is an image—the image of the other. Object *a* is covered over by the other's image and that is necessary if my *semblable* is to arouse my desire. It is a necessary condition because object *a* is the cause of desire.

Let us now consider Lacan's reading of Freud's text "Instincts and their Vicissitudes." This text interests us because object *a* (in this case, the gaze) is the object of the scopic drive. As you are probably acquainted with this article, I'm not going to summarize it. But I would like to make a few comments about it based on Lacan's reading of it. In this article, Freud distinguishes four aspects of the drive: the impetus, source, object, and *Ziel*—which Lacan divides into two English words, "aim" and "goal." The impetus has the character of activity in the drive. The drive is indestructible, and thus its impetus is always there, demanding satisfaction at all times. The drive is given its character by its impetus. According to Freud, the drive is indestructible in its impetus.

Let us turn to the distinction between the aim and the goal. The satisfaction of the drive lies in reaching its aim. The aim is always satisfaction obtained by suppression of the state of excitement that exists in the source of the drive. There is a tendency toward a zero point of activity, but this is impossible to achieve because it is not compatible with life. Satisfaction, then, is paradoxical because the tendency toward the zero point is a tendency reaching beyond the pleasure principle to the realm of the impossible. Lacan defines the real as impossible, but impossible in what way? Impossible to bear. That is what makes the satisfaction of the drive so paradoxical as revealed in symptoms.

The aim is always satisfaction, and the goal is but a means to obtain this aim. The source is the so-called erogenous zones located in the holes of the body surface, which have a rim-like structure. The body's rims are connected to the outside world or, in another sense, to the Other. According to Freud, "the object [*Objekt*] of the instinct is the thing in regard to or through which the instinct is able to achieve its aim. It is what is most variable about an instinct and is not originally connected with it, but becomes assigned to it only in consequence of being peculiarly fitted to make satisfaction possible" (*Standard Edition,* **14**, 122). The drive, then, can be satisfied by any object, but I do not mean an object that can be consumed like an apple or reached like a target. If an object is fitted to the drive, it is the drive that makes this an appropriate drive object. What turns an object into a drive object is the turn the drive makes before returning to the subject. It is the impetus of the drive that turns around the object in its return to the subject.

Following Freud, Lacan calls the drive a montage, assemblage, or construction. But to see the functioning of the drive, we must return to Freud. You know that Freud grammatically deconstructs the drive, dividing it into three elements: first, activity and passivity; second, subject and object as they structure sentences; and third, the three forms of the verb, active, passive, and reflexive. Now, in relation to these three elements Freud talks about two vicissitudes: reversal into its opposite, and the turning of the subject upon him or herself. The reversal into its opposite is very easy to see: for instance, to torture and to be tortured. The reversal of activity and passivity can be seen in the scopic dimension: to gaze and to be gazed at. The example Freud gives of the second phenomenon discussed here—the turning of the subject upon him or herself—is that of masochism and sadism, masochism being equated with sadism directed against oneself. The turning of the subject upon him or herself can be related to exhibitionism, which includes the subject's gazing at his or her own body. Freud says the exhibitionist wants the other (someone similar to himself) to reenact or double the same gesture, but Freud shows that both vicissitudes coincide— the transformation of activity into passivity, and the turning of the subject upon him or herself.

The following distinctions follow from the active/passive schema: to torture someone and to be tortured by someone; to gaze as a voyeur and to exhibit oneself. Freud analyzes the force of the verb in setting the drive's mechanism in motion, and establishes a grammar of the drives. His model is perversion, and he begins with masochism and sadism.

The declension proceeds from the active instance, "s/he tortures," to the reflexive instance, "s/he tortures him or herself," and culminates in the passive, "s/he is tortured." These are the three positions of this grammatical declension: the first offers an instance of sadism, the second an instance of masochism, and the third, which occurs in the sado-masochistic dimension, an instance of obsession.

But there is a problem concerning the scopic drive. Freud remarks that the reflexive "he tortures himself" occurs before the active instance, which can be demonstrated by studying little boys. Freud states that a little boy gazes at his sexual member, obliging him to introduce a third element into the scopic drive: the penis. Tellingly, the penis takes the place of the object of the drive.

When referring here to the scopic drive, let us use *it* as a replacement for the penis. In the first position, s/he *gazes*; in the second, s/he gazes at *it*; in the third, *it* is gazed at by the Other. Freud remarks that what is most important about this construction and deconstruction of the drive is that these three logics are always operative: the drive is obliged to satisfy all three logics at the same time. Lacan proposes an expression to discuss these logics: he says that what is important in the drive is making oneself think. In this "making oneself" we have the verbal formula of the drive.

What do we see in the third logic? We see that the grammatical subject of the sentence has disappeared only to be replaced by an object, and this alteration is very important to the satisfaction of the drive. In the drive's satisfaction, the subject is reduced to an object. We can look at other drives to find similarities. For instance, if we replace the gaze in the oral drive with the act of sucking, we end up with Freud's little boy engaged in the following progression: he sucks an object, he sucks himself, and he is sucked. And—in a sentence that incorporates all three aspects—he gets himself sucked. If we substitute fantasies of plagiarism, we can see the same dynamics at work. Kris discovered as much in the case of an hysteric that dealt with the issue of plagiarism related to the oral drive. If we replace the act of sucking with the attempt to plagiarize, we end up with the plagiarist's desire to suck up someone's ideas or with his fear of having his ideas sucked up by another.

Kris' patient believed he was unable to create ideas by himself. He was sure that everything he wrote was an instance of plagiarism. Kris decided to determine whether or not it was really plagiarism by reading the patient's work. He decided that his patient's claims were false, and said so to his patient. He told him that his ideas had nothing to do with the work of the professor about whom he kept talking. But immediately after leaving his analyst's office, the patient went to a restaurant to eat fresh brains precisely to prove something to his analyst. For this patient, then, eating fresh brains was a symbol related to plagiarism and the oral drive. This fantasy has little to do with the real, a realm which is not crucial here.

The gaze also has connotations for the anal drive. Lacan says that the anal drive has a lot to do with shit. So we can replace the verb "gaze" with the verb "shit": we can say that the subject shits out an object, or shits her or himself out, or is shitted out. Obsessive neurotics feel that they are being shit out all the time, which is a manifestation of guilt. A very common obsessive symptom is the belief that every gift given is reduced to shit. To the obsessional, the Other rejects the subject like a shit.

Let us now examine object *a* in order to connect it with the subject under consideration. But first we must ask exactly what object *a* is in regard to the subject and the Other. Jacques-Alain Miller has explained this connection by saying that object *a* is a part of the Other, but not an element of the Other. In Seminar XI, Lacan tries to demonstrate the connection between the object and the subject by placing the subject in relation to the Other.

In one of his diagrams, Lacan places the subject in one circle and the Other (*Autre*) in the other; object *a* falls between the subject and the Other:

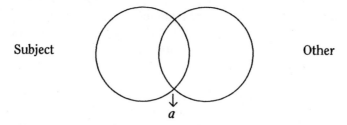

This illustration shows that object *a* doesn't belong to the subject or the Other (*Autre*, or simply A). Lacan's subject is defined as a want-to-be; the gaze-as-object *a* is its being. Thus we determine the subject as a want-to-be, in both senses of the word "want" (want as lack and want as desiring). Object *a* is a being that lacks consistency, a being we cannot grasp or see, but which is, nevertheless, a being. This is very strange since it is the cause of the subject's desire. This object, which condenses jouissance, is the object of the drive. In *The Interpretation of Dreams*, Freud theorizes that for the subject this being is lost in hallucination. Lacan states that, for the subject, this being is lost—cut off—only to slip out through the field of the Other. But if it slips out through the Other, that does not mean that the Other possesses it like other objects. Its slippage through this field explains why each person is attracted by his *semblable* or partner. If it were only one object among others, object *a* would not be the cause of desire.

The gaze as object *a* or cause of desire can be represented, and we can see how this can be accomplished. For instance, a beam of light—a glint in someone's eye, a reflection in someone's hair, a jewel which shines—can

represent a gaze which is not in you. In many representations in the philosophical tradition, light is equated with the gaze. It is common knowledge
that, in such philosophical traditions, many comparisons have been made
between light, vision, and knowledge which, in retrospect, evoke Lacan's
notion of the gaze. In Freud's work, the whiteness of Frau K.'s body evokes
the gaze which attracts Dora for, as we know, the object of Dora's attraction
was Frau K., and her white skin, which I am identifying as a manifestation
of the gaze, added to that attraction. In another example, a spot of light can
represent the object, cause of desire, as a presence that makes one feel
gazed at. Feeling oneself subjected to the gaze can not only produce desire
but anxiety, which is another manifestation of object a.

In Seminar X (*L'angoisse*), Lacan says that the gaze is always present
in manifestations of anxiety. Without object a, he says, there is no anxiety.
The model Lacan gives of the gaze at the height of anxiety is the moment
when Oedipus realizes what he has done. When he perceives the crime he
has committed, Oedipus tears his eyes out of their sockets; according to
Lacan, this prototype of anxiety shows him being gazed at by his own eyes
from afar. This gives us the classic figure of anxiety: his being gazed at by
his own eyes, torn from their orbits, but still staring at him. His own eyes
were the cause of his downfall. He wanted to know what had happened, but
ended up seeing something he could not bear. Lacan defines that as the
emergence of an impossible gaze staring at the subject.

We can see something of the phenomenon of the double when we gaze
in the mirror but don't recognize ourselves. There is an odd moment of
anxiety which is also present in the uncanny. In both experiences there is a
presence that makes us feel gazed at when nothing is there. But in such
circumstances, something is functioning: the screen of the image is filled,
and we can catch glimpses of the gaze that fills us with anxiety. But we
know that it is not only the image that screens the object, because there
must also be the symbolic order.

The function of the screen is to erase the gaze from the world, from
the world's show, from the Other as reality, with all the significations that
help constitute our environment. The object is erased in this representation, which means that there is a screen which hides the gaze, and this is
illustrated by the spot. Lacan says that the spot can represent the screen; at
the same time the screen hides the gaze. "Spot" can also be translated as
"stain." We can use "stain" or "spot," but I think "spot" is more interesting
in English because of the relation between the terms "spot" and "spotlight,"
which illustrate the representation of the gaze. The spot hides and reveals
the gaze. A spot can be an eyewitness of a crime, as it is for Lady Macbeth,
who pleads, "Out out damned spot" when trying to erase a spot of blood
which refuses to go away. In that scene, the screen fails to serve its function

because she does not succeed in erasing the spot, a symbol for her ensuing madness. Here the spot symbolizes the gaze which determines the subject as a receptacle of anxiety, caused by being gazed at.

How can we understand the gaze in the psychoanalytic sense? The most obvious place to observe it is in psychosis where there is a failure of the gaze. For neurotics the gaze as an object has no consistency, no substance. It does not appear; it cannot be seen. But for psychotics, the gaze can sometimes be felt and seen because the screen fails, which is another way of saying that the Oedipus complex fails. In psychosis there is something that shows the subject that the object is not lost. The gaze, then, which is absent for neurotics, is not lost for psychotics, a fact that becomes more evident if we consider the difference between the real and reality.

What is the real? When I talk about reality, I am discussing the reality of our perceptions and images. But even in the imaginary register, reality is structured by the symbolic order, since both the symbolic and the imaginary compose it. The real as a body of experience is excluded from reality. The imaginary gives shape and form to things we can perceive through our representations or signifiers. We know that reality, which is not the same for each person, is structured by the symbolic order. Whereas the real is not normally part of reality, in psychosis object a (normally not part of reality) returns to the field of reality. In neurosis, the mechanism of repression implies the loss of the object. Total satisfaction becomes impossible because the object that could satisfy the drive has been lost. But in psychosis this is not the case; the object can appear as a gaze staring at the subject or as an hallucinatory voice.

What we see in psychosis is a disorganization of the visual field. In cases of such disorganized confusion, the gaze as object a in the scopic field often appears to the subject in a magnified series of multiplying gazes. For instance, one delusional patient went out in the street believing that everyone was looking at him because he was a homosexual. In another instance, a schizophrenic patient who hallucinated that everything from eyes to atoms was staring at him, was obliged to put on dark glasses to avoid their scrutiny. In a psychiatric hospital, a group of patients tried to hide themselves from the hallucinated gaze by staying in their beds because they thought there were spies everywhere staring at them. This symptom, which Freud called the delusion of being observed, appears at the beginning of paranoia. A persecutory delusion develops around the gaze, but it is not very easy to distinguish this kind of phenomenon from a phobia. Analysts occasionally have patients who are unable to leave their homes, not because of phobic fears, but because they cannot bear the Other's gaze.

I'm going to conclude by relating an anecdote about how the gaze, though not apprehensible, can be deduced from certain neurotic symptoms in cases of hysterical blindness. Picture this: a man was going up the stairs in a restaurant when suddenly his eye met his analyst's eye. Their eyes met as his analyst was coming down the same steps he was going up. The patient, immediately struck by blindness, was obliged to grab hold of himself rather than continue. His vision returned little by little, but in a very peculiar way, like a curtain going up in a theater that stops in the middle of its ascent. The curtain remained half raised while he ate at the restaurant. Until he finished his meal and left the restaurant, the analysand could see nothing in a part of his visual field. He remained blind in one sphere of his visual field until he walked out into the street; at that point his symptoms disappeared.

To the analysand, this episode was related to a dream with a strong erotic tonality he recounted in which he and his analyst were eating together. His dream fulfilled the wish to have a drink with his analyst. In fact, he wanted to have a drink with his analyst as soon as his analysis was over. That was what he said he wanted to do. To "have a drink" in French is *prendre un verre*. The patient's symptom, blindness, appeared precisely when he met the Other's gaze. The symptom was sustained by the expression *prendre un verre*, in which the term *"verre"* is ambiguous. The signifier representing the gaze is present in *"verres,"* which is French for glasses (a metaphor for drinks) and lenses (or eyeglasses). The signifier represents the gaze present in the lenses of the analyst's spectacles. The scopic drive manifested itself in the symptom, where there was a "getting oneself seen"—he was blind and did not see. In the manifestation of the scopic drive, this hysterical subject saw nothing because he was reduced to an object. At that exact moment, he was the gaze. In this symptom we see the object. Is it part of the Other or part of the subject? We know that if, in his symptom, the analyst represents the Other for him, the gaze exists between them. In the symptom he is reduced to an object. The subject disappears; in this hysterical reaction he disappears literally because he no longer sees.

On this subject, read Freud's interesting article, "The Psychoanalytic View of Psychogenic Disturbance of Vision," which talks about hysterical blindness. There he explains hysterical blindness as a repression of sexual scoptophilia. Scoptophilia is the activity of the drive and the gaze related to it. Freud says that the repressed drive takes its revenge for being held back from further psychical extension by becoming able to extend its dominance over the organ that is at its service. In other words, the drive finds satisfaction in the symptom, bringing on an unbearable jouissance—blindness. According to Lacan, the drive is the only vehicle for transgression. Thus it is interesting in this particular case that scoptophilia is represented by a curtain which stops in the middle of its ascent. Why?

It was exactly at that instant that the analysand's eye alighted on his analyst's crotch. He was going up the stairs and his analyst was coming down them, when suddenly the drive was repressed.

Note

1. *"Semblable"*, in French, means fellow man or being, someone who seems [*semble*] to be like you; it also means similar.

THE PHALLIC GAZE OF WONDERLAND

Richard Feldstein

By temperament Nora was an early Christian; she believed the word. There is a gap in 'word pain' through which the singular falls continually and forever; a body falling in observable space, deprived of the privacy of disappearance; as if privacy, moving relentlessly away, by the very sustaining power of its withdrawal kept the body eternally moving downward, but in one place, and perpetually before the eye. Such a singular was Nora. There was some derangement in her equilibrium that kept her immune from her own descent (*Nightwood* 51).

Falling Through the Hole in the Other

Intrigued by a white rabbit that is perilously late for a very important date, Alice follows its pied piper's song to Wonderland. Driven by exploratory desire, she chases the rabbit into a hole in the symbolic chain and, relocated on the underside of discourse, falls through a gap in symbolic consistency. But why say that Alice falls through a hole in the symbolic Other rather than through "a large rabbit-hole under the hedge," as it is described in the text (*Wonderland* 2)? Numerous writers have described this hole as an aspect of nature or as a product of fantasy that lands the protagonist in a wondrous world which captivates her imagination. Because Carroll indicates that Alice falls into an extended daydream before waking at the end of the novel, literary critics have read the rabbit-hole as a space of imaginary transformation where dreams transport Alice from the surface world to the shamanistic land down under. But here let us define this hole

149

as a gap in the Other, a site coded by the signifier's logic even as it is covered over by the production of fantasy.

But before developing the implications of such a strategy, I would like to look at what the text tells us of Alice's descent. Finding herself situated in this transformational space, Alice quickly learns that the symbolic knowledge acquired above ground is immediately useful in interpreting her adventures in Wonderland. This realization occurs at the outset of the story as soon as she is released from the gravitational pull of earth-bound experience. Then she floats down a tunnel marked by a sequence of signifiers— with its jars of orange marmalade, cupboards, bookshelves, and other representatives of domesticity that line the sides of the well where she experiences extended free-fall before landing on a heap of dry leaves.

Although Wonderland is most often celebrated as an imaginary extravaganza, it is the signifier's influence which determines structure and transvalues experience. Why else would Alice bother to curtsy as she fell? "Fancy *curtsying* as you're falling through the air!" (Carroll's emphasis, 2). Why take the "opportunity for showing off her knowledge," even if there were "no one to listen to her" (2)? Why, in the midst of descent, recite her lessons as if she were in the middle of taking a test? And, most importantly, why are the sides of the well filled with signifying grids like "maps and pictures hung upon pegs" that provide little help in orienting Alice to her present situation (2)?

Subject to the dictates of desire, Alice falls into a representation of the unconscious, which according to Lacan presents the discourse of the Other. A signifying chain, the unconscious is structured like a language, that is, structured initially by a series of unbound floating signifiers. When falling through the Other, Alice imitates one of these free-floating signifiers which structure the field of language, not through the meaning-making process but by the introduction of innumerable drifting signifiers that exist in oppositional relation to other signifiers. As Lacan says in "The Subversion of the Subject and the Dialectic of Desire in the Freudian Unconscious," "the signifier is constituted only from a synchronic and enumerable collection of elements in which each is sustained only by the principle of its opposition to each of the others" (304).

At the outset these untied elements float until they become fixed in a unified field of meaning, quilted by a *point de capiton* or "master signifier" that gives coherence to a differential series which would otherwise slide inexhaustibly in metonymic progression. According to this logic, Alice drifts downward until her fall is brought to an abrupt halt at ground level where she *begins* to suture herself to a master signifier that retroactively quilts all other signifiers to it, and thus enables her to begin the process of making sense of this nonsensical dimension confronting her. Actually Alice's entire

journey—from the initial encounter with the harried rabbit through her sojourn with the Mad Hatter and March Hare to her interaction with the King and Queen of cards—can be understood as an attempt to make sense of Wonderland, to find a nodal point or *point de capiton* which knots meaning retroactively. In so doing, *capitonnage* provides an identity for the subject structured by the "fish hook" that casts all previous signifiers in relation to it.

Through this process Alice tries to make sense of a nonsensical situation in which animals don clothes and speak as if they were human. For those that people Wonderland utilize language to become speaking beings that signify. Alice's attempt to make sense of what the animals say and to compose significance from the strange sequence of incomprehensible situations is tied to her perceived identity. This identity is a construct created from experiences on the surface world that have been transposed to Wonderland, a nonunified field of signification which poses itself as a question to be answered through the insertion of a *point de capiton* that places itself in the Other and thereby recasts the synchronous code in relation to a diachronic chain that totalizes meaning. In *The Sublime Object of Ideology*, Slavoj Žižek gives a precise example of an anchoring point which unifies a series of free floating signifiers:

> To grasp this fully, we have only to remember the above-mentioned example of ideological 'quilting': in the ideological space float signifiers like 'freedom', 'justice', 'peace' . . . and then their chain is supplemented with some master-signifier ('Communism') which retroactively determines their (Communist) meaning: 'freedom' is effective only through surmounting the bourgeois formal freedom, which is merely a form of slavery; the 'state' is the means by which the ruling class guarantees the conditions of its rule; market exchange cannot be 'just and equitable' because the very form of equivalent exchange between labour and capital implies exploitation; 'war' is inherent to class society as such; only the socialist revolution can bring about lasting 'peace', and so forth. (102)

In Žižek's example the floating signifiers freedom, justice, and peace are recast by a *point de capiton*, communism, which alters their meaning so that each term is read in relation to this determining signifier. In *Alice's Adventures in Wonderland* Carroll intuitively plays with this logic, for instead of introducing terms like freedom, justice, or peace, the very process of representation itself is called into question as that which seeks a master signifier to structure the meaning-making process. In other words, *Alice* presents an emblematic study of the representation of the representational process itself as it relates to the reconfiguration of Alice's identity.

After Alice leaves the surface world, she descends to a dreamscape that confuses her so much she gropes to understand it by applying previously learned principles to her present experiences before trying to grasp this set of unknown variables on its own terms. Because Wonderland insists on its own problematic discourse, Alice is forced to recognize that nonsense is one of the only consistent variables she encounters. Her adventures are so bewildering, she is left wondering who she is in relation to a new *point de capiton*—Wonderland as a surreal master signifier—which ironically introduces nonsense as the fish hook which unites the irrational aspects of her encounter around its pervasive reappearance as the dominant element in the story. With each succeeding misadventure, nonsense becomes the rigid designator that insists on the logic of illogicality established to deconstruct the logocentric lessons learned in the parallel surface world. These are transferred onto the issues of how logic and identity are unstructured and restructured in her new environment.

In Lacanian terms, this focus on structure entails a study of subjectivity in relation to the signifier, the signified, the big Other (*le grand Autre*), and the small object *a* (*petit objet a*). And it is this relationship of the subject to the intersubjective network that Alice confronts when comparing her experiences from one world to another in a desperate attempt to reconstruct an identity for herself in relation to these new surroundings. In the story Alice plays many parts in the structuralist drama in an attempt to situate herself geometrically within the parameters of her uncharted course. She is alternately a divided subject split between competing desires to live in these two contrasting spheres of existence, a floating signifier drifting through a nonunified field of representation, a signified in search of its meaning, and an outsider to Wonderland who mocks the big Other and shrinks into a *petit autre*.

In chapter 5 the caterpillar, who in another world where the laws of nature apply would metamorphose into a butterfly, becomes a teacher of identity-as-transformation when it asks Alice repeatedly, "who are you?" Actually this refrain of identificatory confusion rings in her head immediately after she descends into Wonderland, before meeting this adviser. As early as chapter 2 Alice exclaims, "how queer everything is to-day! And yesterday things went on just as usual. I wonder if I've been changed in the night . . . But if I'm not the same, the next question is, Who in the world am I? Ah, *that's* the great puzzle" (12). Shortly thereafter she wonders if she is Alice or if she is Ada or Mabel: "no, I've made up my mind about it; if I'm Mabel, I'll stay down here! It'll be no use their putting their heads down and saying 'Come up again, dear!' I shall only look up and say 'Who am I then?' Tell me that first, and then, if I like being that person, I'll come up: if not I'll stay down here till I'm somebody else" (13).

On the surface world Alice believes she *is* Alice, a little girl who lives in a natural universe ordered by perceivable cycles. But in Wonderland she quickly realizes that the sign is raised to the function of the signifier once "the dog goes miaow, the cat goes woof-woof," and the animal is disconnected from its cry (Lacan, "Subversion" 303–304). The signifier's relation to the sign indicates utter contempt for verisimilitude, which allows for a range of objectifications in which animals talk, the Queen and King appear as playing cards, flowers are painted red, and, in the game of croquet, the balls become hedgehogs, the mallets become live flamingoes, and the soldier-cards convulse themselves into arches through which the "balls" travel. All this leaves Alice "wondering if anything would *ever* happen in a natural way again" (Carroll's emphasis, 97). Alice repeatedly ponders her identity confusion caused from this journey through such strange environs. Her enigmatic passage baffles her because Alice is torn between two worlds. So when she asks "who am I," she really means "who am I in this world" where nature is so displaced I am having difficulty grounding my recognition of reality.

In Carroll's emblematic story there is the problem of how to situate the subject in relation to the lack of knowledge produced by nonsensical events that subvert an understanding of Alice's situation. This process begins almost immediately, when she falls through the rabbit-hole, which correlates in the Lacanian schema with the big Other that in the second graph of desire is superimposed over the *point de capiton*:

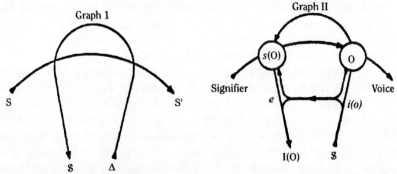

In Lacan's first graph of desire, a mythical intention intersects the signifier's chain S.S' and enacts a *capitonnage* through the quilting process at the upper right point of intersection. The immediate effect of this process is a quilting of the "pure signifier"; its product is the barred S at the bottom left side of the first graph. Lacan superimposes the second graph of desire over the first mapped sequence. Once this is done, it is evident how the mythical, presymbolic intention is transformed into the barred subject which intersects the vector S.S', now conceived as s(O)-O. The superimposed sequence enables us to see that *capitonnage* occurs at the site of the Other, and its effect is s(O), a signified or meaning that is a function of the Other. It becomes apparent that the Other holds dominance in the vector by virtue of its appearing twice, as a doubled referent: on the left as s(O) and on the right as O.

It is through the Other that Alice falls, the Other being a pre-given structural site that proceeds the birth of the subject. It is "the locus in which is situated the chain of the signifier that governs whatever may be made present of the subject," and it determines all codes from which the subject of the signifier receives the messages by which s/he is constituted (Seminar XI, 203). In other words, the Lacanian Other is the symbolic field organized through the chain of signifiers where words guarantee value by the very fact that we speak. Under the influence of the signifier, the subject is constituted in the place of the Other where the I speaks to "the one who hears," only this *one* is not another human being but the structure of language, the signifying chain in the field of the unconscious (Seminar III, 309).

The chain designated as vector S_1-S_2 is shorthand for the Other, which structures the field of the unconscious, determines desire as the desire of the Other, and marks the subject in relation to the signifier. Speech helps to organize the order of the signifier, which is not a space but a place or "locus of the Other, the Other witness, the witness Other than any of the partners" existing beyond any individual personality ("Subversion," 305). In this locus the subject remains submissive "to the law of one and all," the all-encompassing everyone inasmuch as it indicates the chain of signifiers as the site of dispersed desire and regulatory law (Lacan, "Desire in *Hamlet*" 49).

The Other is the first aspect of Wonderland that Alice confronts because it is the initial sign that the extended dream sequence is not entirely her own. At first glance we might assume that, since Alice is dreaming, all aspects of the dream provide representations of her desire. After all it is Alice whose consciousness constructs the zany characters she meets and the weird scenarios that unfold. But if it is accepted unproblematically that all aspects of the dream are hers, we are left with a positivist gesture of full presence wherein the speaker of the consciously enunciated statement is equated with the unconscious subject of enunciation. Given this positivist perspective, we would have to accept what Alice says as equivalent to her desire—to what is said between the lines, to what is requested regardless of the words she uses to articulate her demands. But once the signifier intervenes, the I that speaks is belied by what the unconscious seeks to assert. Furthermore, when Carroll constructs Wonderland as an alternate dimension existing as an aberration of the surface world, he insists on the basic division implied in the splitting of subjectivity. One immediate ramification of this logic is that the Other cannot be reduced to an internalized aspect of subjectivity. It cannot be interpreted solely as a voice articulated from within the subject.

The Other holds a place other than the site of the subject. A self-contained set of signification, the Other insists on the alterity of the unconscious: it has its own demand, its own desire, its own time, and its own linguistic effect, all of which can be understood as impersonal. For whenever we move from the personal, "I believe that you should do this," to the impersonal, "It is imperative that you do that," we witness the linguistic turn indicating our identification with the place of the Other. Alice eventually recognizes this alien intentionality within Wonderland as well as in her introjection of its regulatory processes. She also recognizes—after her initial adventures conclude and she finds the key to the magic garden, enters it, and plays croquet with the Queen—that she is subject to some*thing* in Wonderland that exists beyond the reach of the big Other. This *thing,* which escapes the symbolic by being part of the subject yet more than it, is the remainder left over from the subject's encounter with the Other. It is the *plus de jouir* or object *a* that evades the symbolic castration in which the subject must renounce some primal jouissance and follow the significatory detours of the Other.

Eric Laurent explains that when the subject is structured by the Other there is a loss of jouissance defined as a "desert of jouissance": "in that 'desert,' in that substitution that castration makes (the fact that jouissance is replaced by the Other), there is something left and that's why one accepts castration." That remainder is the *plus de jouir* or surplus jouissance as distinct from the primal jouissance sacrificed to the Other. When Alice looks around the confines of her strange new world, she notices that some aspects of experience remain utterly foreign to consciousness, escaping the subject/Other split. In the Lacanian schema these aspects are comprised of surplus jouissance, the objectal substance which remains after the object is sifted through the symbolic grid. These object *a*'s remain in us yet more than us and therefore cannot be represented as such for they exceed the limits of symbolization.

Thus, it is through symbolic castration at the site of the Other and the loss of jouissance implied by this sacrifice that *plus de jouir* is created and we come to realize that the Other is insufficient onto itself. With this recognition we can understand that the Other is barred because of symbolic inconsistencies in its field tied to what Lacan will later call the process of alienation and separation. During the period that Seminar XI was written, Lacan uses this formulation to replace the graph of desire elaborated in "Subversion of the Subject and the Dialectic of Desire in the Freudian

Unconscious." In both the graph of desire, which elaborates a theory of metaphor and metonymy, and the theory of alienation and separation, Lacan demonstrates how object *a*, functioning in the process of symbolic castration, helps the subject move from the demand of the Other to a recognition of the Other's desire as distinct from his or her own. To do this, the subject must eventually conceive of the Other as barred, inconsistent, or lacking, as Alice begins to do when she descends through the gap in the Other in the first sequence of the story. By the end of the book, after she is accused of stealing the tarts, presents evidence on her own behalf, and disregards the King's injunctions by growing out of the symbolic confines of Wonderland, Alice denies the desire of the Other, detects its limitations, and distinguishes its politicized status as lacking.

Between Two Births

In Lacanian theory there is a term, *traversée du fantasme,* which indicates the crossing of fantasy. This traversal allows the subject to grope with the structural ramifications of fantasy: how the formation of fantasy disguises symbolic inconsistencies in the Other and covers over the multifarious voids in the Other which undermine its authority and call into question its very existence. While bodily jouissance is submitted to the defiles of the signifier, the ego attempts to deny the interpenetration of the symbolic with the real as well as the asymmetrical self-image related to the symbolic mortification of jouissance that results from the interpenetration of the registers. This considered, it becomes apparent that the formation of fantasy in the imaginary is a defensive strategy enabling the compensatory construction of coherent spatial images linked to performative fictions that extend through time in such a way as to provide the illusion of a temporal presence to personality.

In other words, the construction of the big Other presupposes the real of jouissance which destabilizes the signifier, riddling it with inconsistency. Because the significatory process cannot symbolize the jouissance which proceeds it or the *plus-de-jouir* which is sieved through the symbolic cut yet evades the logic of the discursive network, the Other becomes porous with surplus jouissance that remains uninterpretable. To defend against the porousness of the Other shot through with excess jouissance, the ego (that in us which would be "one") resorts to an iconic dumping of fantasy over any disconcerting fragmentation which undermines its unified self-image.

This aspect of Lacanian theory applies to Alice, who has discovered a nonhuman world where the predominant species are talking animals and signifying playing cards. Once in this land of contradictions, Alice recognizes that the Other that has previously structured her symbolic insertion in social tradition is inconsistent with the Other that influences the bizarre intersubjective relations of Wonderland. This is the most immediate ramification of her disconfirming experience in Wonderland. Alice's previous child-like acceptance of her symbolic inscription in Victorian society is challenged once she encounters an Other in which human interaction is displaced by a signifying logic that inscribes talking animals and inanimate cards within textual relations. These creatures are assigned a riddle role to play in the nonsensical drama of their existence. They are provided gamelike rituals to enact, induced to adopt a symbolic mandate in the construction of cultural identity, and, in this way, become historicized subjects whose desire is tied—through a *point de capiton*—to the desire of the Other and their symbolic placement in relation to it. Observing their strange psychodrama, Alice recognizes the symbolic inconsistencies revealed through the comparison of her past and present experiences. As a consequence of this recognition, she begins to subvert the Other's authority by questioning its desire and distinguishing it from her own.

Because Carroll stresses that it is Alice's extended daydream which persists until the end of the narrative, no matter how weird events become, there is every indication that the consciousness which sustains the dream is Alice's. Actually Carroll gives us many ways to read her daydream sequence. For instance, we can interpret the characters who take the stage and enact the drama as a creation of Alice's consciousness, or we can account for such wondrous episodes as the production of Lewis Carroll (Charles Lutwidge Dodgson), who insists that an alien intentionality exists within Alice's consciousness. There is also the option of explaining the interpretative process as a nineteenth-century predecessor of reader-response theory wherein we watch Alice read the text as she encounters it, producing an interpretation of events by reconfiguring herself in relation to this oddly familiar yet often incomprehensible world.

From another perspective, the journey through Wonderland offers Alice an experience very much like a second birth in the cultural mirror where she is spatially recaptured by the field of the Other. Confronted with this bizarre sequence of events, Alice attempts to restructure her imaginary world, and with it, the notion of a unified ego tied to the "jubilant assumption of [her] specular image" in the configuration of an integral sense of self ("Mirror" 2). In other words, once Alice enters Wonderland, the girl's self-image is repeatedly challenged as her body expands and contracts, causing a loss of physical boundaries that radically disorients her. She thus re-experiences symptoms associated with the initial psychodrama that unfolded in front of the mirror where she began the process of cultural birth through the assumption of a self-image that enabled her to conceive of herself as a unity symbolizing her own "mental permanence" ("Mirror" 2). This was done by identifying the body with a statuesque image representing the newly emergent ego in relation to others in an intersubjective network that had not yet fully emerged ("Mirror" 2).

In the initial experience before the mirror, the child constitutes an idealized ego whose foundation rests on a fictional construction of integral boundaries in an identification with an objectified virtual image. In the mirror s/he is presented with a gap between viewer and viewed, the assumption of which position is crucial to the development of the personality. We compensate for this gap and our "anatomical incompleteness" caused by the human "prematurity of birth" by anticipating a future projected mastery over our bodies. To do this, we align geometrical coordinates to construct a totality that compensates for pre-mirror experiences of fragmentation associated with the disjointed body of bits and pieces.

However, in situations where one's unified self-image is severely threatened (having an emotional breakdown, being placed in a concentration camp, or arriving suddenly in a world where animals talk), a process of disidentification can occur. It happens to Alice when she travels to Wonderland and becomes disoriented in the process. Any previously perceived unity dissolves when her body begins to take on strange, incoherent, even unrecognizable shapes that are unrelated to her internalized self-image.

Every time her body grows and shrinks, Alice takes cognizance of these oddities as her original identification in the mirror is replaced by a disidentification wherein she is left emotionally poised between an incoherent abyss and a fictional unity previously concocted to prop up the ideal ego which, with the advent of desire, metamorphoses into the ego ideal.

One reason Alice challenges the creatures of Wonderland to act in accordance with the known laws of nature is to enable her to dramatize herself within the circumscribed locus of a recognizable grid of spatial relations. Since the mirror stage is "a drama whose internal thrust is precipitated from insufficiency to anticipation," the impetus upon whose stage she projects her actions for others enables Alice to reinvent the dramatic aspect of existence, narrativize it, and cast herself narcissistically in the starring role whose totalized perspective is seen and judged in relation to the other's gaze ("Mirror" 4). But since she is faced with a second birth in the mirror that captivates her spatially in a reflection of nonhuman relations, Alice reactivates the memory of her original experience before the mirror, which insists on reasserting its figural foundation each time events turn too bizarre to accept at face value.

But in the second mirror stage Alice's audience is the big Other that structures experience in relation to a *point de capiton* in the signifying system that holds its allegiance to discourse. According to Lacan, discourse

ADVICE FROM A CATERPILLAR

is "the tie that binds" us to the intersubjective network and its symbolic mandate wherein one's cultural destiny is assumed in accordance with the desire of the Other (Seminar XX, 51). For when Alice disidentifies with her original experience before the mirror and attempts to reorient herself to her new surroundings, the initial mirror stage experience is complicated by a secondary symbolic identification with a signifier that is out of kilter with the original process. In this symbolic reidentification the nonsensical "master signifier" of Wonderland represents her to other signifiers that constitute her within a locus beyond the coordinates of subjectivity: beyond her position within the symbolic structure and her inscription within its text, beyond the acceptance of a symbolic mandate, the assumption of assigned roles, and the experience of the two deaths—the first bound to the demise of the biological organism and the second to the inability of the symbolic to contextualize the first.

Wonderland insists that Alice play another part in the script because she must pitch questions to an enigmatic Other that remains incomprehensible to her. She deals with this situation in two ways. First, she tries to master the moment by conjuring memories of past experience and applying them to each situation she encounters. Second, she comes to understand that nonsense has a density which indicates itself as a marker to be read, or, as might be the case, to be eaten as a means to effect bodily transformation and identity reformation. Alice's new world identity, then, is tied to instances of spatial captation in both the first and second mirror stages and to the difference between them as the place of transformation. After Alice falls through the hole in the Other, her personality alters dramatically as she experiences rapid bodily transformation. These transformations repeat so often they become signifiers of flux bound to the repetition of nonsensical, illogical events.

To defend against the radical fragmentation associated with the process of disidentification, Alice tries to impose temporal continuity on a wildcard environment she atttempts to master by appropriating the interpreter's power to dominate the interpreted (Bivona 161). Living in a world decentered by nonsensical game-like rituals, Alice seeks to reestablish "temporal, spatial, political, and interpretive" precedence as a means of asserting her own subjective position (Bivona 161). You might say she supervises her environment. Daniel Bivona goes so far as to label her a "child-imperialist" who wants to make "sense out of unruly matter by extracting herself from that which she would interpret, ultimately an assertion of the 'primacy' of the interpreter over the mere material, the right of Alice the child-imperialist to impose a meaning on the behavior of the illogical 'creatures' " (161). Read in this way, Alice tells us "more about her own ethnocentrism than [. . .] about the behavior of the 'creatures,' " more about this invasive intruder who repeatedly tries to decipher the mastercode of these game-like rituals that offer themselves as a basis for comprehension of such unprecedented situations. Poised defensively in reaction to the unknown, Alice places herself in a position to master her situation by creating dominion over those that inhabit Wonderland, which is, by definition, there to excite wonder rather than to submit itself to any universal systematic interpretative code which would circumscribe it within its parameters.

To the extent that Alice projects rule-governed behavior taught to her on Earth's surface onto the indiscriminate series of ritualistic social structures discovered en route, she remains frustrated. For instance, Alice is frustrated when she assumes she knows how a race is run: there is a starting line, a demarcated finish, a declared winner. But when she participates in the caucus-race where the racecourse is constructed in a circle and the animals begin "running when they liked, and left off when they liked, so that it was not easy to know when the race was over," she becomes confused by this situation (20). She also transfers a notion of English etiquette onto those who attend the "mad tea-party," and she projects a set of predictable semiotic codes for playing croquet (presumably observed through personal experience in the English countryside) onto those in the garden who compete by rituals that "reinforce the power of the King and Queen over life and death" (Bivona 150).

At times Alice does indeed marvel at the wonder of ecstatic transformation, but she often demonstrates the aggressivity Lacan associates with the trauma when the mirror-stage illusion cannot hold and the subject must confront the split between the real and the virtual images perceived in the glass. When previously unobservable aspects of experience emerge within the circumference of mirror relations, they throw into question the performative nature of narrative and the historical conditioning whose authorization becomes suspect. These circumstances emerge for Alice when she intuits that the subject *and* the Other are barred and the object overwritten by a semiotic code incapable of knowing itself. Although passage through Wonderland requires that the subject bow to the dictates of discourse, Alice alone is aware that the symbolic is inconsistent, deadlocked, and ruptured in relation to itself. Being a child, she finds that her experience is directly related to the drives and the alien intentionality of her body, which adheres to an impulsive, unpredictable impetus whose force is substantial. Try as she might, Alice will never make textual relations identical to themselves. Something in the story will always evade the impulse toward conceptual mastery by confronting it with unassimilable phenomena that cannot be geometrically placed and intellectually assimilated.

As a subject who becomes an object of dreams dominated by the desires of the King and Queen of Hearts, Alice tries to renegotiate her transformation from a subject as agent to an object of an alien intentionality that cannot be assimilated by consciousness. Although Alice uses the precepts learned from her mother, father, school and society to read the spatial and temporal implications of the desiring text, it proves to no avail until nonsense itself emerges as a cohesive, dominant signifying function symptomatically indicating its own structural incapacity.

Phallic Rule Forty-two

Nonsense is tied to another type of sense related to a *point de capiton* which exerts its imperialistic influence over the creatures who feel the palpable presence of symptomatic pain caused by their conformity to the royalist time of Wonderland. For even if no one is actually beheaded in the text, when the Queen gives her infamous command, "off with their heads," the threat still exists as an expectation or temporal indicator of anticipatory anxiety to those subjected to it. As early as the initial narrative sequence, Alice confronts the desire of the mother-Other as the "White Rabbit with pink eyes ran close by her" exclaiming "Oh dear! Oh dear! I shall be too late!" (1). When "the Rabbit actually *took a watch out of its waistcoat-pocket*, and looked at it, and then hurried on, Alice started to her feet" to follow its compulsive adherence to the time of the Queen, who presumably had requested the presence of her coterie to play croquet in her garden (2). Leaving a world where her mother and father do not appear in the narrative, Alice becomes captivated by the presence of the Queen who announces herself before she appears in the story. Pressed on by the temporal desire of the Queen before Alice enters the rabbit-hole, the young girl must learn to differentiate her desire from that of the Other if she is to escape the tractor pull of royal desire. It tugs the time of others within a field that orders them in the circumference of the threat "off with their heads" (74).

If the Queen compensates for her own anxiety about the time of the Other by subjugating her subjects to her demands, the King is content to hide his authoritarian designs behind the deflection of the Queen's anger. But in the end he reveals his phallocentric designs, for in the court of justice it is his law that rules, his will which must be obeyed, and his compliance with the Queen's anger that unleashes the power of the drive, causing "the whole pack [of cards to rise] up into the air" and come "flying down upon her" so that Alice emits "a little scream, half of fright and half of anger" as she tries "to beat them off" (116). By the end of the story the putative violence in the statement "off with their heads" manifests as actual aggression directed toward the outsider Alice who refuses to heed the King's commands. Once the King's phallic injunction has been disregarded, his desire is called into question, although he tries to reassert it through an invocation of "Rule Forty-two."

To answer the Other's demand, we do not substitute our own because ours can only be a variant of the demand of the Other. Lacanian analysis is concerned instead with the construction of desire. Marie-Hélène Brousse states that analysis should formulate the subject's desire, "decide it not by the demand of the Other but by the barred Other, by the fact that the Other is barred. In the end you are alone with what you desire or do not desire. You are left with it." The divided, barred subject and the barred, lacking Other are tied to each other via a master signifier, the guarantor of signification, which unifies other floating signifiers by replacing what remains missing as the signifier approaches what is unsymbolizable. In *Alice's Adventures in Wonderland*, the King attempts to insert a master signifier for general consumption at this impossible juncture where the signifier approaches its limit, at the site where there is no sexual rapport, where the sexual relation cannot be adequately signified. There, at the site where his power loses its guarantee, the King makes his claims and tries to defend them by citing "Rule Forty-two."

Rule Forty-two reads, "all persons more than a mile high [are] to leave the court," but its defining point is really a variant of *the unwritten rule* which provides carte blanche to those empowered by it (Carroll 112). On this blank slate the State merely makes up versions of Rule Forty-two to fit a particular purpose for a specific application. Here it pertains to people over a mile high, in this case to Alice, who has grown out of their frame of reference. But had Alice undergone a process of miniaturization and shrunk, Rule Forty-two would have changed its meaning to address that circumstance, condemning her with the same pandemic exactitude. The King himself admits that Rule Forty-two is "the oldest rule in the book" (112). This being the case, Alice argues it should be given chronological priority to underline its importance with a visibility that attests to its significance in the construction of cultural experience: " 'then it ought to be Number One,' said Alice" (113). But linking Forty-two to a chronological structuring principle is absurd because the King invented rule and number to use in accordance with his temperamental desire.

Certifying its stature through a chronological accounting grants Rule Forty-two the pretense of meaning when, in fact, it makes no specific point, provides no perceptual function other than filling a cultural gap with an anointed signifier. The signifier historically sanctioned to fill this gap is the phallus, the "master" signifier which appropriates unto itself the power of initiation into the patronymic empire of signs. But the attempt to certify its stature misses the point that Forty-two is a custom-designed rule applicable to any purpose, giving free reign to significatory possibilities that find their failure in the referent considered. This signifier to which all others refer represents or embodies the subject for all other signifiers. The phallic signifier embodies a lack, erects itself in its place, and assumes the pretense of being the "one" signifier that would "properly" or "fully" represent the subject. But it only misrepresents the subject since its power is established by the insertion of the signifier through a reflexive process created in the objectification of lack and its embodiment in the signifying system.

Through *capitonnage*, the phallus takes its place in a reflexive inversion that like a rock erects its narcissistic effects, an auto-erotic rock that Lacan says symbolizes its rigid emergence over a fluid, nonunified field, a rocky "island which goes down stream adrift" (Seminar IX). The power of this rigid phallic designator rests in its objectification and the ability to institute self-reflection as a dominant psychic process, a determining factor in the construction of identity. Self-objectification involves a reflexive turn so that the subject of need becomes—through this inversion and subsequent obedience to the reflexive signifier—the object of the Other's demand. This is accomplished through converting the battery of floating signifiers through a unified field. In *For They Know Not What They Do*, Slavoj Žižek characterizes the phallus as that which represents for the subject its own ultimate failure: "as the representation of the failure of representation [it is] 'closer' to the subject than all the others . . . [coinciding] with its own impossibility; it is nothing but the void opened up by the failure of its representation" (25).

The phallus that mock-signified Rule Forty-two mimics is the signifier of the Other's desire, marking the site where "logos is joined with the advent of desire" ("Phallus" 288). It designates the split, rupture, or cut caused by the superimposition of the significatory grid over desire and the process of objectification associated with this process; in this respect the phallus provides access to objectified experience associated with viewing life from the site of the Other. A mock-signified of specific meaning, Rule Forty-two represents a phallic inadequation of knowledge (either too little, symbolic castration, or too much, turgid ego-inflation) inasmuch as the rule coerces Alice into accepting the phallic injunction of State signifiers of desire. If Alice were to accept the King's logic, she would become Other-directed, left satisfying a desire foreign to her own needs. At precisely this point of irrelation, patriarchal Rule Forty-two manipulates the structure of discourse by conditioning meaning as an effect of its impetus.

There is a convergence which Alice approaches in her interaction with the King. The convergence is at the juncture where the mirror image, revealing the formless irrationality of the body of bits and pieces, intersects with a significatory *failure of reference* that causes an equivocation in language and an inadequation of knowledge. Such an equivocal inadequation stems from the breakdown of reference in relation to sexuality, the real, and the jouissance which becomes a constituent element in the construction of knowledge. If it is true that there is no *rapport sexuel* (no sexual relation or proportion as a knowable ratio), then the quest for sense reveals the aim for a "unique signification that occupies the place of reference" which does not exhibit any natural tie to it (Miller 29). We witness here a disproportional ratio between the nostalgic wish for a natural tie and the radical alienation that occurs when signification insists upon its privilege precisely where reference desires to become self-identical—at the site of lack where the signifier giveth and taketh away. Here—in a stroke—some*thing* is castrated and filled by the signifier, constituting the subject of the signifier yet simultaneously barring it, creating its displacement in signification along a metonymic traversal of desire.

With this in mind it becomes apparent that once the King decrees Alice must leave the court of justice, she is forced to acknowledge the sacrifice required of her. Because Alice speaks and grows, and grows and dares to speak, she must submit to the phallic monarch who erects his privilege at the site where his power is most vulnerable. The King of Hearts, who pretends to embody the phallus (he is after all a card in a deck and therefore a signifier without being), breaks the injunction that one can *have* the phallus but should never *be* it. We are taught from youth not to identify with the imaginary phallus, but only with the phallus raised to a signifier in its symbolic capacity. We are taught that the imaginary phallus must be sacrificed along with the object of our jouissance and that a substitution should occur raising the phallus to a signifier. But as Alice learns, the phallus holds no privilege other than its customary use in society.

In direct defiance to the King, Alice appropriates for herself the right to *embody* the phallus, which becomes apparent once she grows without eating, now not the dominant component in her feat of transformation. Against the prime dictates of the fathers, Alice becomes the turgid phallus much in the way that Dr. Jekyll is eventually transformed into Mr. Hyde without drinking the formula he created to reconfigure himself. In the court of justice Alice begins to grow without ingesting food. At this point in the narrative she loses the link to biological need, to appetite as that which can be satisfied. So she defies the desire of the Other and enrages the King by *becoming* the phallus, *embodying* the big Other, and assuming its position. But in creating this disrelation to need, Alice reveals the phallus for what it is while she breaks the paternal injunction against identifying directly with the object except through its absence (after it has entered the defiles of the signifier).

From the beginning of the book Alice intuits that the Other is lacking, but by the last scene she is convinced this is the case. Her entire journey can be interpreted as a reading of her relationship to two divergent master signifiers that bind her daylight and daydream identities. She eventually undermines the Other-of-Wonderland by rejecting its values when not addressing herself to it. While she still does, Alice never tires of exposing the hole in the symbolic order and the constructed, produced, contingent quality of the phallic injunction. Throughout her story Alice maintains an ambivalent relationship to the phallic signifier that would petrify her under its mark. This master signifier is instituted as a mythological norm that Alice parodies in the court of justice. There she frees herself to *become* the turgid phallus of nonsensical Wonderland; then she grows in direct resistance to the King's wishes. But as Alice exceeds the frame of reference, she has a direct experience of the unsymbolized trauma that the phallus attempts to displace in the erection of its privilege. With this disconcerting experience she wakes up.

Alice does reveal an element missing from a "universal" foundation laid to prop up the power of the phallic signifier, but she gets too close to the unsymbolizable thing and wakes suddenly from the breakthrough in anxiety. Because she experiences the interpenetration of the symbolic by the real, Alice approaches the point where conceptualization is barred, acknowledges the glaring inconsistencies in the Other, and seeks a way out of her dilemma. But before she does so, Alice is held captive by the gaze of Wonderland, which is linked to the drives, more specifically to Alice's desire to find wonders that puzzle her as she examines her incomprehensible situation. In surrealistic Wonderland Alice is subject to bizarre creatures and uncanny scenarios that unfold on the other side of the gaze, in an imaginary world that pictures Alice for herself as if she were in a dream. In other words, her entire journey only takes shape once Alice imaginatively *pictures* herself in her daydream as part of Wonderland.

As long as Alice projects herself pictorially for the gaze, it is through the eyes of the world that she sees herself in this new psychical locus. As long as she is content to do so, Alice is caught there, "manipulated, captured in the field of vision," situated structurally in the picture while her attention remains captivated by the Other (92). An experience of the gaze activates something real "at the level of the point of light, the point at which everything that looks at me is situated" (Seminar XI, 95). But at the reflexive level of being seen, a geometrically constructable relation paints Alice in its purview. Thus, a predisposition to be seen in a world of light and color positions Alice in Wonderland, the point of placement being structural. For she is graphed in a grid of relations as a screen between the gaze and the picture within which parameters she is geometrically inscribed. But Alice is positioned by the Other only as long as her desire is identical to the site from which she observes herself, a place sanctioned by symbolic relations as a coded, validated point of view and means of seeing. After Alice defies the King, everything changes for her as she enacts a crisscrossed identification with both the upper and under worlds. This allows for one final cataclysmic body disturbance before daylight consciousness is restored.

The Gaze of Wonderland

The screen which separates the gaze from the signifiers of representation is not an optical space that is geometrically traversable. Antonio Quinet describes the screen as that which erases "the gaze from [. . .] the world's show, from the Other as reality, with all the significations that help constitute our environment" (cf. "The Gaze as an Object" in this volume). When Alice follows the rabbit to Wonderland, the object world is screened in such a play of light and shadow, veiled so the gaze is partially blocked. In fact the whole of Alice's dream sequence is a mark indicating structurally where she is pictured within a being-seen that screens her from the real whose direct apprehension is anxiety-provoking and whose effects and retroeffects are disquieting. Thus caught, her desire threads light from object to object, linking them in a network of perception. In the picture world of Wonderland Alice marks her place as a screen between the gaze and geometrically delimited space. She does this by masking observable aspects in the field of inquiry, thereby creating further misalignment of the imaginary, symbolic, and real whose circuits are alternately jammed, imaginarily masked, jammed, symbolically mediated, jammed—in alternation, in succession, both at once.

The gaze-as-*objet a* in the scopic dimension functions to symbolize nothing; rather it performs the Other's desire for the subject. Because the gaze is a function of the presence of others looking at us, the lack created through the bipolar splitting of subject and object focuses the attempt of signification to negotiate this lack by instituting a symbolic geometry to gauge experience. Lacan describes the gaze as the underside of consciousness—which is *un*conscious yet which exerts very real effects that produce counter desires to elide it. We know the perspective: the universe is looking at us; some part of us is looking at ourselves. This perspective yields a "bipolar reflexive relation" to the object world in which the primal object born of the split in us is symbolized by the bar that cuts across the subject ($). Every time the gaze falls upon us, we face a psychic rupture indicating the site from which the gaze is cast upon us. For the desirous gaze is born of an experience in which "no food will ever satisfy the oral drive," no light ever flood the visual field of comprehension because the object is a void "which can be occupied" (Seminar XI, 180).

The gaze is not seen, but imagined. The effects of its splitting (and the repetition related to it) enable the binding of the ego with fantasy, which tries to recapture through memory a nostalgic continuity that cuts across lack, bridges the gap, elides the gaze, and prevents the annihilation of the subject. This fantasy is implicated in the structure of the Cartesian cogito, which sees itself seeing itself. In this way the imaginary fantasy of seeing oneself seeing oneself is substituted for lack, as the bipolar reflexive relation establishes the fantasy of the ego as the ground of certainty, the support, the base, the envelope that allows consciousness to idealize itself rather than to acknowledge its relation to an incomplete text (Seminar XI, 83–85).

After falling through the void, Alice pictures herself in an environment that has some continuity with past historical models of experience, which illustrate the disrelation of knowledge to wonder and the anamorphic distortion that accompanies the imposition of *logos* on desire in the world down under. For much of the time Alice tries to deny there is a limit to her knowledge even though she cannot grasp the meaning of the real. To compensate for this inability, Alice creates a screen from her beloved Dinah's image, the cat that reappears down under in the guise of the smiling Cheshire Cat, one of the few creatures that is kind to Alice. The Cheshire Cat appears and disappears, like fantasy itself around the cut of symbolic castration, which is symptomatic of some knotting of the symbolic to the real. Here some out of kilter aspect of ourselves is raised to the symbolic, a network of inconsistencies we escape through the production of fantasy. In *Wonderland* the production of fantasy is conceptualized in the appearance and disappearance of the Cheshire Cat and its grin.

"Why is this cat smiling?"

Possibly because its smile stands as an enigmatic product of fantasy that summons up pleasurable affect related to Dinah, and beyond that, to the hope of relatedness itself. Alice creates such relatedness by asserting a dual referentiality—to the world above and the one down under—which enables her to chart unchartable aspects of Wonderland that resist reference to the world above. Alice not only tries to elide the gaze, but to defy the signifier's injunction to submit to Rule Forty-two or, more broadly, to the discourse of Wonderland.

The Cheshire Cat provides an example of how to defy the gaze when it materializes—partially—at the Queen's croquet match. For only the Cheshire Cat's head appears in disrelation to its body. As it materializes, the Cheshire Cat refuses to kiss the King's hand. This gesture so disconcerts the King he declares his intention not only to execute the unmannerly cat, but "to fetch the executioner myself" (79). Because the cat manifests as a partial cat (the head already separated from the body), a dispute is engendered between the executioner, the King, and the Queen, who cannot decide on a logic to implement for its execution:

> 1. The executioner's argument was that you could not cut off a head unless there was a body
>
> 2. The King's argument was that anything that had a head could be beheaded. . . .
>
> 3. The Queen's argument was that if something wasn't done about it in less than no time, she'd have everybody executed (80)

The Cheshire Cat terminates their discussion by fading away while they speak, dissolving into a _____ upon which fantasy is projected—a fantasy of relation, of love, of the fantasmatic attempt to bridge the gap of impossibility and recover jouissance lost to the phallus. This jouissance is both renounced and relocated in the fantasy of Alice's Cheshire Cat/Dinah.

Fantasized images are projected onto the veiled site of symbolic castration. These images evoke imaginary attempts to produce transformation where there had been alienation and separation, in the gaps where the symbolic is knotted to the real. Besides the Cheshire Cat's materialization and dematerialization around significatory lack, there is the transformation of the "dreadfully ugly child" into "a handsome pig," the dramatic alteration of Alice's body as she shrinks and grows, and the transformation of Alice into a body part/part object that is unrelated to a unified field of signification capable of constituting a coherent identity (56). There are other transformations: of the surface world into Wonderland, of its zany creatures into talking beings, and, in the last scene, of the cards into leaves. The impetus for transformation transfigures the geometric landscape.

We evade the gaze by creating a transformational two-step at the site of stumbling where there is a glitch in significatory relatedness. There we reexperience the cut of culture under whose representative signifiers we take our positions as subjects represented for other signifiers. We become subjects under the signifier's determination of subsequent self-identifications, which are dependent on the Other's desire to structure, narrativize, and dramatize the subject.

Women under the Gaze

Alice's *Adventures in Wonderland* reveals a structure of fantasy based on the romantic quest for sublime completion in the Other followed by the mocking of that fantasy. The fantasy takes on textual body when Alice

attempts to gain access to the garden, entrance into which promises to produce a transformation of the subject inasmuch as sublime recovery of the
object is possible, that is, recovery of one's subjectivity through a
resubjectification of the self-as-object, which implies taking back oneself from
the Other. Throughout the story Alice is obsessed with finding the coveted
key to open the lock to "the loveliest garden you ever saw . . . [with its] bright
flowers and those cool fountains" (7). The entire journey can be read through
Alice's desire to spatialize herself in this garden of wish-fulfillment. But once
she enters this coveted space, Alice learns that transcendental fantasies of
transformational bliss are crossed over by the master signifier, here depicted
as the Queen's desire, her time, her garden where even the flowers' color is
governed by her declared desire. This desire is the desire of the Other that is
symbolically castrated, barred, displaced elsewhere, so much so that sur-
rounding the Queen is the palpable presence of pain related to her consump-
tive anger that blurts out the oft-uttered threat, "off with their heads."

   With Alice's visit to the Queen, the specter of romanticism is mocked by
the signifier of simulation as the lovely garden belies its appearance and
becomes a replica of the avant-garde preceding itself:

> "Would you tell me [. . .] why you are painting those roses?"
> "Why, the fact is, you see, Miss, this here ought to have been a red rose-
> tree, and we put a white one in by mistake, and if the Queen was to find
> out, we would all have our heads cut off." (71)

   In the garden the flowers' origin is nominal, not natural. They grow
from the superego's dictum, that "*ought* to have been a red rose-tree,"
rather than from organic soil. And when the roses do grow naturally, the
functionary-like cards paint them with the imaginary-symbolic brush of
simulation so that the cards will not "have our heads cut off" (71). In the
garden, flowers are not what they seem to be and creatures cheat in games
of skill in a charade staged so that royalty can mirror itself—its desire/its
ideals—in a contrived production of reality. Others in the garden are implicitly asked to mirror this version of experience and to maintain the
illusion that the Queen does have clothes, that her authority is grounded in
the real by a phallic injunction from a foundationalist text that exists outside its parameters, unlocatable in the gaze of Wonderland.

   The gaze spreads through the spectrum of perspectives; it spreads out
of the object that looks at us from the field of vision. Because it does so, the
gaze induces an effort to codify lack and blunt affects associated with the
phallic ghost that haunts the cut of symbolic castration as a subsequent
repetition borne out of it. For example, if we look at Hans Holbein's painting, *The Ambassadors*, we find a "strange, suspended, oblique object in the

foreground in front of these two figures" that Lacan describes as "frozen" or "stiffened" before the anamorphic object which captivates the domain of appearance as it projects itself through the air. In *Alice's Adventures in Wonderland*, Holbein's flying object expands like the gaze itself, spreading over the field of vision to encompass Wonderland and its comic-book creatures and madcap scenarios that insist that Alice has entered another dimension of experience. Wonderland hovers like Holbein's flying object, a dreamworld down under swirling upon its distorted, desire-infused trajectory. In Carroll's story it is our world that has stiffened into a wooden, clichéd reference point.

When commenting on Holbein's painting, Lacan states that it is only when we disidentify with the object in the frame of reference, "thus escaping the fascination of the picture," can we walk away from its influence, and, looking awry, glimpse the object of desire from another perspective. In Holbein's *The Ambassadors*, when the viewer turns around to look at the object, a skull coheres out of the gestalt related to the "anamorphic ghost" haunting the subject that is annihilated in the "imaged embodiment" of symbolic castration produced at the cut of desire and law. In Carroll's story this "imaged embodiment . . . of castration" reveals something about Carroll's desire as well as "the gaze as such, in its pulsatile, dazzling and spread out function, as it is in this picture" (Seminar XI, 89).

This dynamic is important to consider when examining the depiction of women in Wonderland. Carroll's desire to reduce strong women to vain villains whose hysterical rage knows no bounds is one ghost that haunts the story. For instance, we know that the Queen is a verbal terrorist who assigns signification to the masses. But unlike the Thought Police in *1984*, the Queen's power is hysterized since none of her subjects is ever actually executed. Her words are threats, her will subverted, her decrees described as imaginary rantings in a masquerade of power that has very real effects.

The Duchess is also denigrated as arch duplicity itself, placed in the slave's position to the Queen's supposed mastery. The Duchess's deceptiveness reaches its furthest point of dissembling in the longitude of her "sharp little chin" dug into Alice's shoulder as she explains her position on life:

> never imagine yourself not to be otherwise than what it might appear to others that what you were or might have been was not otherwise than what you had been would have appeared to them to be otherwise (83)

Frightened that the Queen will have her head, the Duchess becomes an eminent scholar in the reading of the Queen's hypercritical desire. She becomes her unofficial interpreter, and her advice is to traffic in appearances, to identify oneself as an image of consumption for the Other, which fits the Other's values and thus asks that desire be transformed through that rerouting.

In Carroll's creation of Wonderland, a fantasy fabricated for consumption has seduced generations of readers. This fantasy openly reduces strong willed women to hysterical, deceptive manipulators of the imagined iconography of the Other. Carroll's fantasy narrative has succeeded in covering over lack and other points of disjunction between the imaginary, symbolic, and real. To those societies which have replicated Carroll's vision, this fantasy takes on mythic proportions as a means to displace lack through the construction of a narrative that projects the gaze of Wonderland, not upon women as women, or children as children, but upon women as emotional children deprived of the right to grow up.

For Alice's part, if she ever did age, she would likely take her place with the other women denigrated in the story, which indicates Carroll's ambivalence towards women. This depiction is further complicated by Carroll's use of a rhetorical strategy that parodies the royalist discourse of the day *as* it belittles women.

At the hole in the Other through which Alice will no doubt continue to fall into Wonderland, we reach the symptom knotted to a geometrical showing that offers us an invitation to lay down our gaze before this testimony to perpetual childhood frozen by a phallic signifier of desire.

Works Cited

Barnes, Djuna. *Nightwood*. New York: New Directions, 1961.

Bivona, Dan. "Alice the Child-Imperialist and the Games of Wonderland." *Nineteenth Century Literature* 42:2 (1986): 143–171.

Brousse, Marie-Hélène. "The Drive (II)." *Reading Seminar XI: Lacan's Four Fundamental Concepts of Psychoanalysis*, eds. Richard Feldstein, Bruce Fink, and Maire Jaanus. Albany: SUNY Press, 1995.

Carroll, Lewis. *Alice's Adventures in Wonderland*. New York: Knopf, 1988.

Lacan, Jacques. "Desire and the Interpretation of Desire in *Hamlet*." *Literature and Psychoanalysis*, ed. Shoshana Felman, 11–52. Baltimore: Johns Hopkins University Press, 1982.

———. *The Four Fundamental Concepts of Psycho-Analysis*. Ed. Jacques-Alain Miller. Trans. Alan Sheridan. New York: Norton, 1977. [Seminar XI]

———. "The Meaning of the Phallus." *Feminine Sexuality*. Ed. Juliet Mitchell and Jacqueline Rose. Trans. Jacqueline Rose. New York: Norton, 1982.

———. "The Mirror Stage." *Écrits: A Selection*. Trans. Alan Sheridan. New York: Norton, 1977.

———. *Le Séminare, Livre III: Les psychoses*. Text established by Jacques-Alain Miller, Paris: Seuil, 1981.

————. *Le Séminare, Livre IX: L'identification.* Typescript of unpublished seminar, 1961–62.

————. *Le Séminare, Livre XX: Encore.* Text established by Jacques-Alain Miller, Paris: Seuil, 1975.

————. *The Seminar of Jacques Lacan: Book II: The Ego in Freud's Theory and in the Technique of Psychoanalysis,* 1954–1955. Ed. Jacques-Alain Miller. Trans. Sylvana Tomaselli. New York: Norton, 1988.

————. "The Subversion of the Subject and the Dialectic of Desire in the Freudian Unconscious." *Écrits: A Selection.* Trans. Alan Sheridan. New York: Norton, 1977.

Miller, Jacques-Alain. "Elements of Epistemology." *Analysis* 1 (1989): 27–42.

Žižek, Slavoj. *The Sublime Object of Ideology.* New York: Verso, 1989.

THE "EVIL EYE" OF PAINTING:
JACQUES LACAN AND WITOLD GOMBROWICZ
ON THE GAZE

Hanjo Berressem

Reading Seminar XI, I was arrested by a short passage on "the evil eye." What follows is an attempt at reading this "fascinatory" passage in the light of excerpts from the *Diary* of the Polish writer Witold Gombrowicz and vice versa.

In Seminar XI, Lacan develops his distinction between the eye and the gaze, the eye standing for the geometral, visual grammar, and the gaze for the subject's position within this grammar. Whereas the eye represents the *cogito*—the conscious, self-reflexive subject and the subject of knowledge—the gaze represents the *desidero*: the subject of the unconscious and of desire. Yet I do not want so much to deal with this visual topography as with a somewhat enigmatic reference to the evil eye that ends Lacan's discussion. In this passage, the relatively clear separation between the structures of the eye and of the gaze is disturbed because Lacan talks of the eye as an organ rather than a geometral convention. The phenomenon of the evil eye embodies the fact that the "eye carries with it the fatal function of being in itself endowed [...] with a power to separate" (Seminar XI, 115). On first sight, this is surprising, because in the earlier discussion, the eye had stood for an objective "inclusiveness," whereas the gaze was related to lack and separation. If before, then, the eye was *juxtaposed* to the gaze, now, the separating function of the eye *relates* it directly to the gaze, and with it to the *desidero*.

This mixing up of the registers makes the passage quite difficult. It is permeated with echoes from Lacan's essays "The mirror stage" and "Aggressivity in psychoanalysis" (*Écrits*) especially in relation to the fact that within the visual register, the gaze symbolizes "object *a*"—the object in its separation from the subject:

> Object *a* is something from which the subject, in order to constitute itself, has separated itself off as organ. This serves as a symbol of lack, that is to say, of the phallus, not as such, but insofar as it is lacking (Seminar XI, 103).

Lacan gives an example he first used in "Aggressivity in psychoanalysis" (*Écrits*, 20) to show that the eye as an organ has a fundamental relation to separation. In the example, *invidia*, envy, which derives etymologically from *videre*, to see, is triggered precisely by gazing at an image of "completeness closed upon itself" (Seminar XI, 116), i.e., the subject gazes at someone else who is—seemingly—in the possession of object *a*. In the example, this object is the object of satisfaction per se: the mother's breast.

The subject's answer to this tableau is an "evil look." This poisonous, and in the final analysis, fatal gaze comes to symbolize the separating function of the eye, "the eye made desperate by the gaze" (Seminar XI, 116). It is this fundamentally and ontologically aggressive and voracious aspect of the eye that painting pacifies, because the painter:

> gives something for the eye to feed on, but he invites the person to whom this picture is presented to lay down his gaze there as one lays down one's weapons (Seminar XI, 101).

It is this element of the *"dompte-regard"* (Seminar XI, 111) in which one has to look for "the taming, civilizing, and charming power of the function of the picture" (Seminar XI, 116).[1]

Painting pacifies by instigating a specific visual economy. On the part of the painter—or more precisely of the Other itself "through" the painter-function—it involves a desire to show his (or himself as) gaze: "a sort of desire *on the part of* the Other, at the end of which is the showing" (Seminar XI, 115). On the part of the viewer, the painting functions quite literally as a "feast for the eyes."

> This appetite of the eye that must be fed produces the hypnotic value of painting. For me this value is to be sought [. . .] in that which is the true function of the eye as organ, the eye filled with voracity, the evil eye (Seminar XI, 115).

Lacan further defines this visual economy by linking the evil eye to what he calls the "terminal time of the gaze" (Seminar XI, 117), which is the time of an incision or breach in the realm of "natural movement." Through this reference, he links it to painting. Unlike animals, who, if they *could* paint, would do so naturally—"If a bird were to paint, would it not be by letting fall its feathers?" (Seminar XI, 114)—"the authenticity of what emerges in painting is diminished in us humans" (Seminar XI, 117); which is to say nothing more and nothing less than that art is artificial. Lacan's objective is the specific structure of this "painterly" artificiality.

As Lacan's example of a film of Cézanne painting shows, the painting is not the result of a natural action but of a terminated gesture. This termination of the gesture which produces "the fascinatory effect" (Seminar XI, 118) "freezes" (Seminar XI, 117) movement.[2] It is by way of this freezing that painting "dispossess[es] the evil eye of the gaze, in order to ward it off" (Seminar XI, 118). There is thus the paradoxical situation that the painter works with a constant arrest of life and movement of himself ("at the moment the subject stops, suspending his gesture, he is mortified" [Seminar XI, 118]) as well as of the gesture, which comes onto the canvas only as its "termination," to ward off and pacify something that similarly "arrests" movement:[3] "the evil eye is the *fascinum* [evil spell], it is that which has the effect of arresting movement and, literally, killing life" (Seminar XI, 118). While banning and pacifying the evil eye, painting is formally relying on its arresting function. In the image of Cézanne painting, one can follow these dialectics of *movement* and *arrest*, in which *arrest* is related to the imaginary, whereas *movement* is related to the symbolic:

> The moment of seeing can intervene here only as a suture, a conjunction of the imaginary and the symbolic, and it is taken up again in a dialectic, that sort of temporal progress that is called haste, thrust, forward movement, which is concluded in the *fascinum* (Seminar XI, 118).

Lacan uses this dialectic of showing and seeing to indicate that in the scopic register, the subject is fundamentally "determined by the very separation that determines the break of the *a*, that is to say the fascinatory element introduced by the gaze" (Seminar XI, 118). While throughout the discussion Lacan plays off the double meaning of fascination as both "charming" as well as "putting under an evil spell," the Latin *fascinum* also means "phallus" or "phallic emblem," a third meaning which perfectly captures the relation of the *fascinum* to lack, castration, and death—and thus to moments of termination.

The symbolic unfreezes the imaginary register, by providing the terminal character of the imaginary relation with a progressive trajectory:

> Let us not forget that the painter's brush stroke is something in which a movement is terminated. . . . the original temporality in which the relation to the other is situated as distinct is . . . in the scopic dimension, that of the terminal moment. That which in the identificatory dialectic of the signifier and the spoken word is projected forward as haste, is here, on the contrary, the end, that which, at the outset of any new intelligence, is called the moment of seeing (Seminar XI, 114).

Because the element of separation determines the subject in the imaginary, every confrontation comes to a grinding halt. In the symbolic, on the other hand, in which the subject is undetermined, the space of play is opened up:

> What I wish to emphasize is the total distinction between the scopic register and the invocatory, vocatory, vocational field. In the scopic field, the subject is not essentially indeterminate (Seminar XI, 118).

It might seem unusual to choose a writer's comments against painting as an example here, but Gombrowicz' polemics in his *Diary*[4]—which is itself highly aggressive, "imaginary," and "specular"—highlight precisely the relation of the rigid realm of the image to the dynamics of the symbolic:

> Compare, in this regard, line and color with the word. The word unfolds in time, like a procession of ants, and each one brings something new and unexpected; he who expresses himself in words is born anew each second; scarcely has one sentence been completed than the next one supplements it, completes it, and behold in the movement of words *the endless play of my existence* [*being*] expresses itself (*Diary II*, 50).

The "frozen" world of the painted image is set off against the "liquid" world of the word:

> Should I cast off the dazzling whirl of form, light, color, that is the world for your lifeless kingdom where nothing moves! (. . .) For the world is form in motion. [. . .] But you, on your canvases, condemn nature to paralysis. (. . .) Why not confess that a paintbrush is a clumsy instrument? . . . It's as if you took to painting explosions of cosmic light with a toothbrush (*Diary II*, 48–49).[5]

Like Lacan, Gombrowicz links the aggressivity which underlies the economy of the imaginary to the *gaze* and the *voracious eye*.[6] The genre in which the gaze of the painter has the closest relation to the subject is of course portraiture, and it is not surprising that this genre is the privileged target of Gombrowicz' polemics. While a portrait should present the "essence" of the model, in Gombrowicz it actually kills and destroys it:

> I wonder if my rebellion against the plastic arts did not begin with my portraits. . . . that stranger's eyes moving all over my form, because of my being sacrificed to those alert eyes [to which I was fed] (*Diary II*, 47).

To Gombrowicz, the painter's gaze is a truly "imaginary" one. Yet this painterly gaze is only one of a whole realm of gazes that encompasses the subject: the gaze of culture. Lacan also mentions this cultural gaze "behind" a painting; in the case of the murals in the Doges Palace, that of those who deliberate in this hall: "Behind the picture it is their gaze that is there" (Seminar XI, 113).

Gombrowicz experiences this cultural gaze as eminently violent:

> You think you are getting close to art voluntarily. . . . In truth, a hand has grabbed you by the scruff of your neck, led you to this painting, and thrown you to your knees. . . . That hand is not the hand of a single man, the will is collective, born in an interhuman dimension, quite alien to you. So you do not admire at all, you merely try to admire (*Diary I*, 25).

Both gazes—that of the painter as well as the gaze of culture—"kill," something which becomes obvious in Gombrowicz' further description of himself being painted.

> He [the painter] was unable to master my form. . . . I assume that if a cliff or a tree could feel something, they would experience exactly these kinds of triumphantly ironic feelings toward the painter *attacking* them with his paintbrush . . . because this very same "thing" rules the painting and rivets us with its relentless thingness. . . . What happened?! He turned me into a thing! . . . And so what if his eyes missed me! . . . He painted me as if it were not I but my shoe that was important (*Diary II*, 47–48).

In the reference to the "Thing," Gombrowicz evokes another of Lacan's topics in Seminar XI, the seemingly natural relation between the Kantian "thing itself" and the subject which Lacan argues against:

> Behind the phenomenon, there is the noumenon, for example. I may not be able to say anything about it. . . . But, then, that's all right, really—everything works out for the best.

> In my opinion, it is not in this dialectic between the surface and that which is beyond that things are suspended. For my part, I set out from the fact that there is something that establishes a fracture, bi-partition, or splitting of being that establishes a fracture to which being accommodates itself, even in the natural world (Seminar XI, 106).

With Gombrowicz, the categorical difference and separation between subject and object instigates a similarly unbearable fracture, especially as the sheer existence of the "Thing" seems to *demand* a broken relation, something which Lacan calls the insistence of the real, or the frightening meeting with the head of the Medusa, which of course also "freezes" the subject:

> The real Medusa's head . . . The revelation of that which is least penetrable in the real . . . of the ultimate real, of the essential object which isn't an object any longer, but this something faced with which all words cease . . . the object of anxiety *par excellence* (Seminar II, 164).

Like Lacan, Gombrowicz anchors his discussion of the difference between the "Thing" itself and its representation in a discussion of painting, because with its specific affinity to hallucination, the primary process, and the real, painting can come to symbolize precisely the replacement of the real by reality:

> Painting . . . I don't know. Maybe I exaggerate this phobia.
> I will not deny that in spite of everything, there is something in a painting, even if it is a faithful copy of nature, that disarms and attracts. What is it? A painted landscape undoubtedly says something else to us than does the same landscape in nature; its effect on our soul is different. But not because a painting is more beautiful than nature, no, the painting will always be incompetent beauty . . . It is possible, though, that this is the reason behind the attraction [fascination]. The picture shows us the beauty that was felt, seen by someone. . . .
> If we consider that the contemplation of an object . . . fills us with the despair of *loneliness*—because then you find yourself alone with the *Thing* and the Thing crushes you—perhaps this fear of the thing [the frightful meeting with the real], as such, would explain the paradoxical phenomenon that an imperfectly painted tree trunk is closer to us than a natural trunk in all its perfection. *A painted tree trunk is a trunk filtered through man* (*Diary II*, 41).

In Gombrowicz' fiction, imaginary and symbolic registers complement each other because all of it describes figures of paranoia. The shift from symbolic to imaginary registers is mirrored in a shift from verbal to visual registers.

The stories of the gradual growth of the paranoiac systems is constantly punctured—as in Lacan's example of the Peking Opera—by arrests of the plot in "gazes" and "tableaux," which symbolize the "terminating" "time of the real." In *Pornographia*,[7] these dynamics are actually embodied by a series of *tableaux vivants*, which freeze live models. This staging of imaginary tropes, however, is countered by the propulsive movement of the symbolic narrative and the process of writing, which is in constant flight from itself, unlike painting, which, as Gombrowicz has shown, cannot escape the representational space of the canvas and is forced to create constant palimpsests.

Not only on a thematic level, however, Gombrowicz' books are full of distorted and paranoiac—read anamorphic—gazes and constantly describe imaginary mirror structures. The narrative itself is subverted by a mirror structure as well, that of the narrator and his alter ego, a split which defines almost all of his novels. In *Pornographia*, this intersubjective system of mirrors actually allows for something Gombrowicz' writing always attempts to provide: the thinking of the repressed in the oscillating, intersubjective void between the subject and his alter ego:

> That must have been what Frederick was thinking. Or maybe, I was only attributing my thoughts to him? And maybe he was attributing his thoughts to me . . . so that each of us was lovingly cultivating his thought, but in the other's mind . . . What a marvelous system of mirrors: he was reflected in me, I was reflected in him—and so, as we wove dreams for each other we came to conclusions which neither of us wanted to admit were his (*Pornographia*, 59).

Notes

1. Unfortunately, the English version translates *charmeur* as fascinating.

2. See in this respect also the Freudian notion of inhibition [*Hemmung*].

3. Because it is exactly "the anti-life, anti-movement function of this terminal point [which] is the fascinum" (118).

4. Witold Gombrowicz, *Diary: Volume I* and *Diary: Volume II*, Northwestern University Press, Evanston, 1988, 1989.

5. See also: "What deception to claim that van Gogh or Cézanne communicated their personalities. . . . A man expressed by an apple! An unmoving apple! If I, a writer and poet, were told that I should communicate via apples, I would sit down and cry in humiliation" (*Diary II*, 50).

6. The shift from the voracious eye of the spectator to that of the painter is parallel to the shift Lacan sees in art history between the kind of painting that pacifies and that in which the *"incomparable monster"* is born, "namely, the gaze of the painter, which claims to impose itself as being the only gaze" (Seminar XI, 113).

7. Witold Gombrowicz, *Pornographia*, Calder & Boyars, London, 1966.

ART AND THE POSITION OF THE ANALYST

Robert Samuels

Why does Lacan turn to the field of art, and in particular to the realm of painting, in his elaboration of the theory of object *a* and the gaze in Seminar XI? We know from later texts that Lacan equates this object with the position of the analyst in the discourse of the analyst. May we infer that Lacan ties the presence of the analyst to the presence of the art object?

To begin to respond to this question, I will re-translate a poem by Aragon that one finds twice in Seminar XI (17 and 79):

> Vainly your image comes to meet me
> And enters me where I am only the one who shows it
> You, turning towards me, You would like to find
> On the wall of my gaze, only your dreamt of shadow
>
> I am the miserable one comparable to mirrors
> That can reflect but cannot see
> Like them my eye is empty and like them inhabited
> By your absence which makes it blind*

In this poem, we find not only the outline of Lacan's theory of art and the gaze, but also his conception of the position of the analyst.

For what the first stanza indicates is that the subject vainly searches for his own image or shadow in the other. This represents what Lacan

---

*This poem, from Aragon's *Fou d'Elsa*, is entitled *"Contre-chant."*

articulates as the imaginary order of consciousness and narcissism, which
is structured by the mirror stage of specular reflection and representation.

Thus, as in the myth of Narcissus, the subject wants to see only the
perfect reflection of his self as a unified and totalized entity. Lacan calls this
specular image of the other an illusion, because it is based on an ideal
representation of space and form. We can also point out that it is the
narcissistic relation between the ego and the image of the other [i(a)] that
serves to regulate the pleasure principle of consciousness. This means that
what the ego wants to see in the other is only a stable and identifiable form
that reinforces the ego's sense of unity and coherency.

In the beginning of most analyses, it is evident that the subject places
the analyst in this ideal position of reflection and reciprocity. The analyst is
supposed to see what the analysand sees, understand what the other says,
and love what the subject loves—which is, after all, his or her self. The
analyst is thus taken as a pure mirror of reflection that reinforces the
subject's sense of understanding and comfort. This is what Lacan calls ego
analysis or self psychology.

Opposed to this mirror relation of reflection and reciprocity is the
position of the analyst as the blind spot in the field of the ego's consciousness and representations. To elaborate this notion of analysis, we can turn
to the second stanza of the poem, which states that the mirror (or analyst)
can reflect, but cannot see. In other words, the mirror is blind because it is
filled with the absence of the subject.

Lacan argues that, in all painting, this blind spot or absence is present
in the central field of the picture. In other words, every representation
contains within itself a vanishing point, which indicates the limit of the
field of vision and consciousness, just as there is always a vanishing point
on the horizon of our field of perception. It is this point or limit that we can
equate with Lacan's notion of object *a*.

In this sense, the absence which blinds the mirror represents the limitation of the subject's imaginary world of consciousness and narcissism. In
fact, Lacan argues that object *a* has no specular image and thus represents
the other side of vision and consciousness.

In the structure of the analytic setting, when the analyst is placed
behind the analysand who is lying on the couch, the analyst is abstracted
from the subject's field of vision and therefore can become the gaze or blind
spot for the analysand. It is, in fact, this presence of the gaze that causes
the inversion of the subject's consciousness and narcissism. For while my
consciousness is based on the illusion of my seeing myself see myself, the
gaze represents the fact that I am seen.

Lacan illustrates this by turning to a passage in *Being and Nothingness* where Sartre demonstrates the presence of the gaze. Let us pretend

that I am the subject of consciousness that Sartre is talking about. I enter a park, and I see the trees that I always see, the fountain that I recognize, and the crowds that are always there. In short, all is familiar and the entire scene is regulated by my intentionality and my point-of-view. However, suddenly, a face appears that turns towards me and stares at me. Now I am the object of the Other's gaze and the target of unknowable desires and judgments. I am no longer the eye or 'I' of consciousness, that is, I am no longer the one that sees what I want to see, but rather I am seen in a way that I don't want to be seen. Here we find a reversal of perspectives and a de-centering of my field of vision.

What ties this presence of the gaze and the reversal of consciousness to art is Lacan's argument that, in many forms of painting, one can find evidence of the gaze and the upsetting of the laws of perspective and representation. In other words, the art object can show us what we don't want to see, by forcing its gaze upon us.

One example of this is Hans Holbein's painting *The Ambassadors*, which presents in the forefront of the picture an elongated object, which only becomes recognizable as a skull when one walks away and looks from a certain angle. According to Lacan, this skull represents the "annihilation of the subject" of consciousness within the central field of the picture. The presence of the limit of the subject is thus inscribed within the representation. However, one must point out that it is not the vanishing point that is absent in the picture, for in fact it is there; what is absent, or rather what vanishes, is the subject.

We can write this relation between the point of the gaze and the vanishing of the subject as: $a \rightarrow \$$. This means that the presence of object a causes the division of the subject ($\$$). This is, in fact, a formula that is part of the analyst's discourse; the presence of the analyst causes the fading of the subject and the emergence of the unconscious.

Furthermore, in his reading of this painting, Lacan adds that the skull represents not only the annihilation of the subject, but also the lack of the phallus in the real. We must keep in mind that, according to Lacan, the phallus is the signifier (S_1) of sexuality and thus we find in the presence of the skull or gaze proof of the absence of the phallus, i.e., the menace of castration. The painting therefore presents an object that has no signifier and cannot be a source of identification for the subject. This is inscribed within the analyst's discourse, where Lacan places the signifier in the position of loss below the subject:

$$\frac{\$}{S_1}$$

This means that the encounter with object *a* causes a loss of the signifier of identification and sexuality.

Now if we argue that in the act of creation, the artist produces this same object, are we saying that there is no difference between art and analysis? No, for there is another part of the analyst's discourse which is missing in the production of art. In the discourse of the analyst, Lacan adds that knowledge (S_2) is placed in the position of truth below object *a*:

$$\frac{a}{S_2}$$

This indicates that there is a discourse of truth and a truth of discourse that is generated through analysis.

We can now return to our original question, by responding that art represents the presence of the object without analysis, and without the placing of knowledge in the position of truth. However, is this the whole truth of analysis? Of course not, because the truth is never whole.

THE RELATION BETWEEN THE VOICE
AND THE GAZE

❖

Ellie Ragland

Seminar XI elaborates the idea of an order of the real to answer Lacan's question concerning what sustains the identity of the field of jouissance. In one definition, the real is that which results from the trauma of loss. Losing satisfactions has the effect of constituting marks on the body, the marks we call erogenous zones. While we know that signifiers constitute the field of language in an imaginary/symbolic network of images and words, we know less about the object *a* Lacan called an excess in jouissance, an excess that stops the sliding of signifiers, thereby fixing a limit to meaning in the real.[1]

$$\frac{S_1}{\$} \longrightarrow \frac{S_2}{a}$$

If we grasp the idea of the *a* at the level of real impasses, functioning as a nodal point (or a knot of meanings) unassimilated in knowledge as such, we start to see how Lacan could argue that "representation" plays its role in the constitution of meaning by trying to cover over or veil something unrepresentable. But the cover does not work consistently or totally. That is, something disruptive or excessive always returns to perforate meaning with an enigma. Lacan viewed this excess as having its own meaning, as that which makes something palpable (or positive) out of the *seeming* negativity or nothingness of impasses or fadings.

There is no linguistic order *qua* unified system, then. Only the *field* of language *in which* we try to satisfy the "drive" for recognition and realize the particularity of our desire. But drive always disrupts language in ways we cannot account for, and thus usually dismiss as "meaning nothing." And desire works by precise combinations of signifiers that constitute the meaning of unconscious desire, which is, nonetheless, enigmatic to conscious thought. Thus, Lacan argues that language is driven by an excess in jouissance itself, denoted by object *a*. Insofar as the three jouissances—of meaning (the symbolic), body (the imaginary), and the physiological organism (the real)—all seek to maintain consistency (i.e., to close out the conflicts of the real that disrupt the conscious *illusion* that the body, being, and language work in harmony with one another), object *a* marks a limit point.

But what is object *a*? At the most primordial level, *a* denotes anchoring buttons of the real, or those parts of the body that *seem* to be attached to an organ or produced by an organ. But, in fact, they are perceptually detachable from the organ and from the body. Lacan lists these objects as the breast, the feces, the (imaginary) phallus, the urinary flow, the phoneme, the voice, the gaze, and the nothing (*le rien*).[2] In between the primordial lost object and the organ mistaken for the thing itself—the object *a* cause-of-desire—there are myriad lure objects we use in trying to concretize our desire by fetishizing things, people, or acts. Layer upon layer of heterogeneous associations build up sublimated meaning, "implicated assumptions" about what will appease lack and fill void space.[3] Let's consider the feces, for example, as an object-cause-of-desire. More precisely, Lacan connects the feces to the social gaze and the scopic drive, referring in one instance to this example: the source of the artist's colors is found in the hues of excrement, rather than Freud's literalist reference to dirt as a symbol of excrement.

One could say that "invisible objects"—the particular effect of color on a given person, for instance—continually float in the air of all human action and exchange, creating the static of desire which, in turn, serves as the motivating force behind the partial drives. And the aim of the drives is to refind the partial objects, Urcause-of-desire which, although few in number, then act as non-specular nodal points. Lacan called them the lining of the real. More to the point, vast collages of associative meanings build up montages that constitute the drives. Thus considered, the drives are not blind instinctual forces, but a concrete network of heterogeneous objects and signifiers that desire fetishizes.

The symbol, however, is not object *a*. It is, rather, the base unit of meaning out of which the signifying chain is built. Although symbols stand for the Thing itself—i.e., the act they represent—they can only be approximated by words and images. But how are these pieces of the world taken in?

How are they transformed from the material of the world into subjective networks of meaning? Object relations theorists argue that this process of transformation, of interjection and projection, is driven by fantasy. But such theorists never say what enables primary fantasies to reconstitute themselves into meaning. Lacan answered Freud and post-Freudians on the issue of what constitutes drive, thereby showing that symbols are first *in-corporated* by two processes, separation and alienation.[4] And whether primary cuts are incorporated (*Bejahung*), or spat out (*Ausstossung*), they leave a mark at the level of bodily effect (the real). What Lacan called object *a* is a symbol denoting both an empty *place* in being and body and the "object" that one chooses to stop it up because this void place produces anxiety. The cut (the mark of an effect of loss) appears in words and images as a unary trait, tying loss [S($\cancel{A}$)] to the objects of the world. Thus phenomenological objects which *seem* to be "out there" are not in and of themselves the things that cut or splinter the symbol Lacan (re)-defined as *not being dual*. Rather, the signifying symbol, which is neither transcription, coded expression, nor fixed semiotic reality, opens up complimentarities by attaching itself where something is lacking. One cannot say, however, that the symbol reflects the crossroads of psychoanalysis and phenomenology. Object *a* tries to eradicate the effects of a real hole in being, showing that the limits of meaning lie in jouissance, S($\cancel{A}$), not in symbolism.[5]

Although desire is the desire to close out the effects of loss—for both sexes—closure is never achieved because the very desire to re-press means that something is already pressing back. And this internal pressure (the *Drang*, the Freudian drive) comes from the primordial objects-cause-of-desire that give rise to an excess in desire that Lacan called jouissance. This concrete basis of jouissance gives new meaning to the lethal enjoyment people take from repeating scenarios that end in similar impasses. Object *a*, as a fundamentally lost Ur-object, resides at the center of the fantasies from which each person constructs desire around substitute objects that can never fill up a real void in being. This point will be important further on when we see that Lacan read dreams backwards, retroactively, into a flow of fantasies that coalesce around sublimated *objects* in which bits and pieces of the real dwell.

In Seminar XI Lacan developed his theory of the gaze as one of the partial objects that cause desire. Linking the gaze to the stain, which he described as "marking the pre-existence to the seen of something that is given-to-be-seen," he advanced the argument that something ex-sists prior to object *a* taken as object-cause-of-desire (74). This something is the void thought of as a point of blackout, the point at which we do not see the world as clearly as we think we do: our blind spots. In fact, we see ("think") against a surface of blackness whose meaning ("implicated assumptions") is the radical loss that produces anxiety: i.e., the void itself as a place that gives rise to all (*tout*) or nothing (*rien*). Not the least of the questions this theory answers is the enigma of why children begin to fear sleeping in the dark at around age four or five, at the same time that they come to know lack as the lack of Oneness with the mother. Marcel Proust's torture at turning out the light, watching the shadows cast by the lamp while praying for the benediction of one last kiss from his mother before sleep, is enshrined as poetic knowledge. In psychoanalytic parlance, one might call *Remembrance of Things Past* a knowledge about jouissance.[6] Life informs literature, not the reverse.

In the gaze, a point of light is reflected against a dark backdrop. Something is given to be seen, something which Lacan equates with the *awareness* of consciousness. This awareness is like daylight that startles one on awaking in a strange bed, unsure for a moment of what constitutes "I" as an identity. Or conscious awareness also resembles the experience of waking up in the middle of the night, confused about where (who) one is. The strange unconscious aspect of these moments is simply this: they demonstrate that the "I" is not an inherent or innate unity. It is a signifier that constitutes itself in words, images, and bodily sensations that coalesce kaleidoscopically against the backdrop of "systems" that seem fixed because they are unified. Lacan looks at the interface of light and darkness in the gaze at the level of the real, then, not as a Lockean kind of metaphor. He emphasizes that one only "sees" something as it really is *when it is illuminated*. What we generally call consciousness, in other words, is simply our subjectively programmed identifications with words, images, and effects in our bodies that we mistake for objective knowledge.

As partial objects-cause-of-desire, both the gaze and the voice drive language. As such, they continually perforate our myriad illusions of consistency. Let us take another literary example to make the point. In Edith Wharton's *House of Mirth* the heroine Lily Bart is not *just* an imaginary object ("piece of meat") of the male desiring gaze as today's feminists portray her.[7] At the level of the real, she is what Lacan called an extimate object. That is, she is an *object* of her own *subject*(ive) gaze whose meaning is that of the interjected ideals and judgments that form a fictive self. Lily's particular tragedy lies in her being unable to find a place within the social signifying chain she inhabits. Having never identified with the signifiers in the Other that would let her accept one of the possible positions designated for her by society—wife, mistress, mother—she cannot find "a way to be." The point is not that she will not, but that she *cannot*. In Lacanian terms, she is an hysteric, a woman who does not identify with the signifier woman, a female person split in psychic identification between identification with her father and rejection of her mother.

At the level of the real where Lacan shows the voice and the gaze as driving language, anchoring it in the demand for love, each person's demand bears the particular coat of arms of his or her subjectivity and symptoms. And the real of impasses (contradictions, suffering, and joy) are also specific to that person's jouissance. Insofar as the real inhabits language itself, Lily Bart is caught in the stasis of her own hysteric's gaze. Finding no symmetry in the world of social norms between her biological gender and her desire, she dramatizes the Oedipal trauma. Recast by Lacan, the trauma concerns how one assumes knowledge of sexual difference at the level of being.

The voice and gaze add a dimension to language that neither linguistic nor philosophical theories of knowledge account for. Lacan's genius was to discover the drive in these objects that cause desire. Although we use language to try to encapsulate the desire experienced in the jouissance of the voice or the gaze, we never capture the essence we seek except in brief moments. Lacan named this effort to grasp jouissance a demand (*demande*) for something more. But there is no acoustic mirror of a maternal voice commensurate with the mother teaching the child language as post-structuralist film critic Kaja Silverman understands Lacan. That is, in his epistomological shift between "mind" and jouissance, gaze and voice are not flattened into some equation of the mother with language. In *The Acoustic Mirror*, Kaja Silverman writes: "The mother is the first language teacher, commentator, and storyteller—*the* one who first organizes the world linguistically for the child, and first presents it to the Other. The maternal voice also plays a crucial part during the mirror stage defining and interpreting the reflected image, and 'fitting' it to the child. Finally, it [the maternal voice] provides the acoustic mirror in which the child first hears itself."[8] When the voice and gaze are, as Lacan teaches, partial objects that *cause* the desire that commands the partial drives, they cannot be one with a person's speech or intellectual vision of life.

In the *Four Fundamental Concepts of Psychoanalysis*, Lacan stuns his listeners with his image of the mirror other as a wall (79). With this topological reality, he leads us away from the imaginary towards the real where the mirror/mother is only one organizer of the world of speech and "self image" for her child. In the real, the mother's discourse produces something other than gestures; it gives a direction to the child's desire. Lacan's first paternal metaphor—

$$\frac{\text{Name-of-the-Father}}{\text{Desire of the Mother}} \cdot \frac{\text{Desire of the Mother}}{\text{Signified to the subject}} \longrightarrow \text{Name-of-the-Father} \left(\frac{\text{Other}}{\text{Phallus}} \right)$$

—is a rewriting of Freud's Oedipal formula. The precise way in which each person identifies with the difference between the sexes produces neurosis, psychosis, or perversion. But the language that comes from the mother, father, nurse, siblings, relatives, and others represents only one side of what orders meaning (the Other). The other meaning system—the energetics of jouissance—is inseparable from the desire that supports the drive to maintain consistency. In this sense, jouissance is a libidinal glue that solders associational meaning clusters in Borromean signifying chains. Having first theorized the real of the voice and the gaze in 1960 as two of four principle objects (cause of desire), it is logical that Lacan would connect them to the maternal voice and gaze at the level where a primordial jouissance makes of the child a phallus—a desired object—constituted by the mother's desire (as fulfilled [or not] by the father). As such, primordial maternal desire places drive *in* language for all humans, ensuring that it never serve as a simple linguistic mirror organizing the world.

Now I shall try to answer the question I posed at the beginning: what grounds an identity of jouissance? Desire grounds an identity of jouissance. That is, psychic energy is created out of the absolute kernel of jouissance in desire that gives rise to the fantasy of oneness that drives language:

$$(\$ \lozenge D) \qquad \text{drive as the demand for jouissance}$$
$$\uparrow$$
$$(\$ \lozenge a) \qquad \text{fantasy as subjective organization of language}$$
$$\uparrow$$
$$a \qquad\quad \text{desire as cause}$$

Gender, a position in language, is chosen in response to one's mother's desire vis-à-vis the father's name (which constitutes the difference Lacan names castration). But while gender position responds to unconscious desire, sexuality responds to the partial drives: oral, anal, scopic, and invocatory. So there is a split within a given individual between object love and object desire.[9] Indeed, Lacan qualifies his idea of the gaze in an effort to show how desire becomes drive: "There is no need for us to refer to some supposition of the existence of a universal seer [that sees us]. If the function of the stain [blackness] is recognized in its autonomy and identified with that of the gaze, we can seek its track, thread, or trace, at every stage of the constitution of the world, in the scopic field" (74). Although cultures invent and then invoke truths, myths, or folklore as natural truths to explain the function of the gaze, a much simpler concept will do: that of the stain. But what does it mean to say that the gaze and the stain are identified one with the other; and moreover, that the stain is autonomous? Perhaps we can understand Lacan's discovery here if we return to the "exemplary dream of the burning child" recounted in Seminar XI.

Here Lacan speaks of a dream Freud had recounted, telling a story that a patient of his had heard at a lecture. A child, a son, who had been sick with fever for a long time, died. Before burial, his corpse was being watched by an old man who fell asleep at his post. The father had also fallen asleep in the room adjacent to the one in which was his son's body. In reality, a lit candle beside the corpse had fallen over and the wrappings on the dead boy's arm had caught fire. The father's dream occurred after these events. In the dream, his son appeared near his bed, took him by the arm and whispered reproachfully, "Father, can't you see that I am burning?" (57–58). Lacan asks: What awakened the father? Freud said the "reality" of the noise of an overturned candle setting fire to the dead boy's bed had awakened the father. Lacan disagreed, pointing out that Freud had used this particular dream to confirm his thesis regarding dreams: that they are realizations of desire. The father's awakening could not have been caused by an external, physical event, Lacan insisted, if the purpose of dreams is to realize a desire not realized in daily life. *"What is it that wakes the sleeper?* Is it not, *in* the dream, another reality?" (58).

Lacan goes on to develop his theory that dreams are imaginary scenarios that, nonetheless, move virtually alongside the unspeakable real which causes one to awaken in order not to know it. If, as Lacan teaches, sexuality *is* the reality of the unconscious, what the father cannot bear to see is that his son represents *burning* with sexual desire. So the dream tells the story of the real—of the son *in flames*, touching his father. Is it his son's burning desire the father cannot bear to see, or what that desire awakens *in him*? He awakens from his dream to consciousness. Indeed, the consciousness regained on awakening offers a place of comfort where one can repress, deny, and refuse to see the reality of the unconscious story told against the blackness of the given-to-be-seen.

When consciousness turns back upon itself in "that form of vision that is satisfied with itself in imagining itself as consciousness . . . *as seeing oneself. . .* an *avoidance* of the function of the gaze is at work there," Lacan says (74). We misrecognize, idealize, and refuse to see ourselves as we are. So when we think we've got "it" at the level of understanding, we have already missed the point. The *truth* is that we lie, painting ourselves as we should be, not as we really are. In referring to the "burning child" as a paradigmatic dream, Lacan tells us not only what actually wakes one up, but also puts dream images into perspective as a subject's accession to the "imaginary forms offered him by the dream, as opposed to those of the waking state" (74). Put another way, Freud erred in his interpretation of this dream because he reduced the father and the child to persons identified with their social roles. The father's dream, says Freud, is a pleasurable

wish or fantasy in which his son's life is prolonged. Freud's interpretation of
the dream is of a piece with his notion of the Oedipus complex as the basis
of family structure where mother, father, and child are real people whose
desires are conscious, not unconscious. By taking the image to be the thing
itself, Freud takes the dream's meaning as being straightforward. The father
loves his son and wants him alive. There is no unconscious desire here. So
Freud fails to see what the dream really shows the father: the son's *form* as
a horribly gruesome burning body that takes his father by the arm, touching him.

In dreams imaginary forms—representations—do not quite succeed in
suturing the real. The gaze and the voice are not tamed in dreams, as they
are in life. Freud's dream interpretation transforms the little boy into a
loving son who takes his father by the arm, as he had in life. Such an
interpretation makes of this nightmare a father's memory of simple pleasure. Lacan argued that Freud's interpretation is founded at the same level
as the misrecognition (the imaginary of perception) that thinks things *are*
as they appear to be. Such misrecognition constitutes the "illusion of consciousness"; the belief that one sees (knows) oneself as one is by identifying
with visible forms and objects, as well as with the ideas one already possesses. But "the gaze is elided" in the illusions of consciousness (83). The
real is ignored. And because the gaze is not distinguished in its *function*
from the eye's function—which is to see—its function has not been understood. But the gaze is so essential to "knowing" that Lacan calls it the
"underside of consciousness [which is] irremediably limited . . . a principle,
not only of idealization, but of *méconnaissance, a scotoma*" (82–83). So
powerful and primordial is the gaze in its *function* of covering over the void
that resides in consciousness that Lacan describes the human subject as
suspended from the gaze "in an essential vacillation" (83). Moreover, its
constitutive privilege—

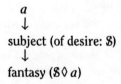

—"derives from its very structure" (83).

But before trying to define the structure of the gaze by making a
distinction between the imaginary and the real, let us go back to the even
more primordial structure Lacan provided in making a distinction between
the stain and the gaze. If the stain marks *something* as existing prior to the
seen of a "given-to-be-seen," then *its* function is "both that which governs

the gaze most secretly and that which always escapes from the grasp of that form of vision that is satisfied with itself in imagining itself as consciousness" (74). While it is difficult to comprehend the stain (or spot) as a *function* that grounds the gaze, this particular function of the gaze grounds Lacan's later use of the topological structure of the Borromean unit. Indeed, the gaze imposes a materiality of libidinal meanings in meaning itself, placing the roots of the Cartesian *cogito* in the real long before language segments the biological organism Lacan called flesh. Once a person is alienated into language, the experience of a oneness between body and desired objects is lost forever. The only grounding left is jouissance functioning in the three orders, producing jouissance of being, body, and meaning.[10]

As infants stitch together a "good enough" unity out of words, sounds, images, and other stuff of the world, they gradually sense that they are "beings who are looked at," as Merleau-Ponty put it. More radical still, Lacan places humans at the same level as things: "That which makes up consciousness institutes us by the same token as *speculum mundi*" (75). We are seen, not seeing; objects, not subjects of free will. The gaze that circumscribes us "in the first instance makes us beings who are looked at, but without showing this [to us]." Lacan asks a poignant question: Can there be any satisfaction "in being under that gaze [of judgment]?" (75).

If one reflects on Lacan's question from different angles, we can perhaps advance in our understanding of what the primordial objects are for Lacan. Feminist film theory, for example, attributes the gaze to the male who looks at the woman and desires her, placing woman in the imaginary order of the lure object. But instead of grasping that the imaginary object is a veil, a stand-in for something else, post-structuralist feminists identify the *visible* object of desire with the invisible object, cause-of-desire. Based on this error, feminists portray Lacan as excluding women from the symbolic order. At this ideological juncture, feminist theory makes the error of conflating Lacan's symbolic order with language and with the voice (three quite distinct concepts in Lacan). It is not a large leap from this error to the idea that Lacan, like Saint Paul in the *New Testament*, wanted women to be silent. The Lacanian concept of the non-existence of an essential Woman comes to mean that women should neither exist nor have a voice. Yet, nowhere in Lacan can one find such theoretical linkages.

The gaze—"that which makes us consciousness"—(75) belongs to neither male nor female. The gaze is first constituted in what Jacques-Alain Miller has called the pre-symbolic real (R_1). Miller's division of the real into pre-symbolic (R_1) and post-symbolic (R_2) clarifies Lacan's effort to describe an Ur-lining of the real where the subject is first constructed as an object-cause-of-desire. Thus the common property of these pre-specular objects is the absence of reflective alterity that is taken on later in the mirror stage.

They make us take note of discontinuities in conscious life. Splitting our seemingly unified identifications with language and images, these objects of the pre-symbolic real bring the *cut* itself into perception, and the cut produces a strange effect on perceptual consciousness, a redoubling of being in the forms that produced us in the first place, but without alterity. The forms out of which consciousness is first constructed are lost at the level of memory, then. Humans undergo this loss prior to any identification of the world with the cohering associations we call consciousness. Lacan called these associations the Borromean unit:

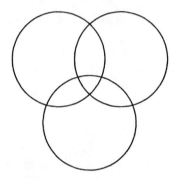

Enlaced with one another, they constitute what he called the signifying chain. This is what *we* call mind. Moreover, the topological "forms" which shape our "illusions" of consciousness in the pre-symbolic imaginary (symbolic-imaginary) and our perceptions (real) of the world, are like the "drive" Lacan describes as having no ascertainable head or tail. One can say that memory is catalyzed by effects from the three orders. Yet we (mis)take memories for a "natural" consciousness.

In Lacan's theory of the voice, there is no hierarchy in which a male uses language in the symbolic to render a female silent in the imaginary. Perhaps the feminist misinterpretations of the voice and the gaze arise out of confused readings of *Encore* where Lacan describes the masculine (phallic) fantasy of constituting a law of the whole wherein one is excluded from castration and thus permitted satisfaction at will. But Lacan depicts this ($\exists x \overline{\Phi x}$) fantasy as a lie on which masculinity is based. Lacan's sexuation symbols give us a logical subject, not a biological one. Thus, a biological female, like a biological male, can imagine herself to be all, can fantasize herself as an exception to the rule of castration. She can invent herself in myths of a clan of women untainted and untouched by the male gaze or voice. But paradoxically such theories place these women in a masculine position in terms of the logic of sexuation. Indeed, most belief systems, not only feminist, confuse biological anatomy with gender. Such an error becomes comprehensible when one grasps that we take the imaginary visible at face value, as the thing itself. Lacan's sexuation tables demonstrate something new which questions our reduction of truth to the visible. Because we are defined as sexual subjects in relation to the phallus and castration, there is no fixed relationship between one's gender and one's biological sex in the unconscious. Nor is there a preordained formula for a sexual relation, only an impasse between the sexes. What we take for relationships relies on the myth of a "natural" relation between the sexes. But in the unconscious, in the realm of fantasy, one identifies, not with gender, but with the gaze that first structured one as a subject of desire, seeking to retrieve a lost jouissance.

The real, biological voice is not language, then, but inhabits language in such a way as to tie desire to jouissance. Lacan argued in the third period of his teaching that the pre-specular objects *could* serve as the means of knotting the orders and, thereby, prevent a psychotic break, as in the case of James Joyce. In *Le Sinthome*, for example, he uncovered what has come to be called his second theory of the paternal metaphor.[11] There he advanced the idea that James Joyce's particular *sinthome* in *Finnegan's Wake* is the voice functioning as a knotting agent, a means of binding the orders together in the absence of a signifier for the Father's Name that perforce joins doubt and dialectic together in language. The voice prevents Joyce from experiencing a psychotic break, while at the same time shattering his language into bits and pieces of poetry.

In reality, we are left with the objects cause of desire as that which institutes consciousness as desire. Although the Ur-objects that cause desire are in and of themselves indivisible, absolute, they nonetheless function as stoppers to the void of loss at the center of all being and knowing:

$$\frac{S(\text{Ⱥ})}{a}$$

In this way desire enters the symbolic order in the partial drives circulating around partial objects, fetish objects that lure one in the imaginary. Because lure objects never deliver the satisfaction implicit in them, but only titillate, Lacan shows where object relations theorists err in taking the imaginary object (breast, mother, transitional object such as blanket, and so on) for the thing in itself. Rather, where an object is sought, there is an empty place that ultimately cannot be filled, causing a dissatisfaction that is finally unappeasable. Because the "object" itself has been already constituted in the "drive" that pushes the subject toward an opaque image of it, the unconscious desire (the aim) to achieve a harmonious mesh of object and satisfaction (the goal) only reveals a gap between the goal and the object. Moreover, the heterogeneous multiplication of desirable objects aimed at by any of the four partial "drives" named by Lacan—oral, anal, scopic, and invocatory—keeps one from recognizing the relation of desired objects to the Ur-objects that leave their mark in the drive montage. Yet, at one level, drive functions by an imaginary relation between organ and lure object where object *a appears* to be the visible thing, separable from the organs that *seem* to produce it. Thus object *a* is a semblant. But, in the real, drives produce repetitions that constitute jouissance as the libidinal glue of consistency. At this level, the gaze and the voice are not language or signifiers. Yet, they enter the register of language, but in the timing of desire and by the logic of jouissance. Where there was one thing, another thing is substituted, while jouissance imposes drive energy on language.

In this formula—2/1—*das Ding* (or primary jouissance) precedes the word which kills or defers the possibility of immediate satisfaction. One must negotiate in language for libidinal satisfaction: A (the Other)/$ (lack). In Lacan's first theory of jouissance, object *a* stands for the difference between a quantity of language and a quantity of libido.[12]

$$\frac{A \quad a}{J}$$

Yet one cannot actually "quantify" jouissance, although a part of *a* is translatable in particular features of fetish objects and in symptoms. But part remains either forever lost or untranslatable. Some post-structuralist critics have mistakenly labeled this lost part described by Lacan as Platonic, as the fantasized ideal form of Plato's shadows on the wall of his cave.[13]

I shall use two concrete examples to argue that Lacan's theory of loss is not metaphorical: I'll speak first of my daughter and then refer to an anecdote on page 75 of Seminar XI. When my daughter was nine years old, she telephoned me in Paris from the USA, where she was staying for the brief period of my absence with her grandmother. She had called to tell me she had "anxiety" (which we renamed "homesickness" in the course of the conversation). But when she first called, she could not yet talk about her feelings of homesickness. She could only say that she couldn't sleep. Gradually, as we talked about other things, she said something that didn't belong to the imaginary register of her narrative. She said, "I can't sleep because I have no place." I replied in the realm of narrative, "But Grandma has two bedrooms right across the hall from you, or you can sleep on the cot in the same room with Grandma and Grandpa." She answered: "I don't have my bed, my house, my friends, my animals, or Daddy nearby." By "place" she did not actually mean geographical space, or an actual bed. She was referring, rather, to a place in the gaze. By my daughter's losing her grounding in the familiar—Mommy, her house, etc.—she was confronting the real void in being: $S(\cancel{A})$. Anxiety *has* an object, Lacan discovered: the positivized real of the void which has a literal weight, be it the heaviness of depression or the piercing pangs of anxiety.[14] The void is *not nothing*, then.

The example with which I shall try to demonstrate that the Lacanian void is not an ideal Platonic form, takes on theoretical meaning in terms of the Moebius strip, whose outside is continuous with the inside, although it intersects with itself at some point, making an interior 8 (156). Lacan says of the figure 8: "This *image* enables us to figure desire as a *locus of junction* between the field of demand [*demande*] in which the synapses of the unconscious are made present, and sexual reality. All this depends on a line that I will call the line of desire linked to the drive in demand, and by which the effects of sexuality are made present in experience" (156). The intersection of drive (demand rendered in language) and desire appeared in my daughter's demand for a place *to be* within the field of familiar gazes. In the desire to make oneself seen (*se faire voir*) that Lacan equates with consciousness, one sees how Oedipal desire is sublimated into the drive to be recognized, loved. In this context, desire in all its forms might be called sexual insofar as the reality of the unconscious is sexual. But a sexualization of the drives is at issue here, not a reduction of sexuality to genital sensations or to sex acts *per se*. If unconscious desire *qua* meaning is sexuality itself, we are far afield from Freud's concept of sexuality as copulation or developmental stages. Lacan described sexuality as the presence of desire in experience. But desire is evasive and evanescent because the real objects that cause it are but metonymic residues of lost libido whose traces subtend demand. Thus, all demand is linked to desire, and all desire to the desire to be loved (154).

The lacking element in my daughter's telephone "call"—loss of the gaze against which she usually constituted an image of herself—is not Platonic at all. She found herself confronted quite literally with the blackness of the stain and attendant anxious feelings of loss. Lacan calls the Platonic perspective the fantasy of an absolute being to whom the quality of being all-seeing is imputed. "The world is all-seeing," he says, "but it is not exhibitionistic—it does not provoke our gaze. When it begins to provoke it, the feeling of strangeness begins too" (75). And strangeness is concretely linked to loss taken as an effect in the body created by the loss of objects with which one has identified. Such identifications literally give individuals a position in the symbolic world of others. A "homesick" child does not use language in the figural, metaphorical sense as Derrida would claim. Whether I speak of my daughter encountering being apart from her mother, or Marcel Proust hoping for one more kiss from his mother before sleep, such moments confront the void in representation itself: $S(\cancel{A})/a$. Usually we have the illusion that things are what they seem, that the visible is the thing itself. My daughter's words—"I have no place"—meant that nothing, Mommy, for instance, is missing as long as things are in their familiar place. Yet the voice enables us to call up the gaze against which we reconstitute ourselves in memory, the gaze of judgment and idealizations that gives us a place in our fantasies. There we are suspended from the gaze that functions as a position marker in the real.

But here we encounter a paradox. The *a* keeps us from seeing our-selves as we are at the same time that it offers a *semblance* of being that people identify with narcissistically. In Lacan's words:

> What specifies the scopic field and engenders for us the satisfaction proper to it is the fact that, for structural reasons, the fall of the subject always remains unperceived, for it is reduced to zero. Insofar as the gaze, *qua* object *a* may come to symbolize this central lack expressed in the phe-nomenon of castration, and insofar as it is an object *a* reduced, of its nature, to a punctiform, evanescent function, it leaves the subject igno-rant as to what there is beyond [the] appearances, an ignorance so charac-teristic of all progress in thought that occurs in the path constituted by philosophical research (76–77).

Object *a* symbolizes the fact that there is an empty place in representa-tion that shows up in being, knowing, desiring. In the real of desire, the subject, as a response of the real, is an object trying to fill up its own holes. Perhaps one can sense the bodily concreteness of the Lacanian object *a* if one grasps what *a* denotes: the difference between language and libido. And since these objects are all linked first to the mother as the primary object of jouissance—and only secondarily to the father *qua* language, image, and *effect* in the real—they retain the mark of incest as a forbidding (or not) of excesses in jouissance.

The first set of splits or cuts—primary separations from maternal ob-jects—constitute what we experience as an imaginary body. And its palpable scars give rise to object *a* as any fantasy object by which individuals imag-ine themselves as whole. Lacan calls this level of visual apprehension the stain, or the psychic point in the scopic function where the split between the gaze and vision is found. This split enables us to add the scopic drive to the list of the drives. Lacan points out that Freud had already placed the scopic drive to the fore in "*Triebe und Triebschicksale*," showing that this drive is not homologous with the others.[15] And indeed this drive most completely eludes the term "castration" (78). Put another way, the visible seems adequate to itself. Not only does the body look whole, so does the world and the things in it. Thus, people identify with the illusion of the whole, rather than the reality of lack.

But, in fact, the figure of the "burning child" in the dream is not a cut-out or a paper doll, but a voice from the real that brings the gaze to bear on an image, showing the temporal side of the drive. When any subject, in this case the boy's father, encounters the traumatic real, language and images are detotalized. When an *a*—such as the child's voice in the father's dream—falls out of the temporal Other, it brings a desexualized part of jouissance with it. This indivisible, organ-like quality of the *petit a* is an irreducible and untranslatable kernel of being. There sexuality joins hands with death, not only around the fact of castration (the experience of lack one has in reference to the phallus), but also in relation to separation (or the experience of the cut). Castration and separation bring inconsistencies into our lives, cutting into jouissance. We see that unities or apparent totalities are only logical consistencies.

The father in Freud's dream had tried not to see his son as sexual when he was alive, thus giving a seeming stability to the set family fiction where the child is "this," the Mommy "that," the Daddy "that," and so on. Thus, the child's *voice* comes as a firebrand, as a piece of anxiety dropped from the hole in the Other into the father's unconscious, opening up a beyond in the dream image, a void that makes the image tell a disquieting truth: Our knowledge is grounded in objects that are not themselves grounded. Human illusions of a natural consistency of consciousness are just illusions, always susceptible of being subverted. And dreams, in particular, demonstrate this.

Dreams, like painting and music, embody the gaze as the intervening *cause* that points to something beyond the horizon, some stain against which we can see ourselves being seen. I shall give a concrete example. A tornado destroyed my brother's beautifully cultivated garden of 100 pines, a trout stream, and a greenhouse, ripping all the trees apart. Afterwards, he could only repeat one sentence in a robot-like voice: "we can see the highway." The uncharacteristic flatness of his voice imposed a strange effect on his language, a haunted, dead tone that split the facade of grammatical unity by some Other kind of knowledge. I kept wondering why his affect and speech were disunified, why he didn't utter some version of "I am devastated. The financial cost of the destruction is enormous. The symbol of what we built together in our marriage is gone, etc. etc. etc." Instead, my brother spoke like a dead man only the words: "we can see the highway."

And then I understood. He felt himself looked at by the stain beyond the gaze. He felt the blackness of the void staring at him, showing him to himself, unprotected, "poor" like any creature faced with death. In other words, it is not the world that is all-seeing, exhibitionistic. The world itself is not pansexual, either. But when the essential emptiness of the world gives itself to be seen, one experiences the uncanny. One literally encounters the holes in being.

In the field of dreams, on the other hand, the image is characterized by what *it shows*. The impasse of the real causes the drive to aim at making itself—oneself—seen, heard, flushed away, clung to, annihilated. *"It* [the dream] *shows* . . . the absence of horizon, the enclosure (the frame) of that which is contemplated in the waking state, and, also, the character of . . . contrast, of stain . . . [It shows] that, in the final analysis, our position in the dream is like our position in the drive—that of someone who does not see. One follows" (45). In chapter 8 of Seminar XI, the sardine can that does not see Lacan means something nonetheless because it places him against the background of the world, showing him his *place* in the story of the desperate lives of the fishermen. Caught between the gaze and vision, Lacan saw himself being seen within the web of gazes and signifiers, beyond the *image* of the sardine can, between the screen of the scene portrayed (the picture) and the stain (96–97).

His concept of the gaze is neither a metaphor nor an idealist view, Lacan says. Rather, the subject is always already *there* (*Fort!*) as an irreducible thing, an object. And the key to grasping this difficult concept is not in terms of mimicry, but in terms of the masquerade. The "lure" that plays between the eye and gaze is visual and verbal. Yet, what one wants to see or hear is never "it." At least "you never look at me from the place from which I see you. Conversely, *what I look at is never what I wish to see"* (103). There is no (sexual) *relation* of one person to another, no pregiven unity, no forgiveness clause for human imperfection (or lack), only the masquerade that seeks to deny loss and cancel the pain of anxiety produced by the void. Life plays between the voice and the gaze, yielding deception, frustration, the domestic quarrel, the disembodied voices droning on and on in Jean Giraudoux's play even after *Sodom and Gomorrah* are burned.[16]

Notes

1. Jacques Lacan. *Le Séminaire de Jacques Lacan, Livre XX: Encore* (1972–73). Text established by Jacques-Alain Miller (Paris: Editions du Seuil, 1975).

2. Jacques Lacan. "The Subversion of the Subject and the Dialectic of Desire in the Freudian Unconscious." *Écrits*, trans. Alan Sheridan (New York: W. W. Norton, 1977): 315.

3. In May 1993, mathematician Chris Anderson described implied associations of meaning as "implicated assumptions." One could take this definition into the area of Lacan's topology where the meaning of *a* between intersected orders can only be guessed.

4. Bruce Fink. "Alienation and Separation: Logical Moments of Lacan's Dialectic of Desire." *Newsletter of the Freudian Field* 4:1–2 (1990): 78–119.

5. Marc V. Howlett. *"L'Objet <D>." L'Ane*, **36** (1988): 32.

6. Proust, Marcel. *Combray* (New York: Appleton-Century-Crofts, 1952).

7. Ellie Ragland. "The Daughter's Dilemma: Psychoanalytic Interpretation and Edith Wharton's *The House of Mirth*," in *Edith Wharton's The House of Mirth: Case Studies in Contemporary Criticism*. Ed. Shari Benstock (Boston: Bedford of St. Martin's Press, forthcoming).

8. Kaja Silverman. *The Acoustic Mirror: The Female Voice in Psychoanalysis and Cinema* (Bloomington: Indiana UP, 1988): 100.

9. Jacques-Alain Miller, *Sur André Gide*, Séminaire de DEA du Département de Psychanalyse, 1989–90, Unpublished seminar.

10. Jacques Lacan. *"La Troisième"*, given at the VII Congress of the EFP in Rome (1974); *Lettres de l'Ecole freudienne*, **16**, 1975: 178–203.

11. Jacques Lacan. *Le Séminaire de Jacques Lacan, Livre XXIII: Le Sinthome* (1975–76). Unpublished seminar.

12. Jacques-Alain Miller. "To Interpret the Cause." *Newsletter of the Freudian Field* 3: 1–2 (1989): 30–50.

13. Plato. *The Republic*, Book VII. Trans. W.H.D. Ross (New York: New American Library, 1984): 315–341.

14. Jacques Lacan. *Le Séminaire de Jacques Lacan, Livre X: L'angoisse* (1962–63). Unpublished seminar; Jacques-Alain Miller "Language: Much Ado About What?", *Lacan and the Subject of Language*. Eds. Ellie Ragland-Sullivan and Mark Bracher (New York: Routledge, 1991): 21–35.

15. Sigmund Freud. "Instincts and Their Vicissitudes" (1915). SE XXIV: 111.

16. Jean Giraudoux. *Sodome et Gomorrhe* (Paris: Éditions Bernard Grasset, 1947).

THE LAMELLA OF DAVID LYNCH

Slavoj Žižek

In chapter 15 of Seminar XI, Lacan introduces the mysterious notion of the "lamella": the libido as an organ without body, the incorporeal and for that very reason indestructible life-substance that persists beyond the circuit of generation and corruption.[1] It is no accident that commentaries on this passage are rare (for all practical purposes nonexistent); the Lacan with whom we are confronted in this passage does not have a lot in common with the usual figure of Lacan which reigns in the domain of cultural studies. The Lacan of the lamella is "Another Lacan," as Jacques-Alain Miller put it, a Lacan of drive not desire, of the real not the symbolic.

How are we to approach this notion of lamella? Let us risk a detour. If, today, the term "post-modernism" is of any theoretical use, then lamella is a post-modern notion *par excellence*—the shift from the Lacan of the symbolic to the Lacan of the real is the shift from modernism to post-modernism. For that reason, one should not be surprised that lamella is the central preoccupation of the person whose work epitomizes post-modernism in cinema, David Lynch. And, in order to expose as clearly as possible Lynch's post-modernism, let us risk an additional detour via those who were, in all probability, the first post-modernists *avant la lettre*: the Pre-Raphaelites.

1

In art history, the Pre-Raphaelites function as the paradoxical border case of avant-garde overlapping with *kitsch*. They were first perceived as bearers of an anti-traditionalist revolution in painting, breaking with the

entire tradition from the Renaissance onwards, only to be devalued shortly
thereafter—with the rise of Impressionism in France—as the very epitome
of damp Victorian pseudo-romantic *kitsch*. This low rating lasted till the
1960s, i.e., until the emergence of post-modernism. How was it, then,
that they became "readable" only retroactively, from the post-modernist
paradigm?

In this respect, the crucial painter is William Holman Hunt, usually
dismissed as the first Pre-Raphaelite to sell out to the establishment, becoming a well-paid producer of sweetish religious paintings (*The Triumph
of the Innocents*, etc.). However, a closer look unmistakeably confronts us
with an uncanny, deeply disturbing dimension of his work; his paintings
produce a kind of uneasiness or indeterminate feeling that, in spite of their
idyllic and elevated "official" content, there is something amiss.

Let us take *The Hireling Shepherd*, apparently a simple pastoral idyll
depicting a shepherd engaged in seducing a country-girl, and for that reason neglecting to care for a flock of sheep (an obvious allegory of the
Church neglecting its lambs). The longer we observe the painting, the more
we become aware of a great number of details that bear witness to Hunt's
intense relationship to enjoyment, to life-substance, i.e., to his disgust at
sexuality. The shepherd is muscular, dull, crude, and rudely voluptuous; the
cunning gaze of the girl indicates a sly, vulgarly manipulative exploitation
of one's own sexual attraction; the all too vivacious reds and greens mark
the entire painting with a repulsive tone, as if we were dealing with turgid,
overripe, putrid nature. It is similar to *Isabella and the Pot of Basil* where
numerous details belie the "official" tragic-religious content (the snake-like
hair, the skulls on the brim of the vase, etc.). The sexuality radiated by the
painting is damp, "unwholesome," and permeated with the decay of death,
and it plunges us into the universe of David Lynch, the filmmaker.

Lynch's entire "ontology" is based upon the discordance or contrast
between reality, observed from a safe distance, and the absolute proximity
of the real. His elementary procedure consists in moving forward from an
establishing shot of reality to a disturbing proximity which renders visible
the disgusting substance of enjoyment, the crawling and twinkling of indestructible life—in short, the lamella. Suffice it to recall the opening sequence of *Blue Velvet*. After the shots that epitomize the idyllic small
American town and the father's stroke while he waters the lawn (when he
collapses, the jet of water uncannily recalls surreal, heavy urination), the
camera approaches the grass surface and depicts the bursting life, the crawling of insects and beetles, their rattling and devouring of grass. At the very
beginning of *Twin Peaks: Fire Walk With Me*, we encounter the opposite
technique which produces the same effect. First we see abstract white pro-
toplasmic shapes floating in a blue background, a kind of elementary form

of life in its primordial twinkling; then the camera slowly moves away and we become aware that what we were seeing was an extreme close-up of a TV screen.[2] Therein lies the fundamental feature of post-modern hyper-realism: the very over-proximity to reality brings about the "loss of reality." Uncanny details stick out and perturb the pacifying effect of the overall picture.[3]

The second feature, closely linked to the first, is contained in the very designation "Pre-Raphaelitism": the reaffirmation of rendering things as they "really are," not yet distorted by the rules of academic painting first established by Raphael. However, the Pre-Raphaelites' own practice belies this naive ideology of returning to the "natural" way of painting. The first thing that strikes the eye in their paintings is the feature which necessarily appears to us, accustomed to modern perspective-realism, as a sign of clumsiness. The Pre-Raphaelite paintings are somehow flat, lacking the "depth" of space organized along the perspective lines which meet in an infinite point; it is as if the very "reality" they depict were not a "true" reality but rather structured as a relief. Another aspect of this same feature is the "dollish," mechanically composite, artificial quality of the depicted individuals: they somehow lack the abyssal depth of personality we usually associate with the notion of "subject." The designation "Pre-Raphaelitism" is thus to be taken literally, as an indication of the shift from Renaissance perspectivism to the "closed" medieval universe.

In Lynch's films, the "flatness" of the depicted reality responsible for the cancellation of infinite perspective openness finds its precise correlate or counterpart at the level of sound. Let us return to the opening sequence of *Blue Velvet*: its crucial feature is the uncanny noise that emerges when we approach the real. This noise is difficult to locate in reality. In order to determine its status, one is tempted to evoke contemporary cosmology which speaks of noises at the borders of the universe; these noises are not simply internal to the universe—they are remainders or last echoes of the Big Bang that created the universe itself. The ontological status of this noise is more interesting than it may appear, since it subverts the fundamental notion of the "open," infinite universe that defines the space of Newtonian physics. That is to say, the modern notion of the "open" universe is based on the hypothesis that every positive entity (noise, matter) occupies some (empty) space; it hinges on the difference between space as void and positive entities which occupy it, "fill it out." Space is here phenomenologically conceived as something that exists prior to the entities which "fill it out." If we destroy or remove the matter that occupies a given space, this space as void remains. The primordial noise, the last remainder of the Big Bang, is on the contrary *constitutive of space itself*: it is not a noise "in" space, but a noise that keeps space open as such. If, therefore, we were to erase this noise, we would not get the "empty space" which was filled out by it. Space itself, the receptacle for every "inner-worldly" entity, would vanish. This noise is, in a sense, the "sound of silence."

Along the same lines, the fundamental noise in Lynch's films is not simply caused by objects that are part of reality; rather, it forms the onto-logical horizon or frame of reality itself, i.e., the texture that holds reality together. Were this noise to be eradicated, reality itself would collapse. From the "open" infinite universe of Cartesian-Newtonian physics, we are thus back to the pre-modern "closed" universe, encircled, bounded, by a fundamental "noise."

We encounter this same noise in the nightmare sequence of *The El-ephant Man*. It transgresses the borderline that separates interior from exterior, i.e., the extreme externality of a machine uncannily coincides with the utmost intimacy of the bodily interior, with the rhythm of heart palpi-tations. This noise also appears after the camera enters the hole in the elephant-man's hood, which stands for the gaze. The reversal of reality into the real corresponds to the reversal of the look (the subject looking at reality) into gaze, i.e., it occurs when we enter the "black hole," the crack in the texture of reality.

2

What we encounter in this "black hole" is simply the body stripped of its skin. That is to say, Lynch perturbs our most elementary phenomeno-logical relationship to the living body, which is based on the radical line of separation between the surface of the skin and what is beneath it. Let us recall the uncanniness, and even disgust, we experience when we endeavor to imagine what goes on just under the surface of a beautiful naked body— muscles, glands, veins, etc. In short, our relating to the body implies the suspension of what lies beneath the surface, and this suspension is an effect of the symbolic order—it can occur only insofar as bodily reality is struc-tured by language. In the symbolic order, we are not really naked even when we are without clothes, since skin itself functions as the "dress of the flesh."[4] This suspension excludes the real of the life-substance, its palpita-tion; one of the definitions of the Lacanian real is that it is the flayed, skinned body, the palpitation of raw, skinless red flesh.

How, then, does Lynch perturb our most elementary phenomenologi-cal relationship to the bodily surface? By means of the voice, of a word which "kills," which corrodes or breaks through the skin surface and di-rectly cuts into the raw flesh—in short, by means of a word whose status is that of a *real*. This feature is at its most expressive in Lynch's version of

Herbert's *Dune*. Suffice it to recall members of the space-guild who, because of their over-indulging in "spice," the mysterious drug around which
the story turns, become distorted beings with gigantic heads, worm-like
creatures made of skinless, raw flesh, indestructible life-substance, a pure
embodiment of enjoyment.

Another case of similar distortion is the corrupted kingdom of the
evil Baron Harkonnen where we see faces whose surface is distorted in an
uncanny way—sewn-up eyes and ears, etc. The face of the Baron himself
is full of disgusting protuberances, "sprouts of enjoyment," in which the
inside of the body breaks through the surface. The unique scene, where
the Baron attacks a young boy in an ambiguous oral-homoerotic way, also
plays on this ambiguity of the relationship of the inside and the surface.
The Baron attacks him by pulling out his heart-cork, so that blood starts
to squirt out. (What we have here is Lynch's typical child-fantasy notion
of a human body as a balloon, a form made of inflated skin, with no
substance behind it.) The skulls of the servants of the space-guild also
start to crack when they run out of spice—again a case of distorted,
fractured surfaces. What is crucial here is the correlation between these
cracks in the skull and the distorted voice: the guild-servant actually
utters unintelligible whispers which are transformed into articulated speech
only by means of the microphone—or, in Lacanian terms, by passing
through the medium of the Other. This delay—i.e., the fact that the sounds
we utter are not speech in an immediate way, but only through the inter-
vention of the external, machine-like, symbolic order—is usually concealed; it is rendered visible only when the relationship between surface
and its beyond is perturbed.

In *Twin Peaks*, the dwarf in the Red Lodge speaks an incomprehensible, distorted English, rendered intelligible only with the help of subtitles
that play the role of the microphone, i.e., the medium of the Other. What
we have here is the hidden reversal of the Derridian critique of logocentrism
in which the voice functions as the medium of illusory self-transparency
and self-presence: the obscene, cruel, superego-like, incomprehensible, im-
penetrable, traumatic dimension of the voice which is a kind of foreign
body perturbing the balance of our lives.[5]

The relationship to surface is also perturbed in the case of Paul's—
Dune's hero's—mystical experience of drinking the "water of life." (Mysti-
cism, of course, stands for the encounter with the real.) Here, again, the
inside endeavors to invade the surface—blood drips not only from Paul's
eyes but also from the mouth of his mother and sister, who are aware of his
ordeal by direct, non-symbolic, empathy. (The ruler's counselors, the "living computers" who are able to read others' thoughts and see into the
future, also have strange blood-like stains around their lips.)

Finally, there is the voice of Paul Atreid himself, which has a directly physical impact. By raising his voice, he is able not only to derange his adversary, but even to blow up the hardest rock. At the end of the film, Paul raises his voice and shouts back at the old priestess who tried directly to penetrate his mind; as Paul himself says, his word can kill, i.e., his speech is not only a symbolic act but can directly cut into the real. The disintegration of the "normal" relationship of bodily surface and its underside is strictly correlative to the change in the status of speech, to the emergence of a word which operates directly at the level of the real.

3

There is another crucial feature of this last scene. The old priestess reacts to Paul's words in an exaggerated, almost theatrical way, so that it is not clear if she is reacting to his actual words or to the distorted, overblown way she perceives his words. In short, the "normal" relationship between cause (Paul's words) and effect (the woman's reaction to it) is perturbed here; it is as if there is a gap separating them, as if the effect never fits or corresponds to its alleged cause. The usual way to read this gap would be to conceive of it as an index of woman's hysteria: women are not able to perceive clearly external causes, they always project into them their own distorted vision of them. Michel Chion, however, provides here a true stroke of genius and proposes a rather different reading of this disturbance.[6] One is tempted to "order" his rather non-systematic way of proceeding in his book on Lynch, by arranging it into three consecutive steps.

1) Chion's starting point is the gap or discord between action and reaction that is always at work in Lynch's films: when a subject—as a rule a man— addresses a woman or "electrocutes" her in some other way, the woman's reaction is always somehow incommensurate with the "impulse" she receives. What is at stake in this incommensurability is a kind of short-circuit between cause and effect: their relationship is never "pure" or linear. We can never be quite certain to what extent the effect itself retroactively "colored" its own cause. We encounter here the logic of anamorphosis presented in an exemplary way in Shakespeare's *Richard II* (Act II, Scene II) by the words of the Queen's faithful servant Bushby:

> Like perspectives, which rightly gaz'd upon,
> Show nothing but confusion; ey'd awry
> Distinguish form: so your sweet majesty
> Looking awry upon your lord's departure,

Finds shapes of grief more than himself to wail;
Which, look'd on as it is, is nought but shadows
Of what is not.

In her answer to Bushby, the Queen herself locates her fears in the context of causes and effects:

. . . conceit is still deriv'd
From some forefather grief; mine is not so,
For nothing hath begot my something grief;
Or something hath the nothing that I grieve:
'Tis in reversion that I do possess;
But what it is, that is not yet known; what
I cannot name; 'tis nameless woe, I wot.[7]

The incommensurability between cause and effect thus results from the anamorphic perspective of the subject who distorts the "real" preceding cause, so that his act (his reaction to this cause) is never a direct effect of the cause, but rather a consequence of his distorted perception of the cause.

2) Chion's next step consists of a "crazy" gesture worthy of the most daring Freudian interpretation: he proposes that the fundamental matrix, the paradigmatic case, of this discord between action and reaction is sexual (non)relationship between man and woman. In sexual activity, men "do certain things to women," and the question to be raised is: *is woman's enjoyment reducible to an effect, is it a simple consequence of what men do to her?* From the good old days of Marxist hegemony, one may perhaps be reminded of the vulgar, materialist, "reductionistic" endeavors to explain the genesis of the notion of causality on the basis of human practice, of man's active relating to his environs: we arrive at the notion of causality by generalizing the experience of how, every time we accomplish a certain gesture, the same effect occurs in reality. Chion proposes an even more radical reductionism: the elementary matrix of the relationship between cause and effect is offered by the sexual relationship. In the last analysis, the irreducible gap that separates an effect from its cause amounts to the fact that *"not all* of feminine enjoyment is an effect of the masculine cause." This "not-all" has to be conceived precisely in the sense of the Lacanian logic of not-all (*pas-tout*)[8]: it in no way entails that a part of feminine enjoyment is not the effect of what men do to a woman. In other words, "not-all" designates inconsistency and not incompleteness: in the reaction of a woman, there is always something unforeseen. A woman never reacts as expected—all of a sudden, she does not react to something that, up to

that time, infallibly aroused her, yet she is aroused by something that a man does in passing, inadvertently. Woman is not fully submitted to the causal link. With her, this linear order of causality breaks down—or, to quote Nicholas Cage when, in Lynch's *Wild at Heart*, he is surprised by an unexpected reaction of Laura Dern's: "The way your mind works is God's own private mystery."

3) The last step is in itself twofold: a further specification or narrowing-down, followed by a generalization. Why is it precisely woman who, by way of her incommensurate reaction to man's impulse, breaks asunder the causal chain? The specific feature which seems reducible to a link in the causal chain, yet actually suspends and inverts it, is *feminine depression*—woman's suicidal propensity to slide into permanent lethargy. Man bombards woman with shocks in order to stir her out of this depression.

4

At the center of *Blue Velvet* (and of all of Lynch's opus), there is the enigma of woman's depression. That the fatal Dorothy (Isabella Rosselini) is depressed goes without saying, since the reasons for it seem obvious: her child and husband were kidnapped by cruel Frank (Denis Hopper), who even cut off her husband's ear, and he blackmails Dorothy by exacting sexual favors as the price for keeping her husband and child alive. The causal link seems thus clear and unambiguous. Frank is the cause of all troubles, he broke into the happy family and provoked the trauma; Dorothy's masochistic enjoyment is a simple after-effect of this initial shock—the victim is so bewildered and thrown off by the sadistic violence she is sub-jected to, that she "identifies with the aggressor" and sets out to imitate his game. However, a detailed analysis of the most famous scene from *Blue Velvet*—the sadomasochistic sexual play between Dorothy and Frank, ob-served by Jeffrey (Kyle MacLachlan) while he is hiding in the closet—requires us to reverse the entire perspective. The crucial question to be asked here is: *for whom* is this scene staged?

The first answer seems obvious: for Jeffrey. Isn't it an exemplary case of a child witnessing parental coitus? Isn't Jeffrey reduced to a pure gaze present at the act of his own conception (the elementary matrix of fantasy)? This interpretation can be supported by two peculiar features of what Jef-frey sees: Dorothy stuffing blue velvet into Frank's mouth, and Frank put-ting an oxygen-mask on his mouth and then breathing heavily. Aren't both of these visual hallucinations based on what the child hears? When eaves-dropping on parental coitus, the child hears hollow speaking and heavy, gasping breathing; he or she imagines that there must be something in the father's mouth (perhaps part of the sheet, since he is in bed), or that he is breathing through a mask.[9]

Yet what this reading leaves out is the crucial fact that the sado-masochistic game is thoroughly staged and theatrical. Both of them—not only Dorothy who knows that Jeffrey is watching since she put him in the closet—act (or even overact) as if they knew they were being observed. Jeffrey is not an unobserved, accidental witness to a secret ritual; the ritual is, from the outset, staged for his gaze. From this perspective, the true organizer of the game seems to be Frank. His noisy, theatrical manner, bordering on the comical and recalling the movie-image of a villain, bears witness to the fact that he is desperately trying to fascinate and impress the third gaze. In order to prove what? The key is perhaps offered by Frank's obsessive repeating to Dorothy: "Don't you look at me!" Why shouldn't she? There is only one answer possible: *since there is nothing to see*. There is no erection to see, since Frank is impotent.

Read this way, the scene acquires quite a different meaning: Frank and Dorothy feign a wild sexual act in order to conceal from the child the fact that his father is impotent; all Frank's shouting and swearing, his comical-spectacular imitation of coital gestures, is designed to mask its opposite. In traditional terms, the accent shifts from voyeurism to exhibitionism: Jeffrey's gaze is but an element in the exhibitionist's scenario. Instead of a son witnessing parental coitus, the father desperately attempts to convince his son of his potency.

There is, however, a third possible reading, centered on Dorothy. What I have in mind here are not anti-feminist commonplaces about feminine masochism, claiming that women secretly enjoy being brutally mistreated, etc. My point is rather the following: what if—bearing in mind that, with woman, the linear causal link is suspended, and even reversed—*depression is the original fact*? What if depression comes first, and all subsequent activity—i.e., Frank's terrorizing of Dorothy—far from being its cause, is rather a desperate "therapeutic" attempt to prevent her from sliding into the abyss of absolute depression, a kind of "electroshock" therapy which endeavors to attract her attention? The crudeness of his "treatment" (the kidnapping of husband and son; the cutting off of the husband's ear; the required participation in the sadistic sexual game) simply corresponds to the depth of her depression; only such rude shocks can keep her active.

In this sense, Lynch can be said to be a true anti-Weininger. In Otto Weininger's *Sex and Character*, the paradigm of modern anti-feminism, woman proposes herself to man, endeavoring to attract and fascinate his gaze and thus drag him down from spiritual heights into the lowliness of sexual debauchery. For Weininger, the "original fact" is man's spirituality, whereas his fascination with woman results from his Fall; for Lynch, the "original fact" is woman's depression, her sliding into the abyss of self-annihilation and absolute lethargy, whereas man, on the contrary, proposes himself to woman as the object of her gaze. Man "bombards" her with shocks in order to arouse her attention and thereby shake her out of her numbness—in short, in order to reinclude or reinstate her in the "proper" order of causality.

The tradition of such a stiff, lethargic woman aroused from her numbness by a man's call was alive and well in the nineteenth century. Suffice it to recall here Kundry from Wagner's *Parsifal* who, at the beginning of Act II and Act III, is awakened from a catatonic sleep (first through Klingsor's rude summons, then through Gurnemanz's kind care). And from "real" life, consider the unique figure of Jane Morris, the wife of William Morris and the mistress of Dante Gabriel Rosetti. The famous photo of Jane Morris from 1865 presents a depressive woman, deeply absorbed in her thoughts, who seems to await man's impulse to shake her from her lethargy; this photo perhaps offers the closest approach to what Wagner had in mind when he created this figure of Kundry.[10]

What is of crucial importance is the universal, formal structure at work here: the "normal" relationship between cause and effect is inverted. The "effect" is the original fact, which comes first, and what appears as its cause—the shocks which allegedly set in motion the depression—is actually a reaction to this effect, a struggle against depression. The logic is once again that of a "not-all." "Not-all" of depression results from the causes which trigger it; yet at the same time there is nothing, no element of depression, which is not triggered by some external active cause. In other words, everything in depression is an effect—everything except depression as such, i.e., except the *form* of depression. The status of depression is thus strictly "transcendental": depression provides the *a priori* frame within which causes can act the way they do.[11]

It may appear that I have simply reproduced the most common prejudice about female depression, i.e., the notion of a woman who can be aroused only by a man's stimulation. There is, however, another way to look at it. Doesn't the elementary structure of subjectivity consist in the fact that not-all of the subject is determined by the causal chain? Isn't the subject the very gap that separates the cause from its effect? Doesn't it emerge precisely insofar as the relationship between cause and effect cannot be accounted for?[12] In other words, what is this feminine depression that suspends the causal link, the causal enchainment of our acts to external stimuli, if not the founding gesture of subjectivity, the primordial act of freedom, of breaking up our insertion into the nexus of causes and effects.[13]

The philosophical name for this "depression" is absolute negativity, i.e., what Hegel called "the night of the world," the withdrawal of the subject into itself. In short, woman, not man, is the subject par excellence. And the link between depression and the bursting of the indestructible life-substance is also clear: depression and withdrawal-into-self is the primordial act of retreat, of acquiring a distance from the indestructible life-substance, which makes it appear as a repulsive scintillation.

5

In conclusion, emphasis should be laid on the inherent political dimension of this notion of enjoyment, i.e., on the way the lamella, this kernel of enjoyment, functions as a political factor. Let us approach this dimension by way of one of the enigmas of cultural life in post-Socialist Eastern Europe: why does Milan Kundera even now, after the victory of democracy, suffer a kind of excommunication in Bohemia? His works are rarely published, the media pass over them in silence, and everybody is somehow embarrassed to speak about him. In order to justify such treatment, one rakes up old stories about his hidden collaboration with the Communist regime, about his taking refuge in private pleasures and avoiding the righteous battle à la Havel, etc. However, the roots of this resistance are deeper—Kundera conveys a message unbearable to "normalized" democratic consciousness.

In a first approach, the fundamental axis that structures the universe of his works seems to be the opposition between the puffy, pretentious pathos of official Socialist ideology and the islands of everyday private life, its small joys and pleasures, laughter and tears, beyond the reach of ideology. These islands enable us to assume a distance that renders visible the ideological ritual in its vain, ridiculous pretentiousness and grotesque meaninglessness: it is not worth the trouble to recalcitrate against the official ideology with pathetic speeches on freedom and democracy. Sooner or later, this leads to a new version of the "Big March," of ideological obsession. If Kundera is reduced to this attitude, it is easy to dismiss him by confronting him with Vaclav Havel's fundamental "Althusserian" insight into how the ultimate conformist attitude is an "apolitical" distance which, while publicly obeying the imposed ritual, privately indulges in cynical irony. It is not sufficient to ascertain that the ideological ritual is a mere appearance which nobody takes seriously; this appearance is essential in its very capacity of appearance, which is why one has to take a risk and refuse to participate in the public ritual. (See Havel's famous example, from his essay "The Power of the Powerless," of a common man, a greengrocer, who of course does not believe in Socialism, and yet, when the occasion demands it, dutifully decorates the windows of his store with official Party slogans, etc.)

One therefore has to go further by taking into account the fact that there is no way to simply step out of ideology. The private indulgence in cynicism and the obsession with private pleasures are all ways in which totalitarian ideology is at work in "non-ideological" everyday life; life is determined by ideology, and ideology is "present in it in the mode of absence," if we may resort to this syntagm from the heroic epoch of structuralism. The depolitization of the private sphere in late Socialist societies is "compulsive," marked by the fundamental prohibition of free political discussion; for that reason, it always functions as an avoidance of what is truly at stake. This accounts for the feature which immediately strikes the eye in Kundera's novels: the depoliticized private sphere is in no way the free domain of innocent pleasures. There is always something damp, claustrophobic, inauthentic, and even desperate in this striving for sexual and other pleasures. In this respect, the lesson of Kundera's novels is the exact opposite of a naive reliance on the innocent private sphere: totalitarian Socialist ideology vitiates from within the very sphere of privacy in which we take refuge.

This, however, is far from being all there is to it. We must take another step here, since the lesson we learn from Kundera is even more ambiguous. Notwithstanding the dampness of the private sphere, the fact remains that the totalitarian situation gave rise to a series of phenomena attested to by numerous chronicles of everyday life in the Socialist East. In reaction to totalitarian ideological domination, there was not only a cynical escape into the "good life" of private pleasures, but also an extraordinary flourishing of authentic friendship, visits, dinners, passionate intellectual conversations in closed societies—features which usually fascinated visitors from the West. The problem, of course, is that there is no way to draw a clear-cut line between the two sides: they are the front and back of the same coin, which is why, with the advent of democracy, they *both* disappear. It is to Kundera's credit that he does not conceal this ambiguity: the spirit of "Middle Europe," of authentic friendship and intellectual sociability, survived in Bohemia, Hungary, and Poland only as a form of resistance against totalitarian ideological domination.

Perhaps yet another step can be ventured here. The very subordination to the Socialist order brought about a specific enjoyment, not only the enjoyment provided by our awareness of living in a universe in which there is no uncertainty since the System has (or claims to have) an answer for everything, but above all enjoying the very stupidity of the System—relishing the emptiness of official rituals and the worn-out stylistic figures of the predominant ideological discourse. (Suffice it to recall here the extent to which certain key Stalinist syntagms became ironic figures of speech even among Western intellectuals: "objective responsibility," etc. "Stalinism" confronts us with what Lacan designated as the imbecility inherent in the signifier.) The contemporary Russian composer Alfred Schnittke succeeded in exposing this feature in his opera *Life with an Idiot*. The opera tells the story of an ordinary married man (known as "I") who, as a punishment imposed by the Party, is forced to bring someone from an insane asylum to live with his family. The idiot, Vava, who has the appearance of a normal, bearded, bespectacled intellectual and prattles meaningless political phrases all the time, soon shows his true colors as an obscene intruder by first having sex with I's wife and then with I himself. Insofar as we are living in a universe of language, we are condemned to this imbecility: we can assume a minimal distance from it, thus rendering it more bearable, but we can never get rid of it.

The ambiguity of Kundera's universe in which Socialist "repression" creates the conditions for authentic happiness is perhaps best rendered at the end of *The Unbearable Lightness of Being*. Philip Kaufman's unjustly depreciated film version of the novel resorts to a temporal displacement that successfully condenses the end of Kundera's novel. Late at night, the hero, a dissident doctor exiled to the Czech countryside, returns home with his wife from a dance in a small nearby town; the last sight of them is a point-of-view shot of the dark macadam road illuminated by the lights of their truck. The film suddenly cuts to California a couple of weeks later; their friend Sabina, who lives there as a sculptor, receives a letter informing her of their death in a traffic accident while returning home from a dance, and comments that "they must have been happy at the time of their death." The film then cuts back to the previous scene, a simple continuation of the point-of-view shot, from the driver's seat, of the road into which our gaze penetrates.

The sublime effect of this last shot results from a temporal displacement: it hinges on the coexistence of the spectator's knowledge that the hero and his wife are already dead, with their forward-moving gaze on a strangely illuminated road. The point is not only that the allure of this strange illumination acquires the meaning of death, but rather that this last point-of-view shot belongs to people who are still alive, although we know that they are already dead. After the flash-forward to California informing us of their death, the hero and his wife dwell in the domain "between two deaths"—the same shot which was, prior to the flash-forward, a simple point-of-view shot of living subjects, now renders the gaze of the "living dead."

Notes

1. See pp. 197–198. For a reading of this passage, see chapter 5 of Slavoj Žižek, *Tarrying with the Negative*, Durham, Duke University Press, 1993.

2. The same procedure was applied by Tim Burton in the outstanding credits-sequence of *Batman*: the camera errs along nondescript, winding, unsmooth metal funnels; after it gradually backs off and acquires a "normal" distance from its object, it becomes clear what this object actually is: the tiny Batman badge.

3. The counterpart to this Lynchian attitude is perhaps the philosophy of Leibniz: Leibniz was fascinated by microscopes because they confirmed to him that what appears from the "normal," everyday point of view to be a lifeless object, is actually full of life. One has but to take a closer look at it, i.e., to observe the object from absolute proximity: under the lens of a microscope, one can perceive the wild crawling of innumerable tiny living things. Cf. chapter 2 of Miran Bozovic, *Der grosse Andere: Gotteskonzepte in der Philosophie der Neuzeit*, Vienna and Berlin, Turia und Kant, 1993.

4. The exception is provided here by the naked body of Isabella Rossellini towards the end of *Blue Velvet*: when, after the endured nightmare, she leaves the house and approaches Jeffrey, it is as if a body belonging to another, dark, nightly, infernal realm all of a sudden found itself in our "normal" daily universe, out of its own element, like a stranded octopus or some other creature from the deep sea—a wounded, exposed body whose material presence exerts an almost unbearable pressure on us.

5. It was Chaplin's Great Dictator which already bore witness to a homologous disturbance in the relationship between the voice and the written word: the spoken word (the speeches of the dictator Hynkel) is obscene, incomprehensible, and absolutely incommensurate with the written word.

6. See Michel Chion, *David Lynch*, Paris, Cahiers du Cinema, 1992, especially pp. 108–117 and 227–228.

7. For a more detailed reading of these lines from *Richard II*, see chapter 1 of Slavoj Žižek, *Looking Awry*, Cambridge, MIT Press, 1991.

8. As to this logic, see Lacan's Seminar XX.

9. In the analysis of films, it is therefore crucial to expose homogeneous, continuous, diegetic reality as a product of "secondary elaboration," i.e., to discern in it the part of (symbolic) reality and the part of fantasy hallucination. Suffice it to recall *Home Alone*. The entire film hinges on the fact that the boy's family—his proper intersubjective environs, his Other—and the two burglars that threaten him when the family is away *never cross paths*. The burglars enter the scene when the boy finds himself alone, and when, at the end of the film, the family returns home, all traces of the burglars' presence almost magically evaporate, although, as a result of their confrontation with the boy, practically the entire house should lie in ruins.

The very fact that the burglars' existence *is not acknowledged by the Other*, un-doubtedly bears witness to the fact that we are dealing with the boy's fantasy. The moment the two burglars enter the scene, we change terrain and jump from social reality into the fantasy universe in which there is neither death nor guilt; into the universe of silent slapstick pictures and cartoons, in which a heap of iron falls on your head, yet all you feel is a slight bump; in which a gallon of gasoline explodes on your head, yet the only damage you suffer is that some of your hair is burned. Perhaps this is how one has to conceive of Macaulay Culkin's notorious scream: not as an expression of his fear of the burglars, but rather as an expression of his horror at the prospect of being thrown (again) into his own fantasy universe.

10. One also encounters this motif of a woman shaken out of her lethargic numbness where one would not normally look for it—in Henry James' *Aspern Papers*, for example. The narrator forces his way into a decaying Venetian *palazzo*, the home of two ladies, an old American who was in her youth, ages ago, a mistress of the great American poet Aspern, and her somewhat younger niece. He uses every possible ruse to obtain the object of his desire: a bundle of Aspern's unknown love letters carefully kept by the old lady. What he fails to take into account, obsessed as he is by the object of his desire, is his own impact on life in the decaying palazzo; he brings with him a spirit of vivacity which awakens the two ladies from their lethargic vegetation and even stirs up, in the younger one, sexual lust.

11. The logic here is exactly homologous to that articulated by Deleuze apropos of the Freudian duality of the pleasure (and reality) principle and its "beyond," the death-drive. (What is the depression of Lynch's heroines if not a manifestation of the death drive?) Freud's point is not that there are phenomena that cannot be accounted for by the pleasure and reality principle (it is easy for him to demonstrate, apropos of every example of "pleasure in pain," apparently running counter to the pleasure principle, the hidden narcissistic gain conveyed by the renunciation of pleasure), but rather that, *in order to account for the very functioning of the pleasure and reality principles*, we are obliged to posit the more fundamental dimension of the "death drive" and the compulsion-to-repeat which hold open the space where the pleasure principle can exert its rule. Cf. Gilles Deleuze, "Coldness and Cruelty," in *Masochism*, New York, Zone Books, 1991.

12. This "unaccountability" is what Freud was aiming at with his concept of overdetermination: a contingent external cause can trigger unforeseen catastrophic consequences by stirring up the trauma which always already glows under the ashes, i.e., "insisting" in the unconscious.

13. This suspension of linear causality is at the same time the constitutive feature of the symbolic order. In this respect, the case of Jon Elster is very instructive. Within the framework of the "objective" socio-psychological approach, Elster endeavors to isolate the specific level of mechanism, located between a merely descriptive or narrative ideographic method and the construction of general theories: "A mechanism is a specific causal pattern that can be recognized after the event but rarely foreseen. . . . It is less than a theory, but a great deal more than a

description" (Jon Elster, *Political Psychology*, Cambridge, Cambridge University Press, 1993, pp. 3 and 5). The crucial point missed by Elster is that "mechanisms" are not simply in between, i.e., they do not occupy the middle post on the common scale at whose extremes we find true universal theory with predictive power and mere description. Rather, they constitute a separate domain of symbolic causality whose efficiency obeys radically different laws. The specificity of "mechanisms" consists in the fact that the same cause can trigger opposite effects: if people cannot have what they would like to have, they sometimes simply prefer what they have, or, on the contrary, they prefer what they cannot have for the very reason that they cannot have it; if people follow a certain habit in one sphere, they sometimes tend to follow it in other spheres as well (the "spillover effect"), or, on the contrary, they act in other spheres in an opposite way (the "crowding-out effect"); etc. This fact that we can never ascertain in advance how the causes which determine us will exert their causal power over us has nothing whatsoever to do with insufficient generality and unpredictability due to overcomplexity. What we are dealing with is the specific symbolic causality in which the subject, in a self-reflective way, determines which causes will determine him or her or determines the causes of what will be the causes that determine him or her. On this problematic of the gap between cause and effect, see Jacques-Alain Miller's unpublished seminar *Cause et consentement* (1987–88).

PART V

REPETITION

THE REAL CAUSE OF REPETITION

Bruce Fink

In Seminar XI, Lacan sustains that repetition is one of the four fundamental concepts of psychoanalysis. But if, as Heraclitus says, "you can't step in the same river twice," repetition seems to be something of a misnomer, consisting in the return, not of the same, but of the different—the return of something else, something other. Thus in fact it would seem that there is no return.

For no two "things" are ever identical or exactly the same. The very fact that we can say that the same book hits the same table twice, i.e., two times, means that time has intervened, the two events being situated differently, chronologically speaking, thus constituting separate events involving objects which can be temporally distinguished.

What generally allows us to consider two things or events as identical is the signifier. All *identification*—whether in human experience or at the theoretical level—is based on the taking up of events, objects, etc. into the symbolic order, their being attributed particular words or names. It is because we have the word "blue" as part of our vocabulary that an analysand can realize that the whole series of boyfriends she's had in the course of her life shared a particular trait—blue eyes. A painter might tell us that the range of shades of blue was quite considerable, and a culture that did not have a term that covered as broad a spectrum of shades as does our English word "blue" might find no resemblance between the eyes of the series of boyfriends. But the signifier "blue" allows the English-speaking analysand to establish an identity: all her men have had blue eyes—as did her father, as the case may be.

223

Heterogeneous things may be equated because one signifier covers all
of them. At this level, repetition thus implies the "return" of something
that would be different the second time but for the signifier. You can only
step in the same river twice because you have a word or name for it—the
"Swanee River," for example.

We could imagine the analysand who identified all of her lovers as
sharing the common trait of having blue eyes getting involved with someone else, and bringing him into the series through his characteristic of
being depressed all the time, or of his having tattoos, the analysand associ-
ating them with Joni Mitchell's—"blue . . . songs are like tattoos." It is the
signifier, in its polysemy, that allows for a series to be established (allowing,
as it does, for substitutions), a metaphorical or metonymic series along
which desire can slide, endlessly pursuing difference.

Difference. Substitution establishes an equivalence between things that
are not identical. Thus substitution is not repetition. Substitution implies
dialectization, the ability to associate a term or idea with other terms and
ideas, draw relations among them, and transfer affect from one to another.
Substitution thus relies on difference, though ostensibly it establishes equiva-
lences. In common parlance, "repetition" refers to this kind of "return with
a difference," and psychoanalysis tends to make the analysand aware of ever
more of his or her repetitive object choices, relationships, scenarios, etc. by
serializing them.

Yet repetition, in its Lacanian acceptation, is the return of that which
remains self-identical, and that can only be object *a*. As soon as we enter
the signifying order, difference being at the very core of the signifier, we
cannot possibly control the identity of elements. Only the real can do the
trick.

Let us turn to Seminar XI, chapter 4, "The Network of Signifiers."
Lacan announces his discussion of repetition here as absolutely new, and as
an instance in which he's going to show us all his cards for once:

> Let us take a look, then, at how *Wiederholen* (repeating) is introduced.
> *Wiederholen* is related to *Erinnerung* (remembering). The subject in him-
> self, the recalling of his biography, all this goes only to a certain limit
> which is known as the real. If I wished to provide a Spinozian formulation
> of what is at issue, I would say *cogitatio adaequata semper vitat eandem
> rem*. An adequate or proper thought, *qua* thought [. . .] always avoids
> [. . .] the same thing. Here the real is that which always comes back to
> the same place—the place where the subject, insofar as he thinks, the *res
> cogitans*, does not encounter it. (49)

Repetition involves something which, try as one might, cannot be remembered.

Thought is unable to encounter it; what is that? It is that which is excluded from the signifying chain, but around which that chain revolves. The analysand circles around and around it in attempting to articulate what seems to be at stake, but is unable, unless the analyst points the way, to put his or her finger on it. Consider the plus/minus (+/–) symbolism Lacan develops in Seminar II and the Postface to his "Seminar on 'The Purloined Letter,' "[1] for that symbolism describes the functioning of thought—unconscious thought—in Lacan's theory.

In Lacan's example, the chain cannot hit the number 3 at a certain point. It allows returns to 1 and 2, but not to 3. This is obviously an analogy, but it helps illustrate the point that the real is what always comes back to the same place: the excluded number or letter. It comes back to the place at which the subject, insofar as s/he thinks, the *res cogitans* or thinking thing, does not encounter it — i.e., does not come across it, as it is radically excluded here. Repetition thus involves the "impossible to think" and "the impossible to say."

Automaton, described by Lacan in chapter 5 of Seminar XI, corresponds to the automatic unfolding in the unconscious of the signifying chain (like the alignment of signs that appears in the $\alpha,\beta,\gamma,\delta$ network). It involves "the return, coming back, or insistence of signs by which we turn out to be commanded by the pleasure principle." (54) Thus what is commonly referred to as repetition is nothing but the "insistence of signs." This also corresponds to the level of structure in Lacan's work.

Tuché, on the other hand, involves the encounter with the real, which is beyond *automaton*:

> The real is that which always lies behind *automaton*, and it is quite obvious, throughout Freud's research, that that is the object of his concern.
>   If you wish to understand Freud's true preoccupation as the function of fantasy is revealed to him, remember the development, so central to us, of the Wolf Man. [In the latter's case, Freud asks,] "What is the first encounter—the real—that lies behind his fantasy?" (54)

The real here is the level of causality, the level of that which *interrupts* the smooth functioning of *automaton*, of the automatic, lawlike, regulated stringing together of the subject's signifiers in the unconscious. Whereas the analysand's thoughts are destined to forever miss the real, being able merely to circle or hover around it, analytic interpretation may hit the cause, leading the analysand to an encounter with the real—*tuché*. The encounter with the real is not situated at the level of thought, but at the level at which "oracular speech" yields non-sense, that which cannot be thought.

Re-presentation

In *Beyond the Pleasure Principle*, Freud revises his two-tiered theory of the pleasure principle and the reality principle because of his experience with war-related traumas, experiences which seem to be unassimilable. Lacan mentions dreams in this context, dreams which, while supposedly embodying the dreamer's wish—and thus generally to be associated with the pleasure principle (*automaton*)—nevertheless introduce the traumatic scene in a veiled or disguised form. His comment here is very revealing:

> Let us conclude that the reality system [or reality principle], however far it develops, leaves an essential part of the real imprisoned within the snares of the pleasure principle. (55)

First of all that indicates that the Lacanian real cannot be equated with the reality principle. Lacan reiterates his equation of the primary process with the unconscious—the automatic unfolding of the signifying chain—and proposes that we situate the unconscious between perception and consciousness (56):

Perception	Unconscious	Consciousness
Vorstellung	other scene/Other/repräsentanz	reality principle
real	unconscious thought, stand-in, place-holder	ego
	primary process/pleasure principle	

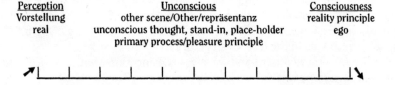

To come to consciousness a perception must pass through the filter of the symbolic order or Other.

In the dream Lacan had that he recounts in this chapter, the knocks at the door are enveloped, as it were, in the primary process constitutive of the dream, so as to allow Lacan to go on sleeping and dreaming. Something from the real appears—we might imagine that it was not even someone who had an appointment with Lacan, but Jane Gallop for example, who went to Paris to see Lacan but never met him, or the concièrge who was inadvertently knocking on the wrong door with a letter addressed to someone else.

Upon awakening, he reconstitutes himself—as ego—around the knocking; he reconstructs his whole representation of the world, his whole representational self, around the knocks. In other words, the end of the schema, consciousness, is not a permanent feature in any sense, but something which must be constantly reconstructed: the ego.

In talking about a different dream—from Freud's *Interpretation of Dreams*—Lacan says:

> The real has to be sought beyond the dream—in what the dream has enveloped, hidden from us, behind the lack of representation of which there is only one representative. (60)

Thus the real cannot be found plainly and simply in a dream—it is always disguised, padded, or clothed. While Lacan seems to perhaps be suggesting prior to that sentence that the real can be directly encountered in a dream—at least more easily than in any other state, certainly not in conscious activity—here he makes it clear that there is no direct encounter with the real even in a dream: the real's representation is lacking and what we find in the dream is its place-holder, its stand-in.

What is representation? This question alone would warrant a book-length study of the French terms *représentation* and *se représenter* and the German term they are generally used to translate, *Vorstellung*. Here representation seems to refer to a presence or image; in English it is usually translated as "idea," but clearly an idea is at the level of thought, thus of the signifier. *Vorstellung* is that which is represented by signifiers; it is not the signifiers themselves. It seems to be a real presence or image which can never be rendered in words.

One might be tempted to think that it is the "true thought" which is missing, but it seems that *Vorstellung* here is more likely at the level of the unthinkable, unnamable, unspeakable.

The dream Lacan is commenting on here is the one Freud recounts where a father whose son has died goes in the next room to sleep, leaving an old man to watch over his son's body. The old man falls asleep, and a falling candle sets fire to the body. The father in the next room simultaneously has a dream that the son is alive, and comes over to him to say, "Father, can't you see I'm burning?"

The real here, as Lacan describes it, is the death of a child—everything implied for a parent, in this case the father, by his child's death. In the dream the child is represented as alive and speaking to the dreamer. This complex series of elements takes the place of the "true referent," so to speak, death. The referent is, in this sense, always absent or missing: unpresented. It is, however, pointed to by a kind of index; a *representative* of that referent appears in the dream. It is represented but never presented.

Repräsentanz—Symbolic

Vorstellung—Real

It is the missing *Vorstellung* (missing in the symbolic, in the representational space of the dream—not something missing in the real) that leads to repetition. It thus seems to be situated at the same level as the lost object—

the object that never *was*, as such, but which is retroactively constituted as having had to have been lost. Lacan translates Freud's *Vorstellungsrepräsentanz* as *représentant de la représentation* or *tenant-lieu de la représentation*, i.e., as representative of (the) representation or stand-in or place-holder for (the) representation. And in Seminar VII, Lacan equates the *Vorstellungsrepräsentanz* with the signifier. Now the signifier *represents* nothing in Lacan's theory—"representing a subject for another signifier," that subject being nothing but a lack or split—rather, it creates *ex nihilo*. Instead of standing in for the thing it represents, in Lacan's work the signifier creates, thereby killing what it purportedly "represents." It stands in for or represents a real that cannot speak for itself.

It is the non-representational nature of the real that brings on repetition, requiring the subject to return to that place of the lost object, the lost satisfaction. Every other satisfaction pales in comparison with the one that was lost, and the subject repetitively returns to the site of that absence in the hope of obtaining the *real Thing*, and yet forever missing it.

Let me try to illustrate my interpretation of *Vorstellungsrepräsentanz* with an example from *Beyond the Pleasure Principle*. Freud's grandson is playing a game with a bobbin or "reel," as it has been translated in the *Standard Edition*, which he throws into his crib, outside of his field of vision, pronouncing one phoneme, and reeling it back out of his crib and pronouncing another. Freud interprets the sounds the child makes as first attempts to pronounce the words *Fort* and *Da* in German—Gone and Here, or There and Here, but what seems essential is the simple difference between the two phonemes: i.e., the very fact that there are two.

Lacan tells us that what the child is *aiming* at in playing the game is that which "essentially is not there *qua* represented." (63) The child is aiming at a *Vorstellung* which is not there, and the binary opposition of phonemes arises to take the place of that particular *Vorstellung*. What is that *Vorstellung*? It seems to have to do with the comings and goings of the child's mother (and Freud views the game as an attempt to master or gain control over the mother's comings and goings), but Lacan stresses that it is the constitution of the child himself as subject that is at stake.

We have here in this game the birth of the signifier (in the form of an opposition between two signifiers, S_1 and S_2), the barred subject, object *a*, etc.

$$\frac{S_1 \ (Fort)}{\math$} \longrightarrow \frac{S_2 \ (Da)}{a}$$

The missing *Vorstellung* seems to be the split subject and the lost object—which Lacan equates here: the reel is both the subject and object *a*. (62) The latter two *will have been* split and lost respectively once *Da* has followed *Fort*, the real being nothing but an after thought.

Note

1. For a much fuller discussion of that symbolism, see my article "The Nature of Unconscious Thought or Why No One Ever Reads the Postface to Lacan's 'Seminar on "The Purloined Letter" ' " in the companion volume to this one, *Reading Seminars I and II: Lacan's Return to Freud*, Albany: SUNY Press, forthcoming. See also Appendices I and II of my *Subject, Object, and Other: Crucial Concepts of Lacanian Psychoanalysis*, Princeton: Princeton University Press, 1995.

PART VI

DISCOVERY AND PSYCHOANALYTIC PRACTICE

INTRODUCTORY TALK AT SAINTE-ANNE HOSPITAL

Jacques-Alain Miller

When Françoise Gorog phoned last week to remind me I was to take part in this seminar at Sainte-Anne, I was with a patient who was making a discovery in the course of his analysis. For my talk today, let me take his discovery as a starting point for some considerations on psychoanalysis.

What was the nature of his discovery? My patient noticed that all the people he had loved, or more exactly, all the people to whom he had been sexually attracted had the same feature. His discovery was the realization of this feature and, as he said, it occurred to him like a flash of light; as a matter of fact, since then he has seen his life in a new light. He feels that in some way he has stumbled on the secret of his life as well as having uncovered the stumbling block in his love life.

Discoveries happen in the course of analysis. In this case, it happened after quite a long time. He had already been with me three years after previous analyses. Thus in spite of the fact that it appeared like a flash of lightning, the discovery was the result of his work. It didn't come at the beginning, and hence we are led to believe that the previous work was necessary to produce the discovery.

It is very difficult to qualify the structure of such a discovery. Discoveries occur in psychoanalysis, if we are to believe what our patients say. Nevertheless, it is very difficult to reconstruct, attribute a structure to, or understand such discoveries. Any reconstruction of their structure is open to question.

There is no one way of understanding this question. The English word "realization" doesn't exactly translate the French word *"réalisation."* The patient's discovery was a realization, and that implies that he became aware of something which was already there; in some way he sensed that he had finally realized something that was already there. That is the strange thing about it; the sense of omni-temporality (not eternality), the sense that something was always there of which he was unaware. He says that he discovered something and we cannot say that he invented it. To discover is to remove a veil from something that was already there. It doesn't imply creation or invention—it is experienced as an uncovering. If we say that during analysis people realize what was already there, what is the meaning of this realization?

It has been interpreted as becoming conscious of something and, when we refer to the unconscious, it seems fitting to say that something becomes conscious which was previously unconscious. We attribute to the unconscious a meaning of which the patient was unaware, assuming that what he didn't know was the content of the unconscious. Thus one way of understanding this discovery is to distinguish degrees of consciousness, the structure of such a discovery implying a move from implicit knowledge to explicit knowledge. As a matter of fact, by simply distinguishing implicit from explicit knowledge, you can already deduce a split which can be taken as a split in the subject. And you can say that this is the true structure of the unconscious, if you qualify the unconscious by its ability to become conscious. Freud has been understood this way.

Let us take a reference, which while perhaps forgotten is nevertheless very much present in French culture. Consider the rewriting of psychoanalysis by Jean-Paul Sartre, in which he identifies the bar which separates the implicit from the explicit with what he calls bad faith. In other words, he equates the unconscious with bad faith, and by this he means that in some sense the unconscious is not unconscious at all: it is merely something that is known without being accepted. It is something that one doesn't consent to; one knows, but acts as if one didn't. That is Sartre's way of understanding the unconscious; it is always possible for the unconscious to become conscious. In some ways, there is a making believe here in which the subject deceives him or herself. Sartre was, in a sense, the first to offer up a philosophy of a split subject—a subject split by bad faith.

The idea of bad faith sounds much more commonsensical than the Freudian concept of the unconscious. Where Sartre says bad faith, Freud says repression. What is the difference between bad faith and repression? We can see that there is a difference if we consider the way in which one gains access to what is under the bar. If the unconscious is merely bad faith, you gain access to what is under the bar by striving to be honest. Or, from a more Heideggerian perspective, by being authentic because authenticity is the opposite of making believe and bad faith. And you may do that through a personal decision—a personal asceticism.

But according to Freud, it's not a matter of being open, nor is it something you can do by yourself. The unconscious is not an asceticism. You need an other. It's quite mysterious, the way you need an other. If we take the example of Freud himself, it looks like he did it alone, but in fact he did it in reference to an other, his friend Wilhelm Fliess. However, the result of the work and the knowledge acquired through the process was Freud's, not Fleiss'. The fact that this process occurs in the patient, not in the dumb analyst, produces something very strange.

In Freud it's not a question of being honest, it's a matter of talking. When my patient says he discovered something, I cannot say anything about it being a matter of consciousness or insight. All I can say is that he said something—if I want to be that pure—or that he said it in a new way. And, after all, analysis is built on a series of formulations and reformulations of the same thing. It's not so strange that Lacan devised or presented us at the end of analysis with what he called "*le bien dire*." The "well-said" or "saying it well" implies that what you are looking for in analysis is to learn to say the same thing better and better until you are satisfied with it. In fact, what we call free association is no different from a "say it again." Every session is a "say it again."

You have been studying Seminar XI, and in that text the function of repetition is already present in the very method of psychoanalysis, in this "say it again; say it better; don't be afraid to repeat yourself trying to say it a little better." By stressing this "say it better," we seem to be indicating that the unconscious is not entirely the opposite of consciousness. Perhaps we can devise another kind of antimony or schema.

Perhaps we believe that the unconscious is something written, the point in analysis being to learn to read what is written better and better. If we consider this "saying it better and better" which we demand of the patient, we could place writing under the bar and reading above it. Reading is speech.

<u>Reading</u>   <u>Speech</u>
Writing   Writing

You speak in analysis, and it is as if you were reading—reading a text better and better. This would make of the unconscious a text, and analysis would not be a matter of what you mean, but a matter of reading well.

In analysis we grant a great deal of importance to slips of the tongue. A slip of the tongue is precisely a moment when it is not what you mean to say but what you don't mean to say that triumphs, as if the text were forcing itself into your speech and making you equivocate. Equivocation is also important in the act of interpretation: making the patient hear what s/he has said by making him or her repeat it. We cut the session or shorten it at some point to make the patient hear what s/he has just said in spite of what s/he meant to say, to make the patient measure the distance between what s/he meant and what s/he in fact said. When we do this, we are trying to show that something s/he said may be heard in another way. That is, we are making him or her read something else in his or her speech, and that frequently involves a reference to the written word in which different meanings may be attributed to the same letters and groupings thereof. This is only understandable by a constant reference of the spoken word to the written word. To separate speech, reading, and writing changes the value of each term.

We can say this in a third way. When you read a text, you are in the realm of meaning and the text as such is like writing—writing which is difficult to read, a transcription of a text which is legible only in parts. This third schema opposes meaning and nonsense, and we could say that in reading a text you give it meaning, but there are parts of it that you cannot read, parts which remain nonsensical. Sometimes, this nonsense manages to show through.

This is the perspective Lacan presents in his preface to the English language edition of Seminar XI. It's not exactly the view he offers in the book itself, which dates back to 1964; his preface was written in 1976, twelve years later. It's from this third perspective that he presents the unconscious in the preface. He says, "when the space of a lapsus no longer has any range of meaning, only then is one sure that one is in the unconscious. One knows."

It is also from this third perspective that he says, "There is no truth that, in passing through awareness, does not lie." As if what counts as truth at this level (under the bar) can only appear as a lie in the upper part of the schema. (This throws into question what we call discovery in analysis. The patient's new awareness is the awareness of a subject who discovers, and I would take this sentence as an index of the problem. Lacan's conclusion, which appears in parentheses in this preface, is that the unconscious is real. We will try to hone in on this strange property of the unconscious.)

Going back to the patient I mentioned earlier, what did he discover? A feature. He named a feature. As you've learned a lot about the Name-of-the-Father, let us speak about the name of the feature. As a function of naming, the feature could give us insight into the nature of clinical knowledge.

It seems to me that in psychoanalysis, clinical knowledge is inductive. Clinical knowledge first appears to be based on induction, not only to the analyst but to the patient as well. It is based on repetition, on the examination of instances in his life, and on the very constitution of the patient. From appearances and instances, the patient moves to a universal generalization. In some ways, what Freud calls "working through" is just such a process of induction. The patient develops what we could present as a sequence of words, let us call them signifiers, which appear to be infinite, potentially infinite. There is always, in the narration of one's life, a strong character of contingency. You experience your life by telling or articulating aspects of it: it was like this, but it could have been like that. I was somebody, but I could have been somebody else. What we have in the end is contingency. That is the meaning in logic of the "possible." It happened like this, but it could have happened like that. In his discovery, however, when the patient named the feature, he had a glimpse of necessity (written under the bar). That is, he glimpsed that, in spite of the fact that he could have been this or that, there was something that was necessarily the way it was. And when you discover—when you glimpse necessity in analysis—it's frequently, I won't say always, a gratifying moment for the patient. Be it hard necessity or horrible necessity, it feels like a victory over the unconscious. So writing and necessity can be situated at the same level: under the bar.

| Possibility | Reading |
| Necessity | Writing |

Lacan provided a play on words involving "necessity"—*"ne cesse"* (doesn't cease or stop)—and Lacan went on to provide the further play on words: *"ne cesse pas de s'écrire"* (always being written, not ceasing to be written). In French this phrase suggests the connection between writing and necessity. It gives analysis the meaning of reading something, something which is constantly being written through one's life.

Another way to schematize this would be to distinguish between variable and constant. There are, indeed, many ways to schematize the difference which this sense of discovery makes necessary. How can we understand and formulate the discovery of the feature? We could say that the patient had previously viewed the various love objects in his life purely as variables, as x's. Many different people may be put in this place because x is nothing but a hole in language. But what appears to be constant is the feature which I will write as a predicate, $F(x)$. The predicate "F" is the constant of this variable, and we could translate his discovery in this way: all the people he had loved, or rather desired, had this feature. It is mere implication, because the patient cannot say that it suffices to encounter this feature for desire to ensue. $F(x)$ is a written formula of constant necessity.

I made you wait before telling you the feature in question. This patient liked women. That's a rather broad feature. He desired women who had something deathly about them, something corpse-like, though perhaps barely noticeable. It seemed to him that this was the formula which gave a kind of necessity to the vagaries of his life. In their physical appearance there might be some slight lack of color, which was in some way attractive to him. Or some kind of enchanting whiteness, which he had discussed before without ever evoking its death-related signification. It could be their way of holding their bodies, some kind of strange rigidity in their way of moving, or a slowness that reminded him of the movement of inanimate objects. Or he preferred "rather skinny ones," for he discovered that skinniness was associated in his mind with death. And sometimes, he lusted after a kind of dirty quality or moral death which the woman represented for him: he loved rather bored and aloof women.

In making this discovery, he realized how he had met his wife, and why he was separating from her. He had met her at a party where she was alone. She was the only one who was alone there. Everybody was enjoying themselves except her; she was the corpse of the party. And it was of the utmost importance to him when he found out, or so he thought, that she had no sexual desire. She made no demands either, no sexual demands, and he was convinced that she experienced no pleasure. He discovered that it was essential to him that she show no sign of enjoyment. When, after having undergone analysis, his wife began to demand sexual activity from him, he wanted to get divorced—she had gone from being a corpse to being a warm body. So he discovered this fixed feature, and the meaning that went with it—death—and had the feeling he had always sought love in the cemetery. That formula was, as such, a blow to him—a love blow, a nonsensical love blow.

Strange as it may seem, as soon as he became aware of this situation, with the awareness that Lacan speaks of in the preface to Seminar XI, he tried to give it the lie. As a way of understanding this phenomenon, Lacan says: "There is no truth that, in passing through awareness, does not lie." In the same session, this patient had a fantasy of immediately finding a plump, lively lady—a choice made in relation to his mother. His mother was the opposite type from a "corpse-like" woman. She had such a lively personality that he described her as an invading force. So though he was looking for a maternal figure to care for him, he nevertheless sought women who were the opposite of his mother, the furthest from this invading person. We can thus consider his object choice as a defense against incest with his mother.

In this discovery, as the subject immediately tried to refute the very law he had just discovered, you can understand in what sense the knowledge obtained from psychoanalytic experience is conjectural knowledge. All previous cases confirmed the law he had discovered, and the patient immediately had this fantasy because he was looking for an example to refute the law. A patient is, in that sense, Popperian. He makes a conjecture, a generalization by conjecture from all previous cases, which always constitute a finite list. He makes a generalization, saying they were all thus, and then immediately looks for a negative test of this generalization. Why else would we analyze ourselves if not to make the future different from the past? My patient was thus looking for a law and then trying to give it the lie.

Along this path we follow the patient from the empirical to the logical. (Necessity does not exist at the empirical level, only at the logical level.) In order to prove that he has discovered something necessary, a test is conducted which shows that something else is possible for him. And that is exactly what this subject immediately tried to do: verify the impossible. Had he managed to verify that something else was impossible for him, he would have demonstrated that the unconscious is real. He would have encountered the fundamental, definitive obstacle which is the only proof that there is something real. Lacan asserts that "the real is the impossible." When he says in his preface to Seminar XI that the unconscious is real, in my view he means that the unconscious is supported by symbolic formulas which demonstrate impossibilities.

In clinical psychoanalysis we are always trying to connect empirical knowledge and logical structure. While we are in search of a law, the patient tries to give it the lie. On this path we follow the patient. As a matter of fact, we obtain these logical structures from the consideration of language by connecting inductive empirical knowledge with fixed, logical, linguistic structure. It is on the basis of these logical structures and their effects on speaking beings that we conceptualize clinical structures using the category $(- \phi$, minus phi) of castration. This is not something we obtain from empirical knowledge; it's something we obtain from logical, linguistic structure.

This is very much present in the case of my patient. There is a sense in which his realization is not a discovery, because he has always recalled a memory from the time he was five years old involving his father. In this memory, or rather screen memory, he was lying in the sun at his father's side. They were both naked and his father was sleeping; the five-year-old boy's penis was erect and his father's was not. This memory remained with him all his life. Through this screen memory we see that he must be the one who has sexual desire. The couple here is not the patient and his mother, nor the patient and many women, but father and son. It appears to be essential to him that this castrated father is at the same time a sleeping father. This may remind us of the defenseless, sleeping father in *Hamlet*, who is so easily killed. The patient's father died at an early age, and was in fact already dead to the patient as his desire was dead. The patient idealized that desire, all the more so in that the form of his ideal was a desireless father. In some way, he transferred this desirelessness onto his love object. The father doesn't sense his son's desire, which perhaps explains the intensity of his sexual life. With his father asleep, the patient could freely engage in sexual pursuits. Perhaps we could understand this better by modifying Freud's famous line "Father, can't you see I'm burning," by saying, "Father, can't you see I'm a man." (Perhaps we could even find some way of adding "on fire.") The patient viewed this as an alternative which always protected him from homosexuality. All of this could also be understood as a defense against incest with his father.

The important thing is that there is only one phallus in the game. The patient's love of death was an incarnation of the phallus—the dead phallus. He always chose women as love objects, as they don't have this organ. But he needed to reinforce "natural castration," as if paternal castration had to double the so-called natural castration of women. We could say that he doubled the castration of the subject with the Other-with-no-lack, so that he finally had the feeling that his love life had been nothing but necrophilia and that jouissance had to be for him alone.

There is another famous case in which this function appears, that of André Gide about whom Lacan wrote in his *Écrits*. In Gide's case, this function is put to use differently. For Gide, desire was also connected with death, and death was present in all of his being for everyone to see. From an early age on he was already called something like "corpse-Gide." He went through life resembling death itself in some way. Lacan shows how in Gide's wife (the only wife he ever had), he had found an angel who remained a virgin and, in so doing, incarnated the dead phallus. She was the only woman in Gide's life and yet embodied the dead phallus which he could never approach. While she was the only woman, Gide had free use of his organ outside of the law with innumerable young boys who represented the exact opposite of this function. He had a very active homosexual life. On the one hand, there was the eunuch woman, the angel he couldn't touch and who he kept in this position his whole life, and on the other hand a multiplicity of young village boys. Gide, Lacan says, spent his youth between death and masturbatory eroticism, which corresponds to those two functions.

In my patient, we see a subject who has in some sense found another way out: masturbation in a corpse. It is as if in his love life, under the spell of the dead phallus, he managed, unlike Gide, to fuck the angel of death on the condition that there be no jouissance, that the angel of death take no pleasure in it. In that sense, he didn't have to worry about not being able to make her come. On the contrary, he managed to convert impotency into a type of potency and to assure his potency thereby.

You may be wondering what the clinical structure of this patient is. Sometimes he is a clear hysteric, because his woman mustn't show any desire, while he must constantly show desire and in a variety of ways in his life. He is essentially a man of capricious desire. But you could also say he is an obsessive neurotic, because he goes to great lengths to kill desire in the other. You could also say that he is fundamentally a pervert because he wants the other to be castrated, not him. But in fact it is not so much the castrated other he wants: he wants an other with no lack, who neither enjoys nor suffers. He doesn't want to divide the other. Thus perhaps we could say that, clinically speaking, he is a painter. For he paints, and in his art he manages to represent, as did Gide, and fix or stop all movement in human beings. In his paintings, there is a play between movement and an immobility that stops the people he represents in strange positions.

By way of conclusion, I would say that the unconscious—which Lacan presented at the beginning of his teaching as symbolic (structured like a language) and elsewhere as imaginary, that is, as a kind of reading of meaning—is presented in the preface to Seminar XI as real, i.e., grounded in the impossible.

I wouldn't say that the unconscious is written law. There are laws, as I have tried to show, but distinct from laws you have causes; and the cause, as Jung indicated, is inscribed exactly where the leap to generalization takes place. Change is possible for a subject in analysis precisely because of the difference between law and cause. Even when the subject has discovered the law of his other, he doesn't stop there, because he still is not sure he has discovered the cause. The cause is what is not written, or perhaps what is not yet read, but, in effect, what is not read is not written.

THE END OF ANALYSIS (I)

Anne Dunand

In my first talk here I will speak of the end of analysis. I will try to show how Lacan conceived of this moment of treatment at the time of Seminar XI.

In my second talk I will discuss the various transformations in Lacan's view of the end of analysis, and the final view evident in his teaching and writing. The very fact that Seminar XI was published in 1973 shows that its author still thought valid what he had outlined ten years earlier, and it is true that, in Seminar XI, Lacan took the first steps regarding the end of analysis that led to his later invention of the "pass" and the positing of the requirements of the final stages of analysis. If there is such a thing as the end of treatment, if analysis is not interminable, if a point can be reached where it can be described as an irreversible process, then its structure has to be defined, and what is expected has to be outlined and specified.

I would like to point out that the continuity from Seminar XI to Lacan's later writings can be seen in the preface, written in 1976, to Seminar XI. There one finds the word "pass" and its connections with Lacan's work. (ix) The "Founding Act of the School," in *Television, a Challenge to the Psychoanalytic Establishment,* was written at the same time as the last chapter of the seminar. In 1967, Lacan wrote "The October 9 Proposition Regarding the Psychoanalyst of the School." In this text, not yet available in English, he states his view of analysis. He invents a procedure to permit a kind of test or testimony. I will not go into that in any detail today because I would rather concentrate first on the pages in Seminar XI where he talks more specifically about the end of analysis. He does so in chapter 1, "Excommunication," and in chapter 20, "In You More Than You." I find it remarkable that Seminar XI is fraught with and framed by, opens with and closes with, notions of what should happen towards the end of analysis. This points out that the unfolding of analysis cannot be detached from the way an analyst has to posit him or herself in relation to the analysand, in accordance with what is to be aimed at, i.e., what is to be done in view of its termination. The very concepts Lacan considers to be fundamental in psychoanalysis are caught up in this framework and in his definition of the end of analysis.

Something to be kept in mind when reading Seminar XI is that in the fall of 1963, Lacan announced he would give a seminar on "The Names of the Father." He gave only one lecture on this subject in November 1963 (cf. *Television*). He never adopted that title again for a seminar. Instead, a few months later, in January 1964, he started the seminar on *The Four Fundamental Concepts of Psychoanalysis*. It has been suggested that Seminar XI should be read in light of the missing seminar on "The Names of the Father." In the meantime, Lacan had taken a radical stand against the International Psychoanalytical Association (IPA). He was forced to leave it, or "excommunicated" as he puts it. But I think of Lacan as having resigned from the IPA because it is quite clear he would have been kept on as a member if he had agreed to modify his way of analyzing and teaching. I think this is a capital point, because it shows he would not compromise on his method of analyzing and teaching, and the main difference between him and the members of the IPA was that he did not accept identification with the analyst as either a means or an end in analytic treatment.

There is an other important issue in Seminar XI and that is that Lacan distances himself from Freud's position. We see an instance of this structural disagreement with Freud when Lacan stresses that Freud is concerned with desire as an object. (13) There Lacan is referring to one of his own earlier conceptions of desire, for he first states that the subject's desire is for the Other's desire. He does not eliminate this view altogether, but certainly modulates its meaning. What an analyst has to bring forth in analysis is the object as cause of desire.

The analyst's position is completely transformed if s/he no longer occupies the place of the desired object but rather the place of the object that causes desire. The encounter with the object is always missed, always fails, and one must separate from the object as cause. As long as the analyst serves as the object of desire, or acts as if s/he were that object, transference can only be a repetition of past events and the end of analysis can only be prepared in terms of identification. But if the analyst occupies the place of the object that causes desire, the aim of analysis is no longer a renewed alienation due to the adoption of an ideal object; it becomes detached from ideals, and leads—via separation—to a detachment from the object. I will not go any further into the subject of alienation and separation here because Éric Laurent is devoting two lectures to it.

In the first chapter of Seminar XI, Lacan refers to himself as having been made the object of a deal. He reduces the IPA's antagonism towards him by framing the problem that is really at stake: "What can, what must be expected of psychoanalysis, and what if this expectation proves to be a hindrance, to what extent does it lead to some kind of failure?" (6) What we might ask regarding the word "failure" here is, "What is it that has to fail?" If the analyst's role (e.g., Lacan's) is to occupy the place of object *a*, what has to fail is the maintenance of the analyst in the position of an ideal. This is why Lacan creates a structure for his school that eliminates such idealization, and when he explicitly compares the IPA to the Church he denounces the religious structure of past psychoanalytic communities. His strivings to construct another basis for psychoanalytic praxis are linked to his desire to create a purely lay group, not only attracting people who are not medical doctors, as Freud had tried to do, but also introducing people who do not practice analysis as a profession, non-analysts.

"If the praxis of analysis does not belong to the religious domain, can it be instated in the scientific field?" (7) Lacan answers that question in very elaborate terms, but his main concern is to raise another question: "What is the analyst's desire?" While this question is left out of science, it is of the utmost importance in analysis. It is because of his desire that Freud was able to create psychoanalysis and encounter the unconscious. And yet this desire has to find its expression and use strictly in language.

The tension between language and the object is developed in these first pages that introduce the four fundamental concepts, as the core of the transmission of psychoanalysis from the analyst to the analysand. What is the analyst's desire, and what does the transmission of psychoanalysis from the analyst to the analysand involve? What does transmission actually effect through the analysis of a subject, if it is not the particular tension between object and language, where a subject has to take a stand at a certain point?

The training of an analyst has nothing to do with age, experience, or a certain number of successful cases. Lacan states that training is complete only when a subject emerges as the agent of a particular desire, the analyst's desire. This has to take place at the end of the treatment.

In the last chapter of Seminar XI one finds a series of queries, one of which is: how can the love object become the object of desire? Such a transformation has to take place during analysis, because the love object is identified with, whereas the object of desire has to emerge as such. A similar point is made in Seminar XX, and I would suggest that in Seminar XI we see some of the main lines Lacan develops later.

What, Lacan asks at the beginning of the last chapter of Seminar XI, is the peculiar truth the praxis of psychoanalysis brings to light? Is the psychoanalyst an impostor? How can object *a* be the equivalent of the search for truth in science, but on a subjective and not on a universal level? How can psychoanalysis have any bearing on sexuality, since it deals with drives only to the extent that they are present in words or propositions? How does one get rid of transference? Does the expression "liquidation of transference" have any real meaning? Does it mean that, at the end of an analysis, there is no unconscious any more, since transference is the enactment of the reality of the unconscious? (146) Or is it the subject-supposed-to-know that must be liquidated as such? (264) Is there a type of transference that does not effectuate this stitching up of the unconscious? What is left over from transference onto the analyst?

To get an idea of what Lacan is aiming at, we have to note that in this chapter there are two definitions of love. One refers to narcissistic love: "as a specular mirage, love is essentially a deception." And at the end we have another definition of love as limitless, because it is outside the limits of the law. As a phenomenon, love, whether narcissistic or not, is always experienced as boundless. Therefore the distinction Lacan makes is difficult to grasp. But, perhaps we can, through an analogy, distinguish two types of satisfaction. In one case, the subject sees him or herself in relation to his or her ideals, and manages to satisfy those ideal images. In analysis, the analyst is at first put in the place of the ideal, and the subject loves the analyst and him or herself, as the ideal ego relates to the ego-ideal. But the subject does not obtain satisfaction in analysis at that level. The analyst has to situate him or herself and regulate transference in such a way that the greatest possible distance is maintained between the ideal and object *a*. No identification with the analyst is thus possible, and the subject experiences a gap; s/he misses the object, becoming the lack thereof. Thus love as narcissistic is watered down.

As an example of an object Lacan chooses the gaze; it is important to note that he states that the gaze is already there, just as he states that the symbolic is already there, determining the subject, subjecting him to the Other's signifiers. Likewise, the subject is also captured by the object of an Other that is already there, that s/he is bent on incarnating.

Going back to Freud's view of hypnosis (in *Group Psychology and the Analysis of the Ego*) as a process of putting a shining object in the place of an ideal, a lot was discovered about the unconscious. But it was only by renouncing hypnosis that analysis could truly get underway, i.e., by not putting object *a* in the place of the ego-ideal, but by separating from object *a*. I would like to emphasize this because a number of people think their analysis is over once they have instated object *a* in the place of their ideal. They cleave to this representation, which is tantamount to putting a negative sign in front of the ideal and acting accordingly, as if they were the cause of their analyst's desire, until they realize that this belief in impersonating the cause of desire is of no substance. In such a case, nothing has really changed: the analyst still embodies object *a*, embodying the patient's object in an inverted hypnosis, to permit the patient to enact his or her relation to such an object. Fantasy has by no means been traversed.

The traversing or crossing of the fundamental fantasy means that object *a* has to be separated either from the patient, or from the analyst where it is first located temporarily. The drive is written $ \mathcal{S} \lozenge D $, and while Freud describes it as a grammatical structure, Lacan reduces it to a formal structure, accurately expressed by silence. It is Lacan's way of describing the drive as a revolving around the object, ever missing its aim, but nevertheless repeating its trajectory in order to obtain satisfaction.

Fantasy is the subject's only way of grasping onto reality. But the drive, embodied in object *a*, is the only extra-analytic access thereto. To make this clear we have to stress the difference between what is achieved by the drive and what is achieved by fantasy. Fantasy is a means of deriving satisfaction from any situation whatsoever, no matter how. The drive is not such a construction, because it is blind and knows not what it seeks. Lacan speaks of its opacity (273). And yet, once the traversing or crossing of the plane of identification has occurred, the fundamental fantasy becomes the drive.

We can see how the end of analysis, in order to fit in with the distinction between the real and reality, must needs be an end without identification: the unconscious can be interminably interpreted, for it is words, words, words. The drive, on the other hand, has to be experienced as an encounter with the real; but in analysis this encounter cannot be just a reminder that a drive exists. It has to be told. It must be signified by an interruption of the session or a sign of acknowledgment by the analyst, consequently creating the subject's question: "Now what? How can I speak of the unspeakable?" One cannot identify with the object; one can only space it out with signifiers around the gap. And this has to be worked through, several times, for, according to Lacan, it is not a mirage or mere illusion, it is the cause of desire. That is the only way of crossing the plane of identification. The analyst cannot be absorbed in the identification.

Furthermore, we must remember that the analyst only holds the place of object *a*, as a semblance of object *a*, modeled on object *a*. Object *a* is not a substance—as is clear in the case of the gaze, for instance, or of no-thing, nothing as an object—it is a logical consistency. The patient always has a tendency to think that the analyst is impersonating demand, which helps him or her materialize the Other's demand and the drive, and to clothe demand with the illusion that what the analyst wants is the subject's castration. It is true that the patient cannot realize what is going on until s/he recognizes his or her own castration ($). There is a difficult point in this operation where the subject is no longer represented by a signifier, but is a void; and where the analyst is just as much of a void, since the subject realizes s/he is nothing but a place holder.

An experience of the loss of all ideals goes hand in hand with the experience of the loss of all desire, since the terms do not hold anything but emptiness. However, from a phenomenological standpoint, desire is represented by anxiety.

Fortunately, as Hume would have put it, habit takes the brunt of this depersonalization, and is helped by a kind of curiosity or "wait and see" approach, that comes with the knowledge that one is hitting on some kind of truth. The drive is not reduced to just staying alive, even if it becomes a very obscure function.

Now when the subject is out of touch with desire, s/he tries to find evidence of desire in the Other, and to understand it as the requited sacrifice of a life. This passage—about which Lacan speaks in Seminar XI when he takes the example of the Holocaust, the horror of the concentration camps, as the offering of a sacrifice to some obscure divinity—is immediately followed by a categorization of three kinds of love: one (derived from Spinoza), *amor intellectualis dei,* the intellectual love of God, founds love as one man's desire, as being his essence. But it is dependent on signifiers: the divine attributes of God. This cannot be the way out for analysis, for we cannot be satisfied with a belief or reference to a proposition based on a negative fact.

The second kind of love is linked to the desire to sacrifice all that is "pathological," i.e., to suppress the object and even murder it. However, Lacan refers to Kant and Sade to show us that this gives the object, inasmuch as it is mettled with the superego or ideal, an outcome that is not ethical but that merely embraces the body of moral laws, forever destined to annihilate the drive; it is a kind of built-in turning around against the object.

Lacan points to another way out: a third kind of love that has renounced its object. A love that carries through what had already started with the paternal metaphor, a first step in the renunciation of jouissance. We can only interpret it as one specific type of sacrifice, that of the previous way of getting some pleasure or jouissance out of the relation that the subject held fast to in fantasy. The subject can then be prepared for another kind of alienation, reversing the former S_1 over $, into $ over S_1, producing the signifier that has led him so far through the deadlock of analysis.

This Lacan terms new-found knowledge, the discovery and exploration of the limits of desire, and the land of limitless love. It is the logical moment where the choice of becoming an analyst can be posited; it is also the moment at which the problem of transmission comes in. What can a subject say of such an experience? Lacan provided a certain number of tools or devices to express it.

In "Analysis Terminable and Interminable," Freud views the end of analysis pessimistically. He suggests that there is nothing that can be done to diminish the length of the process. He gives several examples, one being that of the "Wolf Man" to whom, after a long stalemate in the treatment, he had given one year to terminate; the other being that of Ferenczi, who thought analysis could be made irreversible and definitive, if one had previously analyzed negative transference, by provoking it in analysis itself.

In the case of the Wolf Man, Freud's setting of a deadline suddenly provoked memories, including the famous dream that gave the Wolf Man his name. But, as Freud notes, although the patient got better and was readier to confront difficulties and hardships later on in life, a paranoid fragment of the neurosis was left untouched. In other words, something of the unconscious was unveiled, but a fragment of the real, the core of the unconscious as it were (what Lacanians call object *a*), remained disturbingly active.

As for Ferenczi, Freud stated that, based on his own practice and experience, it was not possible to bring into the transference something that was not there and that the patient never alluded to. Here again we can measure the Lacanian venture against these odds: by impersonating object *a*, the analyst brings into the transference something quite alien to the patient's stream of thoughts, be it conscious or unconscious.

Lastly, Freud warns us that something remains forever out of the reach of analysis, the bedrock of castration, as he calls it. Lacan overrides this objection by setting as a necessary condition the subjectifying of castration. Freud's recommendation to analysts was to go through another round of analysis every five years. What has all of this led up to nowadays? To the setting up of the analyst as a model. Lacan points out this deviation and explains its origin in Freud's view of desire as an object to be attained. Lacan's answer to this is that the analyst must aim at achieving absolute difference, as he puts it in the last paragraph of Seminar XI.

This is what makes the transmission of analytic experience and praxis so difficult. How is one to discern this difference, if it is absolute, i.e., incommensurate with any other experience? How is one to describe it or sketch it as a fact to be contemplated by anyone else?

THE END OF ANALYSIS (II)

Anne Dunand

Strictly speaking, Lacan does not mention the "pass" in Seminar XI; it comes later in his work. Yet, as I pointed out in my talk last week, he was aware of the need to create such a procedure for his school, the *École freudienne de Paris*. In Seminar XI, Lacan alludes to this need: "The context is an urgent one." (31) Urgent in terms of redefining the aims and praxis of psychoanalysis, but also in rediscovering the concepts it cannot do without.

Lacan notes that two different possibilities exist after one has "obtained the satisfaction that marks the end of one's analysis" (viii): (1) A need to grant someone else's urgent request to begin analysis; (2) A choice to run "the risk of attesting to the lying truth."

In the first case, Lacan disconnects the offer of analysis from the offer of Samaritan aid. It does not spring from compassion but from a request, which has to be duly weighed, to encounter truth. What the analysand is offered is an encounter with "the real, [that] shows its antimony to all verisimilitude" (ix), an encounter with that which he has in every way avoided thus far.

In the second case, Lacan refers to another kind of request, which may sound absurd at first, since it is tied up with a pack of lies, "the mirage of truth." (viii)

It is the second task that concerns me here. There would be no "Lacan Seminar in English," and no school for that matter, if we ignored transmission, if we believed that what happens in an analysis were not transmissible, or if we contented ourselves with discovering the difference between meaning and knowledge, knowledge by acquaintance, as Bertrand Russell defines it (to translate *connaissance*), and refused to reduce it to knowledge by description (to translate *savoir*).

There would also be no recounting of clinical cases, regarding particular phases of an individual's analysis in which something changes. People do not change because they are given loads of explanations or interpretations; this merely adds to what they already know without fostering any fundamental changes. People change under the impact of the real, which dislocates the chains of associations they have built around this real. Clinical cases are interesting only inasmuch as they describe the change that occurs in the subject through his or her encounter with jouissance as real.

What can be transmitted if this aspect of psychoanalysis is left out? Psychoanalysis has at least one point in common with culture: if it is not transmitted it ceases to exist. When Lacan laid down the foundations of the pass, he termed the driving force behind such a wish "enthusiasm." The desire to undergo the pass is not pure, just as the analyst's desire is not pure. It doesn't have much to do with the scientific desire to discover the real as written with symbols. Yet it is something of a scientific calling, particularly when it finds its roots in the wish to convey to others how psychoanalysis worked for one individual.

There is a sense of novelty at first, and the freshness of this surprise can be just as exciting as the discovery of a new gene, or of an unknown star. Something prompts us to tell the world about such discoveries. For an individual, analysis presents a wealth of such discoveries, and the world is not the same once they have been revealed. The individual may easily find him or herself in the position of a scientific researcher when s/he tries to add his or her own stone to the edifice of knowledge.

Then why does Lacan situate psychoanalysis outside of science, and why does he, a number of years later, declare that the pass was a failure? How come most of the schools that consider Lacan their founder have so many quarrels over the pass? Why has it become such a sore point, dividing analysts into irreconcilable groups? Some supposedly Lacanian schools have discarded it altogether, while others have suppressed its consequence, namely the nomination for three years of those who undergo the pass to the post of Analyst of the School, with an obligation during that period to account for their experience.

Let us take a close look at what the pass consists of. As proposed in 1967, it does not require the analyst to report on his or her analysands, as is the case in other psychoanalytic schools. On the contrary, the analysand is asked to report on his or her own analysis; s/he has to give an account of the analyst's interventions, handling of the transference, silences, and words, and of how this affected the analysand's relation to his or her unconscious and jouissance. The analysand has to acknowledge the analyst's skill or assess his or her failures, according to his or her own judgment.

The analysand who wishes to go through the pass reports this to a *"passeur,"* a term I have chosen to translate into English by the compound word "pass-bearer," because this particular subject has been designated by his or her analyst as being in the pass at that particular moment; Lacan says that s/he *is* the pass. His or her role is to carry the message s/he has been entrusted with. S/he discloses this message to a group of people, the "Cartel of the Pass." But, in fact, there are two pass-bearers, and they give conflicting or at least dissimilar accounts, since they cannot but filter what has been told them according to their own interests and structures.

The Cartel of the Pass, made up of five persons chosen according to certain criteria that I will not go into now, listens to the pass-bearers' accounts but not the candidate's. I have chosen to translate into English the word *passant* with the word "pass-farer," rather than go on using the word "candidate," because I think it is important to stress not the nomination as Analyst of the School, but the fact that the pass-farer has to reconstruct the pass as a sort of journey. This focuses attention far more on the recollection of the moments of his analysis that have been significant.

So much for a very brief account of the procedure of the pass.

Now let us turn to the operations that have to be accomplished prior to the pass:

1) Traversing or crossing of fantasy.
2) Identification with the symptom.
3) Destitution of the subject.

I will limit myself to these operations here, even though I am aware that they do not exhaust the subject.

1) *Traversing or crossing of fantasy.* "The truth of the subject," states Lacan in the first chapter of Seminar XI (5), "does not reside in himself, but, as analysis shows, in an object that is of its nature concealed." The subject cannot be identified except by his or her particular link to the object. The so-called crossing of fantasy can be the awareness that such an indispensable object necessarily exists, for its existence determines the subject in his or her relation to jouissance and to language. This object is the only attribute of the subject that s/he unconsciously recognizes as such and that determines his or her attitude towards reality. Such an object is a factor of inertia and causes the subject to interpret or even anticipate whatever happens to him or her in the same monotonous way. It is a prefabricated mold that gives all events the same shape.

Fantasy is constructed in such a way as to protect the subject from the Other's desire, and subsequently robs him or her of whatever s/he might experience that does not fit into this mold.

To put it simply, fantasy says, "I know what the Other wants, and I can provide it." For instance, if you take Freud's article, "A Child is Being Beaten," the fantasy, after having been worked through, gradually appears to the subject's mind as stating, "The Other's wish, his desire as far as I am concerned, is to beat me." It is restated by Lacan as the barring of the subject by the chain of signifiers, but what is left out of such a chain is an unfulfilled desire. Object *a* comes to stand for that unfulfilled desire. Having to part from it, when the subject realizes the analyst is only conforming to this pattern, does not mean the subject is deprived of this pattern, but merely that s/he recognizes that all his or her strivings to get hold of such an object are useless; the object is then understood as a lure to keep desire from failing, a gap in meaning filled in with an erroneous interpretation on the subject's part.

I think that we may safely say that, in Lacan's work, "castration" refers to the absence of symbolic inscription of a sexual relationship. There is no guarantee of a sexual relationship with the Other. The Other is barred or doesn't exist as such, and is, consequently, a lacking, desiring Other. Fantasy is a means of stopping up that lack or gap.

The crossing of fantasy can be reduced to discovering that: recognizing the lack in the Other. It brings a subject to realize that the Other, albeit non-existent, requires his or her jouissance. The latter has to be sacrificed as "a thing of nothing," calculated in terms of time and work, and not necessarily a pound of flesh or the sacrifice of a life.

2) *Identification with the symptom*. Here we have to distinguish carefully between symptoms—such as agoraphobia, anorexia, and sadistic or masochistic traits—and the psychoanalytic symptom as a basic structure. The symptom in the latter sense is a clinical category, whereas the fantasy is a trans-clinical category.

Identification with the symptom (valid for obsession and hysteria, though not for perversion or psychosis) requires one to be attentive to how one always manages to obtain the same perception of the real, regardless of the guises in which it presents itself. The symptom is as systematic as Descartes' systematic doubt; it is a method, more so than Descartes', because it is at first unconscious. Being attentive to how it functions on the basis of the intertwining of a certain type of jouissance and certain master signifiers means figuring out retroactively what one had understood or done and being able to anticipate a good deal as well. Since one realizes one is incurable at that level, one learns to make do with it.

Nevertheless, it is not sufficient to say, as a pass-farer to a pass-bearer, "I am an obsessive neurotic," or "I am basically an hysteric." One has to be able to gauge the effect it has on one's perception and, especially in one's role as analyst, how it can limit one's possibilities as far as analytic action is concerned.

3) *Destitution of the subject.* If it is a necessity to be able, at a certain point in analysis, to recognize one's particular relation to castration, it is just as necessary to let go of the particular jouissance castration produces. It is probably the most difficult aim to achieve, since jouissance from castration is a protection against any possible form of castration. In analysis, the subject first has to be instituted, just as the symptom has to emerge and the fantasy has to be constructed. At the end, the subject has to bring about his or her own destitution, and his or her castration really derives from the fact that the Other is barred (what Freud described as the mother's castration). This amounts to the destitution of the subject-supposed-to-know, and it also goes against the satisfaction stemming from transference; it deprives the subject of finding him or herself lovable as an ideal ego contemplated by the ego-ideal.

But it is not the same as narcissistic deflation; it goes much further, entailing a loss of fundamental references. At this stage, ethical principles have to be reconsidered, since they were, up until then, just another way of finding approval or love as compensation for whatever renunciations the subject had imposed upon him or herself. When a subject reaches this boundary s/he can no longer ask him or herself what his or her analyst's desire is, but what range is left to his or her own desire.

In Seminar XI, Lacan emphasizes that desire is not boundless, for it finds its limit somewhere, even though it crosses the threshold of pleasure; the pleasure principle is a principle of homeostasis, limiting the range of human possibilities. (30–31)

Desire, as you know, is indestructible; pleasure is just a child of fortune. Like happiness, it happens or it doesn't. On the other hand, "after the mapping of the subject in relation to object *a*, the experience of fantasy becomes the drive." One may ask oneself how, at the end of analysis, desire and the drive can beget the idea to practice analysis, since they do not blend; rather they maintain an antagonistic relationship to one another. They aim at different levels of the good.

Can we define the particular blend of desire that emerges after analysis? We have a number of paths to follow in Seminar XI: desire for absolute difference, desire akin to the slave's desire, desire of the analyst as a pivotal point in analysis, desire as related to the Other's desire, and the desire of different psychoanalysts to become the unbarred Other (e.g., Abraham's wish to play the part of the perfect mother, and Ferenczi's to become the son and father at the same time).

Inasmuch as desire is framed by words, it is related to the drive—that is the logical structure of demand. (164) Both are related to language, and the drive is a *"konstante Kraft,"* a constant force.

The main difference between these two threads of human life is perhaps the following: the drive achieves satisfaction taking no heed of repression; it mocks repression, as Freud says. Desire is essentially dissatisfaction enjoyed. But neither of these refers to the subject's own good. This stands out even better when we consider the drive, because the object, as far as the drive is concerned, is "strictly speaking, of no importance. It is a matter of indifference." (168)

Desire for an object is conditioned by the object's attributes. Yet it cannot be said that the analyst's desire concerns any particular object in that sense. Should we then consider the analyst's desire as having no object? Lacan designated this desire as a desire to obtain absolute difference, as addressed, as it were, to alterity as such. We can perceive it, using Freud's terms, as one of the features of anaclitic love, where what is sought, as opposed to the case of narcissistic love, is love for something unknown or radically other ("On Narcissism," S.E. XIV, 69). This love of the unknown is radically different from the love addressed to the subject-supposed-to-know. It goes from what is known and has been experienced to love for what is still unknown. It is that kind of love that is at the origin of science. But the subject of desire is evacuated from science, whereas it is the main protagonist in psychoanalysis.

We can attempt to forge a sort of amalgamation between love for what we do not know—the desire for otherness, for what is not yet part of knowledge—and the drive that can exert itself in revolving around any kind of object. We may solder them together; that is the word used by Freud to describe the stuff the drive is made of: the "soldering" together of an object and a drive (*Three Essays on the Theory of Sexuality*, S.E. VII, 125).

PART VII

TRANSLATION FROM THE *ÉCRITS*

POSITION OF THE UNCONSCIOUS

remarks made at the 1960 Bonneval colloquium
rewritten in 1964

Jacques Lacan

Henri Ey—thanks to his authority, which has made him the most influential figure in French psychiatric circles—brought together in his ward at Bonneval Hospital a very broad spectrum of specialists around the theme of the Freudian unconscious (October 30 to November 2, 1960).

The talk given by my students Laplanche and Leclaire promoted at the colloquium a conception of my work, which, since the talk was published in *Les temps modernes*, has become definitive, despite the divergence between their positions manifested therein.

Interventions made at a colloquium, when there is something at stake in the debate, sometimes require a good deal of commentary to be situated.

And when the texts have been thoroughly rewritten, the task becomes an arduous one.

Its interest wanes, moreover, with the time it takes to rewrite them, for one would have to replace it with what takes place during that time considered as logical time.

In short, three and a half years later, though barely having had the leisure to monitor the interval, I made a decision that Henri Ey, in a book on the colloquium published by Desclée de Brouwer, introduced in the following way:

This text summarizes Jacques Lacan's interventions which, due to their importance, formed the axis of all the discussions.

The transcripts of these interventions have been condensed by Jacques Lacan in these pages written at my request in March 1964.[1]

I hope the reader will allow that for me this logical time has been able to reduce the circumstances, in a text extracted from a more intimate gathering, to this mention of them.

(1966)

Remarks made at a colloquium such as this, inviting philosophers, psychiatrists, psychologists, and psychoanalysts on the basis of their respective expertise, fail to agree on the level of truth of Freud's texts.

Concerning the unconscious, one must go straight to the crux of Freud's experience.[2]

The unconscious *is* a concept founded on the trail [*trace*] left by that which operates to constitute the subject.

The unconscious *is not* a species[3] defining the circle of that part of psychical reality which does not have the attribute (or the virtue) of consciousness.

There may be phenomena that are subsumed by the unconscious according to both of these acceptations; the latter remain no less foreign to each other. The only relation between them is one of homonymy.

The importance I attribute to language as cause of the subject requires that I be more specific: aberrations abound when the concept "unconscious" is depreciated by being applied to phenomena *ad libitum* that can be classified under the homonymous species [*espèce*]. It is unthinkable that the concept might be restored on the basis of these phenomena.

Let me specify my own position concerning the equivocation to which the "is" and "is not" of my initial positions might give rise.

The unconscious *is* what I say it is,[4] assuming we are willing to hear what Freud puts forward in his theses.

Saying for Freud the unconscious *is not* what goes by that name in other contexts could be of little value if what I meant were not grasped: the unconscious, prior to Freud, *is not* purely and simply. That is because it names nothing [prior to Freud] that counts any more as an object—nor warrants being granted any more existence—than what would be defined by situating it in the "un-black" [*l'in-noir*].

The unconscious before Freud has no more consistency than this un-black—*viz.* the set of what could be classified according to the various meanings of the word "black," by dint of its refusal of the attribute (or virtue) of blackness (whether physical or moral).

What indeed could the following possibly have in common—to take the eight definitions reviewed by Dwelshauvers in a book that is old (1916),[5] but not so far out-of-date that, were such a catalogue to be prepared anew today, its heterogeneity would not be diminished: the sensory unconscious (implied by the effects of contrast and of so-called optical illusions); the automatic unconscious developed by habit; the co-consciousness[6](?) of split personalities; ideational emergencies of an oriented latent activity which imposes itself [upon consciousness] as in creative thought, and telepathy, which certain people would like to relate to the latter; the learned and even integrated reserves of memory; the passions in our character that get the better of us; the heredity that is recognized in our natural gifts; and finally the rational or metaphysical unconscious that is implied by "mental acts"?

(None of them can be grouped together, except confusedly, because of what psychoanalysts have added by way of obscurantism in failing to distinguish the unconscious from instinct, or, as they say, from the instinctual—the archaic or primordial, succumbing thereby to an illusion decisively dispelled by Claude Lévi-Strauss—and even from the genetics of a supposed "development.")

My claim is that they have nothing in common if one grounds oneself in psychological objectivity, even if the later is derived by extension from the schemas of psychopathology, and that this chaos merely reflects psychology's central error. This error consists in taking the very phenomenon of consciousness to be unitary, speaking of the same consciousness—believed to be a synthetic faculty—in the illuminated area of a sensory field, in the attention which transforms it, in the dialectic of judgment, and in ordinary daydreaming.

This error is based on the undue transfer to these phenomena of the value of a thought experiment which uses them as examples.

The Cartesian *cogito* is the major, and perhaps terminal, feat of this experiment in that it attains knowledge certainty. But it all the better exposes that which privileges the moment upon which it is based, and proves how fraudulent it is to extend its privilege to phenomena endowed with consciousness, in order to grant them a status.

For science, the *cogito* marks, on the contrary, the break with every assurance conditioned by intuition.

And the much sought-after [*recherchée*] latency of this founding moment, as *Selbstbewusstsein* [self-consciousness], in the dialectical sequence of Hegel's phenomenology of mind, is based upon the presupposition of absolute knowledge.

Everything, on the contrary, points to the distribution of consciousness in psychical reality—however the latter's texture is ordered—consciousness being heterotopic in terms of levels and erratic at each level.

The only homogeneous function of consciousness is the imaginary capture of the ego by its specular reflection, and the function of misrecognition [*méconnaissance*] which remains linked to it.

The negation [*dénégation*][7] inherent in psychology in this regard should rather, following Hegel, be chalked up to the law of the heart and the delusion of presumption.

The subvention received by this perpetuated presumption, to consider only what it receives in the way of scientific honors, raises the question of where its value is situated; it cannot come down to the mere publication of more or less copious treatises.

Psychology transmits ideals: the psyche therein no longer represents anything but the sponsorship [*parrainage*] which makes it qualify as academic. Ideals are society's slaves.

A certain kind of progress in our own society illustrates this, when psychology furnishes not only the means, but even defers to the wishes of market research.

When a market study had concluded upon the proper means by which to sustain consumption in the U.S.A., psychology enlisted, enlisting Freud along with it, to remind the half of the population most exposed to business' goal that women only realize their potential through gender ideals (cf. Betty Friedan on the directed wave of the *Feminine Mystique*,[8] in that postwar decade).

Perhaps psychology, through this ironic channel, reveals why it has always subsisted. But scientists may recall that the ethics implicit in their training commands them to refuse all such blatant ideology. The unconscious as understood by psychologists is thus debilitating for thought, due to the very credence thought must lend it in order to argue against it.

Now the debates that have taken place during this colloquium have been remarkable in that they have constantly turned to the Freudian concept in all its difficulty, and have derived their very strength from this difficulty.

That is remarkable inasmuch as psychoanalysts' only endeavor, in today's world, is to enter psychology's ranks. The aversion everything coming from Freud meets with in their community has been plainly avowed, especially by a subset [*fraction*] of the psychoanalysts present.

This fact cannot be excluded from the examination of the issue at hand. No more than can another fact: that it is due to my teaching that this colloquium has reversed the trend. I am saying this not merely to make mention of the fact—many have done so—but also to note that this obliges me to account for the paths I have followed.

What psychoanalysis finds itself enjoined to do when it returns to the fold of "general psychology" is to sustain what deserves to be exposed—right here and not in the far-off realms of our former colonies—as primitive mentality. For the kind of interest that psychology comes to serve in our present society, of which I have given an idea, finds therein its advantage.

Psychoanalysis thus underwrites it by furnishing an astrology that is more decent that the one to which our society continues to surreptitiously sacrifice.

I thus consider justified the prejudice psychoanalysis encounters in Eastern Europe. It was up to psychoanalysis not to deserve that prejudice, as it was possible that, presented with the test of different social exigencies, psychoanalysis might have proved less tractable had it received harsher treatment [*elle s'y fût trouvée moins traitable d'être plus mal traitée*]. I gauge that on the basis of my own position in psychoanalysis.

Psychoanalysis would have done better to examine its ethics and learn from the study of theology, following a path indicated by Freud as unavoidable. At the very least, its deontology in science should make it realize that it is responsible for the presence of the unconscious in this field.

This function was served by my students at this colloquium, and I have contributed thereto in accordance with the method that I have constantly adopted on such occasions, situating each in his position in relation to the subject. The main axis is sufficiently well indicated in the recorded responses.

It would be of some interest, if only to the historian, to have the transcripts of the talks actually given, even if they were cut where blanks appeared due to defects in the recording devices. They underscore the incompetence of he whose services designated him as the person who could highlight with the greatest tact and accuracy the detours of a moment of combat in a place in which ideas were exchanged—his connections, his culture, and even his social savvy [*entregent*] allowing him to understand better than anyone else the recordings with the intonations. His failings [*défaillance*] already ensconced him in the good graces of defection.[9]

I do not deplore the occasion that was missed, everyone having since taken ample advantage of a time-worn practice, carefully reworking his presentation. I will take advantage of the occasion to explain my present doctrine of the unconscious, all the more legitimately as the resistances of a peculiar allocation of roles impeded me from saying more about it then.

This consideration is not political, but technical. It has to do with the following condition, established by my doctrine: psychoanalysts are part and parcel of the concept of the unconscious, as they constitute that to which the unconscious is addressed. I thus cannot but include my discourse on the unconscious in the very thesis it enunciates: the presence of the unconscious, being situated in the locus of the Other, is to be sought in every discourse, in its enunciation.

The very subject of the agent who sustains this presence—if he is an analyst—must, according to this hypothesis, in the same movement be given form [*informé*] and "thrown into question," in other words, experience his subjection to splitting by the signifier.

Hence the sense of an arrested spiral one finds in the work presented by my students, Serge Leclaire and Jean Laplanche. For they limit it to the testing of a spare part [*pièce détachée*].

And that is the very sign that my statements[10] are, in all their rigor, made firstly for the function they only *serve* in their stead.

In the introductory phase, one can illustrate the effect of enunciation by asking a student if he can imagine the unconscious existing in animals, unless they have some degree of language [*à moins de quelque effet de langage*]—human language. If he indeed agrees that that is the condition which would allow him to at least consider the possibility, you have verified that he distinguishes between "unconscious" and "instinct."

Propitious initial omen, for if we were to call upon every analyst as well, regardless of the doctrine he was most trained in, and ask him whether, in fulfilling his role (bearing the patient's discourse, restoring the effect of meaning, throwing himself into question [*s'y mettre en cause*[11]] by responding, as well as by remaining silent), he ever had the feeling he was dealing with anything like an instinct—could he say yes?

Reading analytic writings and official translations of works by Freud (who never wrote the word "official") that use the term "instinct" all across the board, there is perhaps a point in obviating a rhetoric which obturates the concept's effectiveness. The style appropriate for a paper on [analytic] experience does not constitute the whole of theory. But it guarantees that the statements by which analytic experience operates preserve within themselves the backward movement [*recul*[12]] of enunciation in which the effects of metaphor and metonymy are constituted, i.e., in accordance with my theses, the very mechanisms Freud described as those of the unconscious.

But here the question is legitimately raised: are they effects of language or of speech? Let us assume that the question here only assumes the outlines of Saussure's dichotomy. Directed at what interests Saussure—effects on language [*la langue*]—it supplies warp and woof to what is woven between synchrony and diachrony.

When it is directed at what throws us into question (as much as he who questions us, if he is not already lost in the stays of his question), namely the subject, the alternative [language or speech] proposes itself as a disjunction. Now it is this very disjunction that provides us with the answer, or, rather, it is in constituting the Other as the locus of our answer—the Other furnishing the answer in a form that inverts the question into a message—that we introduce the effective disjunction on the basis of which the question has meaning.

The effect of language is to introduce the cause into the subject. Through this effect, he is not the cause of himself; he bears within himself the worm of the cause that splits him. For his cause is the signifier, without which there would be no subject in the real. But this subject is what the signifier represents, and the latter cannot represent anything except to another signifier: to which the subject who listens is thus reduced.

One therefore does not speak to the subject. It[13] speaks of him, and that is how he apprehends himself; this is all the more necessary in that, before he disappears as subject beneath the signifier which he becomes, due to the simple fact that it addresses him, he is absolutely nothing. But this nothing is sustained by his advent, now produced by the appeal made in the Other to the second signifier.

As an effect of language, in that he is born of this original split, the subject translates a signifying synchrony into this primordial temporal pulsation that is the constitutive fading of his identification. That is the first movement.

But in the second, desire—bedding down in the signifying cut in which metonymy is effectuated, the diachrony (called "history") which was inscribed in fading—returns to the kind of fixity Freud assigned to unconscious wishes (see the last sentence of the *Traumdeutung* [*The Interpretation of Dreams*]).

This secondary subornation[14] not only closes[15] the effect of the first in projecting the topology of the subject into the instant of fantasy; it seals it, refusing to allow the subject of desire to realize that he is an effect of speech, to realize, in other words, that he is but the Other's desire.[16]

That is why any discourse is within its rights not to consider itself responsible for this effect—any discourse except that of the teacher when he addresses psychoanalysts.

I have always considered myself accountable for such an effect, and, while unequal to the task of overcoming it [*d'y parer*], it was the secret prowess of each of my "seminars."

For the people who come to hear me are not the first communicants Plato exposed to Socrates' questioning.

That the "secondary" they come out of must be doubled with an introductory,[17] says enough about its shortcomings and superfluities. Of their "philosophy [classes]," most have retained but a grab-bag of phrases—a catechism gone haywire—that anaesthetizes them from being surprised by truth.

They are thus even more easily preyed upon by prestige operations, and by the ideals of high personalism by which civilization presses them to live beyond their means.

Intellectual means, that is.

The ideal of authority with which the medical candidate falls in; the opinion poll in which one finds the mediator of relational impasses; the meaning of meaning[18] in which every quest finds its alibi; phenomenology, a lap that awaits whatever may fall into it—the range is vast and the dispersion great at the outset of an ordered obtusion.

Resistance, equal in its effect of denial despite Hegel and Freud, misfortune of consciousness and discontent of civilization.

A χοινή[19] of subjectification underpins resistance, which objectifies the false evidence of the ego and routes every proof away from certainty and towards endless procrastination. (Should I be opposed by an appeal to Marxists, Catholics, or even Freudians, I promise to request a roll call.)

That is why only the kind of teaching that grinds up this χοινή can trace out the path of what is known as "training analysis" [*analyse didactique*], for the results of [analytic] experience are distorted by the very fact of being inscribed in that χοινή.

This doctrinal contribution has a name—it is, quite simply, "scientific spirit"—and it is altogether lacking in the places where psychoanalysts are recruited.

My teaching is anathema in that it is inscribed in that truth.

The objection that has been raised, concerning the impact of my teaching on the transference of analysts in training, will make future analysts laugh, if, thanks to me, there are still analysts for whom Freud exists. But what it proves is the absence of any doctrine of training analysis that includes the latter's relations with the affirmation of the unconscious.

It will thus be understood that my use of Hegel's phenomenology bore no allegiance to the system, but was intended as an example with which to counter the obvious fact of identification. It is in the way in which one conducts an examination of a patient and draws one's conclusions that a critique of intellectual fables [*bestiaire*] is put forward. It is by not avoiding the ethical implications of our praxis for deontology and scientific debate that the beautiful soul will be unmasked. The law of the heart, as I have said, is a bigger nuisance than paranoia. It is the law of a ruse which, in the ruse of reason, traces out a meander whose current is seriously slowed.

Beyond that, Hegel's statements, even if one sticks to the text, provide the opportunity to always say something Other,[20] something Other which corrects therein the link of phantasmatic synthesis, while preserving their effect of exposing the lures of identification.

That is my *Aufhebung* [sublation], which transforms Hegel's—his lure—into an occasion to point out, in lieu and place of the leaps of an "ideal progress," the avatars of a lack.

To confirm in its function this point of lack, nothing is better at this point than Plato's dialogue, insofar as it falls into the comic genre, does not shy away from indicating the point at which one can do nothing but oppose the "marionette's mask to wooden insults," and remains stone-faced through the centuries, rooted to a hoax, waiting for someone to find a better hold than the one it clings to [*fige*] in its judo match with the truth.

That is why Freud is a guest one can risk inviting impromptu to the *Symposium*, if only on the basis of the short note[21] in which he indicates what he owes to its clear-sightedness [*justesse*] concerning love, and perhaps concerning the tranquillity of its view of transference. No doubt he was the kind of guy who would revive its bacchanalian lines, which no one remembers having said after the drunkenness.

My seminar was not "where it speaks" [*là où ça parle*], as people said jokingly. It brought forth the *place* from which it could speak, opening more than one ear to hear things which, had they not been recognized, would have been passed over indifferently. One of my listeners put this naively, announcing the marvelous fact that, that very evening, or perhaps just the day before, he had come across in a session with a patient what I had said in my seminar—verbatim.

The place in question is the entrance to the cave, towards the exit of which Plato guides us, while one imagines seeing the psychoanalyst entering there. But things aren't that easy, as it is an entrance one can only reach just as it closes (the place will never be overrun with tourists), and the only way for it to open up a bit is by calling from the inside.

This is not unsolvable, assuming the "open sesame" of the unconscious consists in having speech effects, the unconscious being linguistic in structure,[22] but requires that the analyst reexamine the way it closes.

What we have to account for is a gap, beat, or alternating suction, to follow some of Freud's indications, and that is what I have proceeded to do in grounding it in topology.

The structure of that which closes [*se ferme*] is indeed inscribed in a geometry in which space is reduced to a combinatory: it is what is called an "edge" in topology.[23]

By formally studying the consequences of the irreducibility of its cut, one could rework some of the most interesting functions between aesthetics and logic.

One notices that it is the closing[24] of the unconscious which provides the key to its space—namely the impropriety of trying to turn it into an inside.

That closing also demonstrates the core of a reversible time, quite necessarily introduced if we are to grasp the efficiency of discourse; it is rather easily perceived in something I have been emphasizing for a long time: the retroactive effect of meaning in sentences, meaning requiring the last word of a sentence to be sealed [*se boucler*].

Nachträglichkeit (remember that I was the first to extract it from Freud's texts), *Nachträglichkeit* or deferred action [*après-coup*], by which trauma becomes involved in symptoms, reveals a temporal structure of a higher order.

But above all, experience with this closing shows that it would not be gratuitous on the part of psychoanalysts to reopen the debate over the *cause*, a phantom that cannot be exorcised from [*conjurer de*] thought, whether critical[25] or not. For the cause is not, as is said of being as well, a lure of forms of discourse[26]—otherwise it would have long since been dispelled. It perpetuates the reason[27] that subordinates the subject to the signifier's effect.

It is only as instance[28] of the unconscious, the Freudian unconscious, that one grasps the cause at the level at which Hume attempts to flush it out [*débusquer*], which is precisely the level at which it takes on consistency: the retroaction of the signifier in its efficiency,[29] which must be rigorously distinguished from the final cause.

In demonstrating that that is the only true first cause, the apparent discordance of Aristotle's four causes would dissipate; from their terrain, analysts could contribute to this reformulation.

They would have the benefit of being able to use the Freudian term "overdetermination" as something other than an evasive answer. What follows introduces the feature that commands the functioning relationship between these forms: their circular, albeit non-reciprocal, articulation.

While there is closing [*fermeture*] and entry, they do not necessarily separate: they provide two domains with a mode of conjunction. They are the subject and the Other, respectively, and these domains are only to be substantified here on the basis of my theses concerning the unconscious.

The subject, the Cartesian subject, is the presupposition of the unconscious—I have shown that elsewhere.

The Other is the dimension required in order for speech to affirm itself as truth.

The unconscious is, between the two of them, their cut in act.

This cut is seen to command the two fundamental operations with which the subject's causation should be formulated. These operations are ordered in a circular, yet non-reciprocal, relationship.

The first, alienation, constitutes the subject as such.[30] In a field of objects, no relationship is conceivable that engenders alienation apart from that of the signifier. Let us take for granted that no subject has any reason to appear in the real except for the fact that speaking beings exist therein. A physics is conceivable that accounts for everything in the world, including its animate part. A subject intervenes[31] only inasmuch as there are, in this world, signifiers which mean nothing and must be deciphered.

To grant priority to the signifier over the subject is, in my book, to take into account the experience Freud opened up for us: the signifier plays and wins, if I may say so, before the subject is aware of it, to such an extent that in the game of *Witz*, in puns, for example, it may surprise the subject. What it lights up with its flash is the subject's division from himself.

But the fact that the signifier reveals to the subject his own division should not make us forget that this division derives from nothing other than that very same play, the play of signifiers—signifiers, not signs.

Signs are polyvalent: they no doubt represent something to someone, but the status of that someone is uncertain, as is that of the supposed language of certain animals, a sign language which neither allows for metaphor nor engenders metonymy.

This someone could, by some stretch of the imagination, be the universe, insofar as information, so we are told, circulates therein. Any center in which information is added up [*se totalise*] can be taken for a someone, but not for a subject.

The register of the signifier is instituted in that a signifier represents a subject to another signifier. That is the structure of all unconscious formations: dreams, slips of the tongue, and puns. The same structure explains the subject's originary division. Produced in the locus of the yet to be situated Other, the signifier brings forth a subject from a being that cannot yet speak,[32] but at the cost of freezing[33] him. The ready-to-speak [*prêt à parler*] that *was to be* there—in both senses of the French imperfect "*il y avait*," placing the ready-to-speak an instant before (it was there but is no longer), but also an instant after (a few moments more and it would have been there because it could have been there)[34]—what *was to be* there disappears, no longer being anything but a signifier.

It is thus not the fact that this operation begins in the Other that leads me to call it "alienation." The fact that the Other is, for the subject, the locus of his signifying cause merely explains why no subject can be his own cause [*cause de soi*]. This is clear not only from the fact that he is not God, but from the fact that God Himself cannot be His own cause if we think of Him as a subject; Saint Augustine saw this very clearly when he refused to refer to the personal God as "self-caused" [*cause de soi*].

Alienation resides in the subject's division, the cause of which I just designated. Let us proceed to discuss its logical structure. This structure is a *vel*,[35] which shows its originality here for the first time. In order to do so, it must be derived from what is known, in so-called mathematical logic, as union[36] (which has already been acknowledged to define a certain kind of *vel*).

This union is such that the *vel* of alienation, as I call it, imposes a choice between its terms only to eliminate one of them—always the same one regardless of one's choice. The stakes are thus apparently limited to the preservation or loss of the other term, when the union involves two terms.

This disjunction is incarnated in a highly illustratable, if not dramatic, way as soon as the signifier is incarnated [*s'incarne*] at a more personalized level in demand or supply: in "your money or your life" or "liberty or death."

It is merely a question of knowing whether or not (*sic aut non*) you want to keep life or refuse death, because, regarding the other term in the alternative, money or liberty, your choice will in any case be disappointing.

You should be aware that what remains is, in any case, diminished:[37] it will be life without money and, having refused death, a life somewhat inconvenienced by the cost of freedom.

That is the stigma of the fact that the *vel* here, functioning dialectically, clearly operates on the *vel* of logical union, which is known to be equivalent to an "and" (*sic et non*). This is illustrated by the fact that, in the long run, you will have to give up your life after your money, and in the end the only thing left will be your freedom to die.

Similarly, our subject is subjected to the *vel* of a certain meaning he must receive or petrification. But should he retain the meaning, the non-meaning produced by his change into signifiers will encroach on[38] this field (of meaning). This non-meaning clearly falls within[39] the Other's field, though it is produced as an eclipse of the subject.[40]

This [*la chose*] is worth saying, for it qualifies the field of the unconscious to take a seat, I would say, in the place of the analyst—let us take that literally—in his armchair. We have arrived at such a pass that we should leave him this armchair by way of a "symbolic gesture." The latter is an expression commonly used to say "a gesture of protest," and its import would be to challenge the order—so prettily avowed by its crude motto in "Francglaire" (to coin a term), directly issuing from the ἀμαθία[41] a princess perpetrated upon French psychoanalysis by replacing the Presocratic tone of Freud's precept, "*Wo es war, soll Ich werden*," with the croaking strains of—"the ego" (the analyst's no doubt) "must dislodge the id" (the patient's, of course).[42]

The fact that people have objected to Serge Leclaire's claim that the unicorn sequence[43] is unconscious, by pointing out that Leclaire himself is conscious of it, means that they do not see that the unconscious only has meaning in the Other's field. Still less do they see the consequence thereof: that it is not the effect of meaning that is operative in interpretation, but rather the articulation[44] in the symptom of signifiers (without any meaning at all) which have gotten caught up in it.[45]

Let us turn now to the second operation, in which the subject's causation closes, to test the structure of the edge in its function as limit, but also in the twist that motivates the encroachment of the unconscious. I call this operation "separation." We will see that it is what Freud called "*Ichspaltung*" or splitting of the subject, and grasp why Freud, in the text in which he introduces it ["The Splitting of the Ego"], grounds it in a splitting, not of the subject, but of the object (namely, the phallic object).

The logical form dialectically modified by the second operation is called "intersection" in symbolic logic; it is also the product formulated by a belonging *to* ___ and *to* ___ .[46] This function is modified here by a part taken from a lack situated within another lack,[47] through which the subject finds anew in the Other's desire the equivalent of what he is *qua* subject of the unconscious.

In this way, the subject is actualized[48] in the loss in which he surged forth as unconscious, through the lack he produces in the Other, following the course Freud considered to constitute the most radical drive: the "death drive," as he called it. A belonging *neither to* ___ is called upon to fill a *nor to* ___ . Empedocles' act, responding thereto, shows that a will is involved. The *vel* returns in the form of a *velle*.[49] That is the end[50] of the operation. Now for the process.

Separare, separating, ends here in *se parere*, engendering oneself. Let us dispense with the obvious gems we find in the works of Latin etymologists concerning the slippage in meaning from one verb to the other. One should simply realize that this slippage is grounded in the fact that they are both related to[51] the function of the *pars*.

The part is not the whole, as is said, though usually without thinking. For it should be emphasized that the part has nothing to do with the whole. One has to come to terms with it;[52] it plays its part [*sa partie*] all by itself. Here the subject proceeds from his partition[53] to his parturition. This does not imply the grotesque metaphor of giving birth to himself anew. Indeed, language would be hard pressed to express that with an original term, at least in Indo-European climes where all the words used for this purpose are of juridical or social origin. "*Parere*" was first of all to procure (a child for one's husband). That is why the subject can procure for himself what interests him here—a status I will qualify as "civil." Nothing in anyone's life unleashes more determination to succeed in obtaining it. In order to be *pars*, he would easily sacrifice the better part of his interests, though not in order to become part of the whole [*s'intégrer à la totalité*], which, moreover, is in no way constituted by others' interests, still less by the general interest which is distinguished therefrom in an entirely different manner.

Separare, se parare: in order to take on[54] the signifier to which he succumbs, the subject attacks the chain—that I have reduced to a binary,[55] at its most elementary level—at its interval. The repeating interval, the most radical structure of the signifying chain, is the locus haunted by metonymy, the latter being the vehicle of desire (at least that is what I teach).

It is, in any case, through this impact—whereby the subject experiences in this interval something that motivates him Other [*Autre chose*] than the effects of meaning by which a discourse solicits him—that he in fact encounters the Other's desire, before he can even call it desire, much less imagine its object.

What he will place there is his own lack, in the form of the lack he would like to produce in the Other through his own disappearance—the disappearance (which he has at hand, so to speak) of the part of himself he receives from[56] his primal [*première*] alienation.

But what he thus fills up[57] is not the lack [*faille*][58] he encounters in the Other, but rather, first of all, that of the constitutive loss of one of his parts by which he turns out to be made of two parts. Therein lies the twist whereby separation represents the return of alienation. For the subject operates *with* his own loss, which brings him back to his point of departure.

His "can he lose me?"[59] is, no doubt, the recourse he has against the opacity of the desire he encounters in the Other's locus, but it merely brings the subject back to the opacity of the being he receives through [*qui lui est revenu de*] his advent as subject, such as he was first produced[60] at the other's summoning.

It is an operation whose fundamental outlines are found in psychoanalytic technique. For it is insofar as the analyst intervenes by scanding[61] the patient's discourse that an adjustment occurs in the pulsation of the rim through which the being that resides just shy of it must flow.

The true and final mainspring of what constitutes transference is the expectation[62] of this being's advent in relation to what I call "the analyst's desire," insofar as something about the analyst's own position has remained unnoticed therein, at least up until now.

That is why transference is a relationship that is essentially tied to time and its handling. But what is the being that responds to us, operating in the field of speech and language, from just inside the cave's entrance? I would go so far as to give it body in the form of the very walls of the cave which live, or rather come alive with palpitations whose living movement must be grasped now, i.e., since I articulated the function and field of speech and language in their conditioning.[63]

I don't see how anyone can rightfully claim that I neglect dynamics in my topology; I orient it, which is better than to make a common-place of it. (The most verbal is not where people are willing to say it is.[64])

As for sexuality, concerning which people would like to remind me that it is a question of force and that that force is biological, I retort that analysts perhaps have not shed as much light as people at one time hoped on sexuality's mainsprings, recommending only that we be natural, repeatedly trotting out the same bird-brained themes.[65] I will try to contribute something newer by resorting to a genre that Freud himself never claimed to have superseded in this regard: myth.

To compete with Aristophanes on his own ground in the above-mentioned *Symposium*, let us recall his primitive double-backed creatures in which two halves are fused together as firmly as those of a Magdeburg sphere. The halves, separated later by a surgical operation arising from Zeus' jealousy, represent the beings we have become in love, starving for an unfindable complement.

In considering the sphericity of primordial Man as much as his division, it is the egg that is evoked and that has thus perhaps been repressed since Plato, given the preeminence granted for centuries to the sphere in a hierarchy of forms sanctioned by the natural sciences.

Consider the egg in a viviparous womb where it has no need of a shell, and recall that, whenever the membranes burst, a part of the egg is harmed, for the membranes of the fertilized egg are offspring [*filles*] just as much as the living being brought into the world by their perforation. Consequently, upon cutting the cord, what the newborn loses is not, as analysts think, its mother, but rather its anatomical complement. Midwives call it the "afterbirth" [*délivre*].

Now imagine that every time the membranes burst, a phantom—an infinitely more primal [*primaire*] form of life, in no wise willing to settle for a duplicate role in some microcosmic world within a world [*redoubler le monde en microcosme*]—takes flight through the same passage.

Man [*l'Homme*] is made by breaking an egg, but so is the "Manlet" [*l'Hommelette*].[66]

Let us assume the latter to be a large crêpe that moves like an amoeba, so utterly flat that it can slip under doors, omniscient as it is guided by the pure life instinct, and immortal as it is fissiparous. It is certainly something that would not feel good dripping down your face, noiselessly while you sleep, in order to brand it.[67]

If we are willing to allow the digestive process to begin at this point, we realize that the Manlet has ample sustenance for a long time to come (remember that it is among the organisms, which are quite differentiated, that have no digestive tract).

It goes without saying that a struggle would soon ensue with such a fearsome being, and that the struggle would be fierce. For it can be assumed that, as the Manlet has no sensory system, it has for guidance but the pure real. It thus has an advantage over us men who must always provide ourselves with a homunculus in our heads in order to turn that real into reality.

Indeed it would not be easy to obviate the paths of its attacks, which would, moreover, be impossible to predict, as it would know no obstacles. It would be impossible to educate, and just as impossible to trap.

As for destroying the Manlet, one had best avoid helping it proliferate, for to cut it up [*y faire une entaille*] would help it reproduce, and the least of its cuttings to survive—even after having been set afire—would preserve all of its destructive powers. Apart from the effects of a lethal ray, that has yet to be tested, the only way out would be to lock it up, placing it in the jaws of a Magdeburg sphere, for example, which turns up again here, as if by chance, being the only appropriate instrument.

But the *whole* Manlet would have to slip into the sphere, and would have to do so by itself. For to touch it in order to shove a negligible overflowing amount [*un rien*[68]] back in, even the bravest person would be justified in thinking twice for fear that it would slip between his fingers and take up its abode who knows where?

Except for its name, that I will now change to a more decent one, "lamella" (of which the word "omelette" is, in fact, but a metastasis[69]), this image and this myth seem to me apt for both illustrating [*figurer*] and situating [*mettre en place*] what I call "libido."

This image shows "libido" to be what it is, namely an organ, to which its habits make it far more akin than to a force field. Let's say that it is *qua* surface that it orders this force field. This conception is corroborated when one realizes that Freud considered the drive to be structured like a montage, and articulated it in that sense.

Referring to electromagnetic theory, and, in particular, to a theorem known as Stokes' theorem, would allow me to situate the reason for the constancy of the drive's pressure,[70] which Freud emphasizes so greatly,[71] in the fact that that surface is based on a closed rim which is the erogenous zone.

It is also clear that what Freud calls the *Schub*[72] or flow [*coulée*] of the drive is not its discharge, but should rather be described as the turning inside out and outside in[73] of an organ whose function should be situated in relation to the preceding subjective coordinates.

This organ must be called "unreal," in the sense that the unreal is not the imaginary and precedes the subjective it conditions, being in direct contact with the real.

That is what my myth, like any other myth, strives to provide a symbolic articulation for, rather than an image.

My lamella represents here the part of a living being that is lost when that being is produced through the straits of sex.[74]

That part is certainly indicated in the media that microscopic anatomy materializes in the globules expulsed at the two stages of the phenomena organized around chromosome reduction, and in the maturation of a gonad.

Represented here by a deadly being, it marks the relationship—in which the subject plays a part—between sexuality, specified in the individual, and his death.

Regarding what is represented thereof in the subject, what is striking is the type of anatomical cut (breathing new life into the etymological meaning of the word "anatomy") by which the function of certain objects—which should not be called partial, but which stand apart from the others—is determined.

The breast, to take an example of the problems to which these objects give rise, is not merely a source of "regressive" nostalgia, having been a source of highly prized nourishment. It is, I am told, related to the mother's body, to its warmth, and even to tender loving care. But that does not sufficiently explain its erotic value, which a painting (in Berlin) by Tiepolo, in the exalted horror with which it presents Saint Agatha after her ordeal,[75] illustrates far better.

In fact, it is not a question of the breast, in the sense of the mother's womb,[76] though one may mix as much as one likes resonances in which the signifier relies heavily on metaphor. It is a question of the beast specified in the function of weaning which prefigures castration.

Weaning has been too extensively situated, since Klein's investigations, in the fantasy of the partition of the mother's body for us not to suspect that the plane of separation[77] passes between the breast and the mother, making the breast the lost object involved [en cause] in desire.

For if we recall that mammalian organization places the young, from the embryo right up to the newborn, in a parasitical relation to the mother's body, the breast appears as the same kind of organ—to be understood as the ectopia of one individual on another—as that constituted by the placenta at the beginning of the growth of a certain type of organism which remains specified by this intersection.

The *libido* is this lamella that the organism's being takes to its true limit, which goes further than the body's limit. Its radical function in animals is materialized in a certain ethology by the sudden decline [chute] in an animal's ability to intimidate other animals at the boundaries of its "territory."

This lamella is an organ, as it is the instrument of an organism. It is sometimes almost palpable [comme sensible], as when an hysteric plays at testing its elasticity to the hilt.

Speaking subjects have the privilege of revealing the deadly meaning of this organ, and thereby its relation to sexuality. That is because the signifier as such, whose first purpose is to bar the subject, has brought into him the meaning of death. (The letter kills, but we learn this from the letter itself.) That is why every drive is virtually[78] a death drive.

It is important to grasp how the organism is taken up in the dialectic of the subject. The organ of what is incorporeal in the sexuated [*sexué*] being is that part of the organism the subject places[79] when his separation occurs. It is through that organ that he can really make his death the object of the Other's desire.

In this way, the object he naturally loses, excrement, and the props he finds in the Other's desire—the Other's gaze or voice—come to this place.

The activity in the subject I call "drive" (*Trieb*) consists in dealing with [*tourner*] these objects in such a way as to take back from them, to restore to himself, his original loss.

There is no other pathway [*voie*] by which the impact of sexuality is manifested in the subject. A drive, insofar as it represents sexuality in the unconscious, is never anything but a partial drive. That is the essential failing [*carence*], namely the absence [*carence*] of anything that could represent in the subject the mode of what is male or female in his being.

The vacillation psychoanalytic experience reveals in the subject regarding his masculine or feminine being is not so much related to his biological bisexuality, as to the fact that there is nothing in his dialectic that represents the bipolarity of sex apart from activity and passivity, i.e., a drive versus outside-action polarity, which is altogether unfit to represent the true basis of that bipolarity.

That is the point I would like to make here—sexuality is distributed on one side or the other of our *rim qua* threshold of the unconscious as follows:

On the side of the living being *qua* being that will be taken up in speech—never able in the end to come to be altogether in speech, remaining shy of the threshold which, notwithstanding, is neither inside nor out—there is no access to the opposite sex as Other[80] except via the so-called partial drives wherein the subject seeks an object to take the place of the loss of life he has sustained due to the fact that he is sexuated.

On the side of the Other, the locus in which speech is verified as it encounters the exchange of signifiers, the ideals they prop up, the elementary structures of kinship, the paternal metaphor considered *qua* principle of separation, and the ever reopened division in the subject owing to his primal alienation—on this side alone and by the pathways [*voies*] I have just enumerated, order and norms must be instituted which tell the subject what a man or a woman must do.

It is not true that God made them male and female, even if the couple Adam and Eve said so; such a notion is also explicitly contradicted by the highly condensed myth found in the same text on the creation of Adam's companion.

No doubt Lilith was there beforehand, but that doesn't explain anything.

Breaking off here, I leave to the past the debates [at the Bonneval colloquium] in which, concerning the Freudian unconscious, irresponsible interventions were quite welcome, precisely because those responsible for them only came halfheartedly, not to say from a certain side [*bord*].

One of the results was, nevertheless, that the order issued by this side to pass over my teaching in silence was not respected.

The fact that, regarding the Oedipus complex, the final point—or rather the special guest award—went to a hermeneutic feat,[81] confirms my assessment of this colloquium and has since revealed its consequences.

At my own risk, I indicate here the means [*l'appareil*] by which precision could return.[82]

Translated by Bruce Fink[83]

Notes

1. [*VIe Colloque de Bonneval: l'Inconscient,* Paris: Desclée de Brouwer, 1966, 159. All footnotes in square brackets are translator's notes.]

2. [An alternative reading here would be: "To go to the crux of the unconscious, one must begin with Freud's experience."]

3. [*espèce*: "species" should no doubt be understood here in terms of Medieval philosophy, where it is distinguished in ontological discussions from "genus"; the genus here would be psychological reality, and the species that which does not have the attribute "consciousness."]

4. [or "the unconscious *is* what we say."]

5. [Georges Dwelshauvers, *L'inconscient,* Paris: Flammarion, 1916, especially 14–16.]

6. [Cf. Lecture XIX of Freud's *Introductory Lectures on Psychoanalysis.*]

7. [Lacan's translation for Freud's *Verneinung.*]

8. [New York: Dell Publishing Company, 1963; see especially chapter nine, "The Sexual Sell."]

9. [Lacan is apparently referring here to Jean-Bertrand Pontalis.]

10. [*énoncés.* In this translation, statement(s) always corresponds to *énoncé(s)*. Here Lacan's statements serve the function Leclaire and Laplanche failed to serve, even though the latter did the enunciating at the colloquium. *Énonciation* is always translated here as enunciation, though some translators prefer utterance.]

11. [This could also be translated: "situating himself as cause."]

12. [*recul* has many other meanings as well: distance, perspective, backing away (from), recoil, kick, postponement, lagging, reverse movement, switching back, etc. I have interpreted it here as referring to the retroactive effect of enunciation on the enunciated or statement.]

13. [*Ça* is also the French for "id."]

14. [*subornement* also means leading astray and seducing.]

15. [*boucler* also means to buckle or bring full circle.]

16. [I have abbreviated what Lacan says here as it sounds so awkward in English: *soit ce qu'il est de n'être autre que le désir de l'Autre*—"in other words, what he is due to the fact that he is no other than the Other's desire."]

17. [*propédeutique* here refers to college prep classes formerly taken by French high school graduates; thus their *secondary* education was followed by *introductory* classes—classes that introduced them into "higher education."]

18. [In English in the original. The reference here is to Ivor Armstrong Richards and C.K. Ogden's book, *The Meaning of Meaning*, 1923, which is also referred to in "Agency of the Letter in the Unconscious," *Écrits*, 150.]

19. [Common or shared thing or element.]

20. [*Autre-chose* could also be translated more idiomatically as "something Else."]

21. [Cf. *Standard Edition*, XVIII, 58.]

22. [*si le sésame de l'inconscient est d'avoir effet de parole, d'être structure de langage*—this ambiguous part of the sentence could also be translated "if the 'open sesame' of the unconscious is to have speech effects, i.e., to be linguistic in structure," etc.]

23. ["edge" and "rim" are the terms I have most often used here to translate *bord*, a term with topological, corporal, and political meanings; those meanings tend to be inseparable in Lacan's text, and run the gamut from edge, perimeter, rim (as of a bodily orifice or topological surface which closes upon itself), and limit, to border, side (in the sense of front or back, or political position), and margin.]

24. [*fermeture* also means lock, locking, shutting, etc.; in topology it is translated "closure," and a set is said to be "closed" if it contains each of its limit points.]

25. [*critique* should, no doubt, be understood here in the sense of Kant's "Critiques."]

26. [*formes du discours* seems to be modeled on *parties du discours*—parts of speech. Lacan himself says that there would be no being without the verb "to be": *"il n'y a d'être que de parler; s'il n'y avait pas le verbe être, il n'y aurait pas d'être du tout"* (Seminar XXI, *Les non-dupes errent*, January 15, 1974).]

27. [It should be kept in mind that *raison* can also mean ratio or proportion.]

28. [*Instance* is often translated as "agency"; one should keep in mind the element of insistence here.]

29. [I.e., in its capacity as efficient cause.]

30. [In French, *est le fait du sujet* would most usually mean that it is the subject's doing, i.e., that alienation is due to the subject or brought about by the subject, but that makes little sense given what follows.]

31. [*s'y impose* might also be translated "imposes itself therein," "intrudes therein," "forces itself upon the world (or upon physics)," or even "becomes a necessary addition" (to physics' theory of the world, no doubt exploding that theory).]

32. [*n'a pas encore la parole* also means "cannot yet express himself well" or "has not yet earned the right to be paid attention to when he speaks."]

33. [*figer* means to fix (like a fixer in photography or a fixative), congeal, clot, coagulate, etc.]

34. [The French imperfect functions to some extent like the English "The bomb *was to* go off two minutes later," where the verb tense allows one to imagine at least two different temporal contexts: one in which the bomb is set to go off in two minutes, and will go off if we don't manage to defuse it beforehand; and another in which, looking back on the situation, we note that the bomb actually went off two minutes after the moment we are considering (for example, in a documentary, one might hear, "The bomb *was to go off* two minutes later, killing the President and the First Lady"), did not go off at all (e.g., "the documents *were to be* destroyed, but turned up in KGB files rendered public many years later"), or went off, but not at the designated time. Lacan uses this example from Raymond Queneau's *On est toujours trop bon avec les femmes,* Paris: Gallimard, 1971.]

35. [Latin for "or," "either/or," or "alternative."]

36. ["Union" (*réunion*) is one of a pair of terms from set theory, Venn diagrams, Euler circles, etc., the other term being "intersection." Sheridan mistakenly translates it as "joining" in Seminar XI.]

37. [*écorné* also means spoiled, marred, abraded, eroded, chipped away, etc.]

38. [*mordre sur* also means to bite into, gnaw into, make a dent in, etc.]

39. [*relève de*: comes under, is related to, has to do with.]

40. [See the diagrams and discussions provided in Seminar XI, 209–215.]

41. [ignorance, crudeness, inexperience, blunder, etc.]

42. [See Marie Bonaparte's French translation of Freud's *New Introductory Lectures on Psychoanalysis,* the last page of Lecture XXXI.]

43. [See Leclaire's paper in *L'inconscient* and Lacan's commentary in Seminar XI, 212 and 250.]

44. [*articulation* should be understood in the sense of linking up or connection.]

45. Abbreviated version of my answer to an inoperative objection.

46. [Belonging, for example, to both set X and set Y.]

47. [*d'une part prise du manque au manque*—this highly ambiguous formulation could be interpreted in a number of ways (e.g., a part taken from one lack into the other, grasped by the lack in lack, grasped in the lack-to-lack lineup, taken from a lack by another lack); considered in terms of the diagrams Lacan provides in Seminar XI, it seems that the part is "taken" from the place where the two circles representing the subject and the Other overlap.]

48. [*le sujet se réalise*: the subject comes to be, or is constituted, i.e., subjective realization occurs.]

49. [*Velle*—in French *vouloir*—to will, to desire, to want, to wish, etc. Empedocles' will here seems to be Strife, and his act that of flinging himself into Mount Etna's volcanic crater.]

50. [*fin* can be understood here as either terminus or goal.]

51. [*appariement commun*: Lacan continues to play on the word "part" here— "they have in common that they are paired with the function of the *pars*."]

52. [*en prendre son parti* could also be rendered: "come to a decision about it" or "make up one's mind about it."]

53. [*Partition* also means musical score.]

54. [*se parer du signifiant* literally means to adorn or bedeck himself with the signifier; more figuratively it means to take it upon himself, to assume it (like one assumes a responsibility), etc.]

55. [S_1 and S_2].

56. [*qui lui revient*: which accrues to him, or which he recovers, though it should be kept in mind that he did not have it before.]

57. [*comble* also means to fulfill, make good, etc.]

58. [*faille* has many meanings, running from failing, flaw, defect, weakness, and shortcoming to rift and fault (in the geological sense); here the meaning seems to be topological: it is a space that is filled up, the space constituted by the lack in the Other.]

59. [or "is he willing to lose me?", "can he afford to lose me?", "could he bear for me to be gone/dead?"]

60. [*il s'est produit* also means he produced himself, brought himself into being, created himself.]

61. [*scander* is the verb form of "scansion," and is usually translated as to scan or scanning (as in scanning verse). I have opted in all of my translations of Lacan's work to date to introduce a neologism—to scand, scanding—so as to distinguish the far more common contemporary uses of scanning (looking over rapidly, quickly running through a list, taking ultra-thin pictures of the body with a scanner, or "feeding" text and images in digital form into a computer) from Lacan's idea here of cutting, punctuating, or interrupting something (usually the analysand's discourse).]

62. [*attente de* also means waiting for.]

63. [See "Function and field of speech and language in psychoanalysis," *Écrits*, written over 10 years earlier.]

64. [*verbal* could also be understood in the sense of verb-like here, thus word-like; *où l'on veut bien le dire* could also mean where people are willing to say it, or put it into words.]

65. [literally, "which sometimes go as far as cooing [*roucoulement*]"—lovers' warbling words to each other.]

66. [*Hommelette* is a conflation of *Homme*, man, and *omelette*; the ending, "ette," is a diminutive; compare with *femmelette*. Recall the French proverb, "*Pour faire une omelette il faut casser des oeufs.*"]

67. [*cacheter* literally means to seal or to stamp.]

68. [*un rien* could also be translated as a mere smidgen or as a trifling, trivial, or insignificant quantity, but the *rien* or nothing is also one of the "objects" associated with Lacan's object (a).]

69. It seems that those who espouse the virtues of mother's milk [*bon lait*] laugh at my references to . . . metastasis and metonymy (*sic*). But the one whose face is perfect [*parlant*] for illustrating the slogan that I would make its brand name, rarely makes people laugh: laughing cow dung [*la bouse de vache qui rit*].

70. [See "Instincts and their Vicissitudes" (1915); the *Standard Edition* gives "pressure" as the translation for *Drang*, while the *Collected Papers*, translated under the supervision of Joan Riviere, give "impetus"; Lacan's French translation is "*poussée.*"]

71. It is well known what this theorem states about curl flux. It assumes a continuously differentiable vector field. In such a field, since the curl of a vector is based on the derivatives of the vector's components, it can be demonstrated that the circulation of this vector along a closed curve is equal to the curl flux calculated for the surface whose edge is defined by this curve. In other words, by positing this flux as invariable, the theorem establishes the notion of a flux "through" an orificial circuit, that is, such that the original surface need no longer be taken into account.

For topologists: $\int \vec{dl}.\ \vec{V} = \iint \vec{dS}.\ \mathrm{Curl}\ \vec{V}.$

72. [*Schub* is also translated "thrust"—see "Instincts and their Vicissitudes" (1915)—appearing in that essay in connection with images like "successive eruptions of lava."]

73. [*évagination aller et retour*: the figure provided in Seminar XI of the circuit of the drive would suggest that this be translated somewhat differently: "back and forth evagination" or "insertion in and back out."]

74. [*par les voies du sexe*: by sexual passageways, pathways, or means; via sex.]

75. [Saint Agatha was reputed to have had her breasts cut off.]

76. [*matrice* can take on a great many meanings, including womb, die, matrix, register, and mold in the sense of a shaping ring or die in which something is cast; note that *sein*, which I have translated here as "breast," can also mean "womb" or "uterus."]

77. ["plane" to be understood here in the geometrical sense.]

78. [*virtuellement* also means potentially, practically, and for all intents and purposes.]

79. [*vient à placer* suggests a placing or investing of something, in addition to a situating.]

80. [*l'Autre du sexe opposé* could also be translated as the Other of the opposite sex.]

81. [Paul Ricoeur spoke last, and soon published his hermeneutic reading of Freud and the Oedipus complex in *Freud and Philosophy: An Essay on Interpretation* (first published in French in 1965). Cf. Seminar XI, 153–4.]

82. Let it be pointed out, nevertheless, that in restoring here, in an ironic way, the function of the "partial" object, without making the reference to regression in which it is usually shrouded (let it be understood that this reference can only be operative on the basis of the structure defining the object that I call object *a*), I have not been able to extend it to the point which constitutes its crucial interest, namely the object (- φ) as "cause" of the castration complex.

But the castration complex, which is at the crux [*noeud*] of my current work, exceeds the limits assigned to [psychoanalytic] theory by tendencies in psychoanalysis that were claiming to be new shortly before the war and by which it is still affected as a whole.

The size of the obstacle I must overcome here can be gauged by the time it took me to provide this sequel to my Rome discourse and by the fact that, even now as I edit it [for the 1966 Seuil edition], the original version still hasn't been published.

83. [I wish to express my thanks here to Héloïse Fink, who provided a great deal of helpful criticism of this translation, and to Russell Grigg, Henry Sullivan, and Suzanne Barnard who made a number of very useful comments.]

INDEX

Printed in the United States
1350000004B/223-225